Media Diplomacy and Its Evolving Role in the Current Geopolitical Climate

Swati Jaywant Rao Bute
Jagran Lakecity University, India

A volume in the Advances in Electronic Government, Digital Divide, and Regional Development (AEGDDRD) Book Series

IGI Global
DISSEMINATOR OF KNOWLEDGE

Published in the United States of America by
IGI Global
Information Science Reference (an imprint of IGI Global)
701 E. Chocolate Avenue
Hershey PA, USA 17033
Tel: 717-533-8845
Fax: 717-533-8661
E-mail: cust@igi-global.com
Web site: http://www.igi-global.com

Library of Congress Cataloging-in-Publication Data

Names: Bute, Swati Jaywant Rao, 1974- editor.
Title: Media diplomacy and its evolving role in the current geopolitical climate / Swati Jaywant Rao Bute, editor.
Description: Hershey, PA : Information Science Reference, 2018. | Includes bibliographical references.
Identifiers: LCCN 2017023184| ISBN 9781522538592 (hardcover) | ISBN 9781522538608 (ebook)
Subjects: LCSH: Mass media and international relations. | International relations--Technological innovations. | Information technology--Political aspects. | Diplomacy--Technological innovations. | Internet and international relations.
Classification: LCC P96.I53 M425 2018 | DDC 302.23--dc23 LC record available at https://lccn.loc.gov/2017023184

This book is published in the IGI Global book series Advances in Electronic Government, Digital Divide, and Regional Development (AEGDDRD) (ISSN: 2326-9103; eISSN: 2326-9111)

British Cataloguing in Publication Data
A Cataloguing in Publication record for this book is available from the British Library.

All work contributed to this book is new, previously-unpublished material.
The views expressed in this book are those of the authors, but not necessarily of the publisher.

For electronic access to this publication, please contact: eresources@igi-global.com.

Advances in Electronic Government, Digital Divide, and Regional Development (AEGDDRD) Book Series

ISSN:2326-9103
EISSN:2326-9111

Editor-in-Chief: Zaigham Mahmood, University of Derby, UK & North West University, South Africa

MISSION

The successful use of digital technologies (including social media and mobile technologies) to provide public services and foster economic development has become an objective for governments around the world. The development towards electronic government (or e-government) not only affects the efficiency and effectiveness of public services, but also has the potential to transform the nature of government interactions with its citizens. Current research and practice on the adoption of electronic/digital government and the implementation in organizations around the world aims to emphasize the extensiveness of this growing field.

The Advances in Electronic Government, Digital Divide & Regional Development (AEGDDRD) book series aims to publish authored, edited and case books encompassing the current and innovative research and practice discussing all aspects of electronic government development, implementation and adoption as well the effective use of the emerging technologies (including social media and mobile technologies) for a more effective electronic governance (or e-governance).

COVERAGE

- Social Media, Web 2.0, and Mobile Technologies in E-Government
- Public Information Management, Regional Planning, Rural Development
- E-Governance and Use of Technology for Effective Government
- Issues and Challenges in E-Government Adoption
- Online Government, E-Government, M-Government
- ICT Infrastructure and Adoption for E-Government Provision
- Emerging Technologies within the Public Sector
- Frameworks and Methodologies for E-Government Development
- E-Government in Developing Countries and Technology Adoption
- Knowledge Divide, Digital Divide

IGI Global is currently accepting manuscripts for publication within this series. To submit a proposal for a volume in this series, please contact our Acquisition Editors at Acquisitions@igi-global.com or visit: http://www.igi-global.com/publish/.

The Advances in Electronic Government, Digital Divide, and Regional Development (AEGDDRD) Book Series (ISSN 2326-9103) is published by IGI Global, 701 E. Chocolate Avenue, Hershey, PA 17033-1240, USA, www.igi-global.com. This series is composed of titles available for purchase individually; each title is edited to be contextually exclusive from any other title within the series. For pricing and ordering information please visit http://www.igi-global.com/book-series/advances-electronic-government-digital-divide/37153. Postmaster: Send all address changes to above address.

Titles in this Series

For a list of additional titles in this series, please visit:
https://www.igi-global.com/book-series/advances-electronic-government-digital-divide/37153

Political Mediation in Modern Conflict Resolution Emerging Research and Opprtunities
José Pascal da Rocha (Columbia University, USA)
Information Science Reference • ©2018 • 246pp • H/C (ISBN: 9781522551188) • US $150.00

Proliferation of Open Government Initiatives and Systems
Ayse Kok (Bogazici University, Turkey)
Information Science Reference • ©2018 • 231pp • H/C (ISBN: 9781522549871) • US $195.00

Socio-Economic and Education Factors Impacting American Political Systems Emerging...
Pamela Hampton-Garland (University of the District of Columbia, USA) Lisa Sechrest-Ehrhardt (University of the District of Columbia, USA) and Benson George Cooke (University of the District of Columbia, USA)
Information Science Reference • ©2018 • 191pp • H/C (ISBN: 9781522538431) • US $145.00

Handbook of Research on Women's Issues and Rights in the Developing World
Nazmunnessa Mahtab (University of Dhaka, Bangladesh) Tania Haque (University of Dhaka, Bangladesh) Ishrat Khan (University of Dhaka, Bangladesh) Md. Mynul Islam (University of Dhaka, Bangladesh) and Ishret Binte Wahid (BRAC, Bangladesh)
Information Science Reference • ©2018 • 452pp • H/C (ISBN: 9781522530183) • US $245.00

Handbook of Research on Sociopolitical Factors Impacting Economic Growth in Islamic...
Suleyman Ozdemir (Bandırma Onyedi Eylül University, Turkey) Seyfettin Erdogan (Istanbul Medeniyet University, Turkey) and Ayfer Gedikli (İstanbul Medeniyet University, Turkey)
Information Science Reference • ©2018 • 472pp • H/C (ISBN: 9781522529392) • US $275.00

Urbanization and Its Impact on Socio-Economic Growth in Developing Regions
Umar Benna (Benna Associates, Nigeria) and Indo Benna (Muhammad Al-Mana College of Health Sciences, Saudi Arabia)
Information Science Reference • ©2018 • 404pp • H/C (ISBN: 9781522526599) • US $195.00

For an entire list of titles in this series, please visit:
https://www.igi-global.com/book-series/advances-electronic-government-digital-divide/37153

IGI Global
DISSEMINATOR OF KNOWLEDGE

701 East Chocolate Avenue, Hershey, PA 17033, USA
Tel: 717-533-8845 x100 • Fax: 717-533-8661
E-Mail: cust@igi-global.com • www.igi-global.com

This book is dedicated to my father, Shree (late) Jaywant Rao Bute, my mother. Smt. Prema Bute, my dear brother, Sachin Bute, and sister, Kshama Bute Shinde.

Editorial Advisory Board

Table of Contents

Detailed Table of Contents

Can there be a symbiotic relationship between the armed forces and the private conventional news media in a country with a democratic setup? What are the issues that come between these two entities especially in a complex scenario such as Fourth Generation Warfare? The objective of this chapter is to study these challenges in the relationship between the two institutions in the setting of fourth generation warfare in India. It presents areas of divergence that have been critical in the efficient symbiotic functioning of these two institutions.

Diplomacy refers to the professional activity or skills that are used to manage and strengthen the relations on international or global level. E-diplomacy can be termed as the new mode of conducting diplomacy acts with the help of internet and information and communication technologies (ICTs). In general, we often say that diplomacy is maintained of relations through communication. It is the art of conducting negotiations, forming alliances, discussing treaties, and reaching agreements. This can be done with proper communication which helps maintain a social image. Moreover, communication in diplomacy is that tactful move that ensures that the diplomat smoothly handles the relations with the other parties and makes them do what is needed without harming the interests and profits of either of two or more parties. This ensures peace and eliminates the feeling of ill-will. The chapter sheds light on the emergence of e-diplomacy in India, its advantages, use, and the future uses as well.

Most scholars advocate that the people are seeking identity, and for this purpose, they are reinventing ethnicity to establish their ideology. So, they need opponents and create enmities. Among the civilizations, the sectorial powers that represent common ideology within the geography provoke extremism, and through religious and cultural pundits, the extremists are radicalized to disturb the entire world through terrorism.

This chapter attempts to understand the inter-relationship between the media and the national security/foreign affairs sector in Nepal, particularly unfolding the perceptions between each other and the resultant impression in the print media – thereby carrying forward the "securitization" discourse. Through the process of content analysis and expert opinions, this chapter advocates for the "desecuritization" of sensitive issues such as national security and diplomacy, promoting peace and cooperation rather than polarization of ideas and perspectives.

In a globalized world when countries are working together in different areas such as economic, political, geopolitical, defense, security, and science and technology, media plays an important role in keeping them updated about the actual and ground level realities about different countries. This chapter examines how new media is important in international relations and diplomatic affairs, what role new media is playing in international relations, India's relations with South Asian countries and role of media diplomacy, India's relations with international community and role of e-diplomacy, people's participation in discussion and dialogue in international relations and its impact in diplomatic policies, relation between people's participation and deciding policies and national level, increasing role of new media and changing practice of international diplomacy, and foreign policy adopted by governments.

Preface

The constant changing landscape of current practices in media diplomacy in geopolitical climates creates a need for knowledge resources that will empower professionals, academic educators, researchers, and industry consultants all over the world. Media Diplomacy and Its Evolving Role in the Current Geopolitical Climate is a vital reference source that will meet these needs by exploring the latest coverage on all aspects of e-diplomacy, news media, and securitization from different fields, covering topics such as foreign policy, national security, social media, and the digital divide.

This reference source is organized into eight chapters contributed by global experts, drawing on their experiences, observations, and research surrounding foreign diaspora, international affairs, and cyber-attacks. A brief description of each of the chapters can be found in the following paragraphs.

Chapter 1: This chapter explores relation between the conventional news media and the Indian armed forces in context to Fourth Generation Warfare. The author has attempted to evaluate the various parameters that influence the relationship between the two entities in the new milieu of warfare. The study is important due to the following reasons:

1. Redefining security in a globalized and technologically connected world. This new redefinition of security carries a very strong political import – for it requires not just the state's acknowledgment, but also the population's mandate to carry out operations other than war, even within own boundaries.
2. Change in the dynamics and structure of warfare and global impact. In the redefined world order, most conflicts are between established and recognized armies and non-state actors, such as terrorist organizations or insurgent groups. Also, war in any corner of the world directly or indirectly affects all countries as now countries are more dependent and inter-connected to each other for economic and other purposes.

3. The all-influencing and ubiquitous news media. The news media plays a very powerful role in molding public perception and thus, in the armed forces. The Indian armed forces, is a very professional organization that takes great pride in its institution and ethos, which is reinforced by its unique culture that it zealously adheres to. However, with the impact of the traditional news media and new-age communication platforms, such as social media, even the most staunchly traditional bastions of hierarchy, is slowly, but increasingly witnessing inroads of opinionated public perception impacting their operations. This brings out the key question of the chapter: can the media be used effectively as a propaganda tool by the government and the armed forces?

Chapter 2: This chapter highlights that with 1.2 billion population and due to its geographical presence in the map of South Asian continent India is getting attention of international community for business, economy and geopolitical negotiations. In such changing time India has identified the power of Internet and also has adopted new policies to remain updated in changing time. Earlier India had a image of conservative and traditional pattern of governance but by adopting new media for a very sensitive government department India has established a new image that the political leaders of India are not only Internet savvy and have presence on social media and are participating very actively in all issues trending on social media specifically issues related to government. They are very well connected and informed about things happening at global platform. By quickly responding on social media on any issue related to the sovereignty and unity of the country they not only gives a message that how firm they are when things come to national interest and security but also by listening problems of Indian citizens living abroad they shows how sensitive they are towards the minor needs of the citizens. Not only that but when required they are ready to provide any kind of help to the Indian citizen living out of the country. This chapter also highlights the system which Indian government has adopted for E-diplomacy, sensitive areas, precautions and content requirements of such platforms.

Chapter 3: In this chapter author highlights change in communication and information technology all over the world and in Nepal; and how technology is helping in nation development as well as stabilizing the country. He further highlights change which media in Nepal is observing, how new media and technology is helping in improving government system and reducing corruption in governance which is the major barrier in the growth of developing countries like India and Nepal. He explains politics and geopolitics and their changing nature in the South Asian continent, geographical location of Nepal, its closeness to two varied emerging countries India and China, Nepal's social, cultural, political, economic and military relations with both the countries and pressure of International community.

He explains that changing scenario is exploring, giving a new identity and decision-making power to the local people with increased rate of literacy, development and use of technology. Due to presence and direct and indirect dominance of internal and external forces and imposition of political ideologies in the region the people of Nepal now feel that the local culture, own identity has lost somewhere and in the age of information technology when they are more educated, aware, skilled and empowered they want to go back to the roots and preserve the lost identity of self.

At the same time in the changing geopolitical conditions in South Asia region and all over the world the local have feeling of insecurity that their land, resources and people will be used once again by dominating neighboring powers and international forces for their own economic, military and geopolitical interests and benefits and this feeling of insecurity come out time to time through different modes of media. Fragile political system of the country is not able to give them any hope of nation development and assurance of nation's sovereignty, integrity, unity and security.

Chapter 4: This chapter is in the context of use of media in diplomatic affairs in Nepal and its influence on political working system. Nepal is observing changes in its political system and set up very frequently. Year 1990 was the transition time period in the politics of Nepal. Over the years, media was used by different political actors for their own interests, benefits and for political ambitions. This paper highlights the interrelation between politics, media and security and diplomatic issues. This paper analyses Nepali print media and focuses on major issues related to interrelation between media, politics and security and diplomatic issues such as coverage and importance given to security and diplomatic issues in print media of Nepal and the way media handle security issues in reporting it.

Author has given well searched background information on the concept of security, media, national security and diplomatic issues and its coverage in Nepali media, giving reference of security theory to support his arguments. To analyze what impact print media stories on security and diplomatic issues creates the way it is reported in print media in the minds of the readers and what impact and atmosphere the tone and treatment of the stories creates on the community and society at large, the author has conducted interviews with the small sample of academicians, security and foreign policy experts. Additionally, he also analyzed editorial of Kantipur Daily, a highly circulated local language newspaper during the first three years after the People's Movement II (2007-10).

This study reveals that the tone of newspaper reports was highly authoritative in nature and there is a wider securitization of security's discourse in Nepali media as the editorials being declarative or directive in nature rather than being assertive. Author concludes that national security and diplomacy issues can be misinterpreted or manipulated by powerful agents such as media. Therefore, it is needful and essential to use media in sensitizing people by providing right information on security's issues and concerns rather polarizing ideas and perspectives. New media can thus be used to promote people friendly e-diplomacy in geopolitically important countries like Nepal.

Chapter 5: Media plays an important role in international affairs and bilateral relations. In last few years we are observing change in media practices and reporting patterns in contemporary and digital media. Politicians and government officers shaping/making foreign policy has realized that in changing scenario it is necessary to use media and keep people update, get their involvement in making people centric policies. In last few years media practices have changed all over the world which is also affecting the domestic and local media. Media always played an important role in international, bilateral and diplomatic relations. In this age of information technology both contemporary and new media is playing important role in informing and keeping people update about international relations and affairs. Now the practice and patterns of diplomacy is also changing. Countries are deciding strategic and diplomatic relations on the basis of reports in media about the country. In a globalized world when countries are working together in different areas such as economic, political, geopolitical, strategic, defense, security and science and technology. Media plays an important role in keeping people and politicians update about actual and ground level realities of different countries. This chapter examine how contemporary and new media is important in international relations and diplomatic affairs. What role contemporary and new media is playing in international relations? India's relations with south Asian countries and role of media diplomacy. India's relations with International community and role of media, public and digital diplomacy. People's participation in discussion and dialogue in International relations and its impact in diplomatic and foreign policies, people's participation in deciding policies at national, regional and at international level. Increasing role of new media and changing practice in bilateral, multilateral, multinational and international diplomacy. This chapter also explores foreign policy adopted by present Government and role of digital and contemporary media in enhancing and promoting it, making relations more friendly and strong at regional and at international level.

Chapter 6: This chapter highlights evolution and growth of digital diplomacy in India, it's usage, popularity and active participation of political leaders and government officers in making people aware about foreign policy, diplomacy and new amendments, rules and regulations implemented by government to improve transparency in government policies and system for foreign affairs. Author given reference of few international events and crisis when Indian diaspora living abroad approached to government through social media and received timely help. This chapter also highlights how this new practice in diplomacy is changing set definition and working pattern and how users are exploring it more and more and getting benefits, feeling more empowered, how it's changing people's understanding in governance which is more open, approachable and interactive, how people's faith in democracy is increasing and what role it is playing in making democracy more strong and mature. How due to political pressure the officers are more accountable and such act is reducing existing red tappism in system, how politicians are using it to get work done from bureaucrats because normally when things are not happening political leaders are blamed and answerable but sometimes politicians are not responsible but the existing frozen system who do not To act, take action and make things happening, in a way digital diplomacy is removing existing corruption in system and making system and everybody involved in that including political leaders, bureaucrats and higher and lower level officials to be more active, approachable and answerable. Recently during his visit to Prime Ministre of India, Mr. Narendra Modi has mentioned that the External Affairs Minister of India, Mrs. Sushma Swaraj has converted diplomacy into human diplomacy, she is available all the time and respond, approach to everybody who is in need and wants her help in solving problems through her interaction with people on social media such as Facebook and twitter, this chapter highlights this particular aspects which is helping in projecting India's soft image at international level.

Chapter 7: The chapter is divided into four main sections. The first section provides a theoretical framework composed of the Actors Network theory and the digital divide theory. The second section provides a definition of e-diplomacy and traces its history. The third section examines African countries' progressive "appropriation" of this culture; and the fourth section highlights the prospects of e-diplomacy in Africa as well as major challenges faced by African countries in their deployment of digital diplomacy.

Innovation in information and communication technologies have revolutionized international communication, international relations and public diplomacy. Authors writes that phenol e-diplomacy has become a global tradition, involving even poor African nations. He has given reference of two theories Actor Network Theory (ANT) and the digital divide theory to explain the practices which are in use in E-diplomacy sector all over the world. He further explain how digital diplomacy is being defined and used by global powers in their day to day affairs. He has given brief history of inception of concept of e-diplomacy and its increased use over the years. He further examines the status of digital diplomacy in Africa and concludes that few African countries have required infrastructure and resources to boost and use e-diplomacy but there are few other African countries who still do not have required infrastructure and resources and are lagging behind. Digital diplomacy has both prospects and challenges and therefore requires specific strategies by African governments. He writes that the prospects of digital diplomacy in Africa can be seen in a plurality of domains including nation branding, diaspora diplomacy networked diplomacy and information and knowledge management by diplomatic missions. He sees digital divide, lack of public trust in African politicians and policy makers, the top bottom process of foreign policy making and regulations and censorship of social media and internet by African government as some of the barriers in the overall growth of e-diplomacy in Africa. He concludes by saying that despite positive development there are various issues which produces challenges for e-diplomacy which needs proper and effective strategies to deal with.

Chapter 8: The birth of digital diplomacy has opened plethora of opportunities for the people as well as the state, author highlights changes and growth in computer from its inception to till date. In this paper the author has given detail information of evolution of Internet and its use in all areas. Popularity of social media for different purposes, further she writes about use of Internet and social media by non-actors for spreading negative things for which she has given examples of propaganda on social media by terrorist groups and emergence of new practices in international politics such as Russian cyber hacking during 2016 US presidential elections. She further explains how state actors are using Internet digital platforms in International affairs as she writes that tele-conferencing and information, communication and technology (ICT) have radically changed the execution of these businesses, yet the basic components and negotiation to come to mutual conclusion remain imperative. Author highlights that face to face diplomacy has not evaporated from the diplomatic circuits but the utility of ICT in this field has been overwhelming realized with complex challenges and threats beyond the traditional boundaries of state emanating their field of diplomacy and statecraft has to evolve further so that it counters them. She also highlights origin of social media on digital platform and popularity which it has achieved among the masses and growth of contemporary diplomacy to digital diplomacy, expansion of sophisticated diplomacy to digital or E-diplomacy. This change has led communication technologies as a important tool for acquiring diplomatic objectives. She further explains how information revolution has compressed the time and distance.

Chapter 1
Fourth Generation Warfare and the Challenges in Military–News Media Relations in India

Ramakrishnan Ramani
University of Madras, India

ABSTRACT

Can there be a symbiotic relationship between the armed forces and the private conventional news media in a country with a democratic setup? What are the issues that come between these two entities especially in a complex scenario such as Fourth Generation Warfare? The objective of this chapter is to study these challenges in the relationship between the two institutions in the setting of fourth generation warfare in India. It presents areas of divergence that have been critical in the efficient symbiotic functioning of these two institutions.

DOI: 10.4018/978-1-5225-3859-2.ch001

INTRODUCTION

"Every war must end, but this tug of war between the media and the military with the information as its bone of contention has no end in sight. This love–hate relationship between the two is the greatest hindrance in the task of preserving national security," says popular journalist and Nehruvian scholar, Manikonda Chalapathi Rau (Saxena, 1997). A profound statement and one that is increasingly proving correct as Fourth Generation Warfare is ever more becoming a reality of conflict in the subcontinent – cases in point being the 26/11 Mumbai attacks and the January 2016 attack on the Pathankot airbase.

What Is Fourth Generation Warfare?

Major scientific and doctrinal developments spurred by socio-political transformation have constituted significant changes in the way wars have been fought. Most military engagements since the early 1990s (since the fall of the Soviet Union) are typically of the 'Fourth Generation' a generation in which the "tactics of the weak confound the tactics of the strong" *(Wilson, Sullivan, & Kempfer, 2003)*. Today's international environment is defined by this reality. People, the world over, including India are witnessing sub-national 'non-state' actors use guerrilla tactics, insurrection, sabotage and terrorism to subvert nations and challenge the established international system and the very concept of the 'nation-state'.

Fourth Generation Warfare is a transition in the way wars are fought – traditional military might is avoided; the focus is shifted from high technology to ideology. Conflict shifts from simply destroying military targets and regular conventional forces to socio-economic, religious or political centres.

William S. Lind states, "In Fourth Generation war, the state loses its monopoly on war. All over the world, state militaries find themselves fighting non-state opponents such as al-Qaeda, Hamas, Hezbollah, and the Revolutionary Armed Forces of Colombia. Almost everywhere, the state is losing. Fourth Generation war is also marked by a return to a world of cultures, not merely states, in conflict. We now find ourselves facing the Christian West's oldest and most steadfast opponent, Islam" (Lind, 2004).

Fourth Generation Conflicts in India

India has witnessed Fourth Generation Warfare in the form of Guerrilla Warfare and insurgencies since at least the past couple of hundred years. Indian military history is replete with incidents of guerrilla warfare and even insurgencies. The 'Mountain Rat' Shivaji is perhaps the most famous example of this style of warfare. Since the latter days of the British 'Raj', Terrorism, or Extremism as it was more popularly called then, became a not-too-infrequent headline in Indian newspapers.

Since 1967 India has witnessed non-conventional warfare within its boundaries. Starting with the Naxalbury movement in 18 May 1967 till present, India has fought its fair share of Fourth Generation war. Here is a case in point.

Jammu and Kashmir continues to be Pakistan's unsettled issue. In fact, from what India has witnessed over the past 60+ years, it has become its reason for existence. It has tried its hand in wrestling the contested state from the Indian Union through conventional military means in 1947, 1965, and 1999. However, what it has received in return is either an outright defeat or a debatable stalemate – but found no tangible progress. It then resorted to non-conventional means. Since the early years of the 1980s, Pakistan is making attempts to create chaos and disorder to destabilise India – to bleed India by a thousand cuts. Here is a quick look at the various Fourth Generation conflicts India has fought on its soil. India's internal security threats have been cancerous, spreading to over 50% of the districts across all its states either as insurgencies or in the form of terrorism (Vohra, 2008).

During the 1980s, the Khalistan movement in Punjab became the source of enormous loss of human life and socio-economic loss. The violence lasted for over a decade till the government was forced to take a controversial, yet decisive, military action. In the north-eastern arm of India, several states still continue to face unending insurgencies and struggle supported from ideologies across the border. The illegal migration of large masses of people from Bangladesh has created regional demographic imbalance and has become the source of communal tension as reflected in the states of Assam, Bihar and the north-east. Since the 1980s, religion has been leveraged to drive violence across the country – Sikh terrorism in Punjab and Islamic terrorism through various hard-line Wahabi fundamental groups and their networks across India.

Hard core Communist extremist organizations such as the Naxalites, with covert backing of Maoists in China, still continue to embark on violence, not on state security and government personnel, but also on unsympathetic civilians – often villagers and political leaders. Their activities are witnessed across Eastern, Central and South-Central regions of the country. Maoists openly deprecate the state apparatus and call for its downfall. Popular institutions, such as Democracy, are not part of their political system. The previous Congress Party-led UPA government has labelled this issue as the country's greatest internal security threat of the 21st century, after domestically fostered religion-fuelled terrorism (Vohra, 2008). This insurgency that started as a pro-peasant movement has been the source of numerous large and small scale killings, arson and wanton acts of sabotage across regions infested with this problem. Today, this infestation has spread across more than 600 districts – but primarily in the resource rich states of Jharkhand, West Bengal, Madhya Pradesh,

Telangana and Seemandhra, pockets of Maharashtra, and the north-east. The central and state governments have been tackling this issue through multiple channels – military and paramilitary means, people-to-people activities, economic policies, education and through propaganda by leveraging the vernacular mass media.

Another major source of security threat is through the organized crime and mafia groups that are actively supported by Pakistan's ISI networks in India (Gupta & Arvind, 2010). These illegal activities that include drug and arms smuggling, human trafficking, extortion, antique smuggling and so on help fund Islamic fundamentalism. It is a known fact that Islamic extremists not only cross the border to carry out their despicable activities on Indian soil, but have also been recruited and trained indigenously in the country (such as the Indian Mujahideen) with the tacit support of Pakistan's military and ISI.

Factors That Inhibit the Relationship

Covering Fourth Generation Warfare is not the same as covering Conventional Warfare. The rules of the game differ, the operating space is different, the range of weapons used is different, and the existence of conflict too is at different planes – physically and in the minds of the protagonists and the general public. Thus, the challenges of covering this generation of war are multi-fold when compared to covering conventional conflicts where the demarcation is clear – the sides are either 'us/ours' versus 'them/theirs'.

To start with the efficiencies needed to cover the types of engagements in Fourth Generation Warfare from long-drawn guerilla warfare, short, but intense, bursts of terrorist attacks, and attacks on civilian population in cities and villages to focused attacks on military personnel and the intrinsic complexities that come with it, takes much bandwidth from news media organizations – especially regional news media – to deliver what they must (unbridled truth) to their readers and viewers. Above this, they must also meet the business requirements of their establishment to keep the day-to-day operations running. When there is much to be dealt with, is it possible to completely align with the armed forces and cooperate fully as a communications partner?

On the other side, an increasing commerciality of news as a business item and the increasing nature of news media organizations to 'cash' upon opportunities, thus over-playing their role which would hamper the armed forces' overall operational strategy has been observed and reported. While this is one instance, there are other factors that also affect the relationship between the Indian military and the private news media in the research scenario.

OPERATIONAL ISSUES FOR THE NEWS MEDIA

The 'Human' Angle: Covering Human Rights Issues

Any military engagement, especially COIN and Anti-Terrorist operations, would rake up issues of Human Rights violations. The murky nature of such conflicts, the battle ground (often the midst of human civilization), and the association civilian population provide the right scenario for such allegations to crop up. To make matters worse, the armed forces almost never respond to issues like human right violation with sincerity and clarity. In an interview with Col Danvir Singh, (11th June 2016), he stated that one of the reasons why unverified news of human rights violations rage in the news media, especially local media, is due to the challenges about sharing credible and adequate information. When that is not available the new media may, under pressure to deliver and in competition, give out uncorroborated information that causes problems.

The armed forces' engagements with terrorists in Jammu & Kashmir, militants in the Northeast and Naxalites in the districts across Karnataka, Chhattisgarh, Odisha, Andhra Pradesh, Maharashtra, Jharkhand, Bihar, Uttar Pradesh, and West Bengal have been published and broadcasted across all national and regional newspapers and news television channels across the country – albeit with the reports of violations of Human Rights. The Indian armed forces' counter-insurgency and anti-terrorist operations across insurgency prone regions of the country have resulted in widespread human rights 'abuses' that includes extra-judicial killing, third-degree torture, abductions and unlawful detention, mass rape of local women, curtailment of freedom of assemble, speech and movement. (UN Special Rapporteur on Extrajudicial Execution, 2010) These issues are published by the local and national new media organizations.

From the perspective of ethics of the news media, it becomes its duty to bring to the wider attention (and conscience) of the people of the region and of the country any unfortunate violation of human rights. The methods that the armed forces use in quelling such reports include deportation of journalists, intimidation, denial of access to information and location, and even violence. (Hayes, 2012; Chaudhury, 2011) This becomes counterproductive to the larger interests of the armed forces and its COIN strategy.

Threat to Life

One of the primary challenges that a journalist faces when covering an unconventional conflict is the direct threat to his/her own existence. The case of the gruesome killing of Wall Street journalist Daniel Pearl by the Taliban in 2002 is a case in point. There have been more similar deaths since across the world. The killing of the US journalist Steven Sotloff by ISIS shows that covering such type of conflicts are not governable under any accepted international policies on the conduct of handling non-combatants.

India too has seen numerous such incidents right from the days of the Khalistan movement in Punjab, where journalists were forced to accept the dictates of both the military and the militants and write about them much against their journalistic principles. Such cases were galore in Kashmir, Naxalite infested regions and in the Northeast. Journalists walk a very tight rope while trying to balance judicious reporting on the actual on goings in the region. Reports of missing or killed journalists, which appear on various news media platforms, are stark and gruesome reminders that threat to life and limb is a real and present danger to serious journalists on the field.

Conflict in Interest

While the news media is interested in complete coverage and to highlight significant aspects of a conflict, such as the cause and course of engagement, in real time, the military sees the other way. In interest of the overall outcome of an anti-terrorist operation, such as the terrorist operation at The Taj in Mumbai on 26 November 2008, the news media's hunger for exclusiveness and comprehensive coverage stands at logger heads to the military's operational requirement of secrecy. Consequentially, the government slaps communication regulations or even a complete operational coverage blackout in the interests of security (Jeffrey, 2007).

Accessibility Issues

For the news media the ability to cover military operations of this type of warfare depends on factors such as accessibility. In other words, location of the conflict determines how it is covered. Access to insurgency and terrorist leaders, access to field commanders and their plans, even access to the field of operation – either deep in forests or in quarantined concrete jungles, access to the actual action is highly dependent of official authorization. This makes accessibility an issue for effective coverage. Today, there is no working relationship whatsoever and thus, the more isolated the area, the lesser the coverage; the North East region is a classic example of this.

In course of covering conflicts, journalists face impediments caused by the armed forces and the government such as limits to access and broadcast information (censorship). Often the news media has to depend solely on official sources and information. One reason for this state is due to the news media organization's incapability or unwillingness to dedicate expensive resources in gathering more information that are often complex to get, glean, comprehend and convert to usable data especially in the long run.

Armed forces control information that is shared with the news media and feed information as required. This is a core function of COIN operations. However, of late, journalists are becoming bold and are not tagging the official line despite straining their resources to gain complex information (Caparini, 2005).

Efficiency Issues

A couple of years ago, technology was a great challenge for the news media. The 1991 Gulf War and, at home, the Kargil War have proven that the news media organization has come to age technologically, bringing into our living rooms wars fought in jungles, deserts and the icy slopes of the world's greatest mountains. But what continues to plague the ranks of most news media organizations in the country is the serious lack of awareness of military affairs and a strategic awareness of the various conflicts in the country and their roots. It is truly unfortunate that even in the most militancy infested regions such as Kashmir and the Northeast, local news organizations do not have dedicated correspondents with deep knowledge in national security and defence affairs. One of the key reasons for this is the issue of resource bandwidth. Other reasons are rapid organizational requirements and even the educational system in the country could be stated to be cause for such lacunae. Journalists who are not up to speed on such turf will not be able to add value to their reportage and may even be easily manipulated by vested interests of the armed forces or non-state actors. It is often quoted to the extent of being clichéd that "knowledge is power", this is especially true in the profession of journalism as it is supposed to deep dive into issues far more acutely than the common man – its audience – and create awareness. The lack of overarching awareness of strategic issues is a major cause of news media's inefficiencies.

Today, there are notable Defence and Strategic Affairs specialists in the news media, those who had served in the uniform and now face the camera as well as those without first hand 'experiential' knowledge. These journalists offer expert opinion and comment on strategic issues. However, to cover long drawn engagements such as Naxalism, not every regional news media can afford an expert. Also, when an attack breaks out, often the 'first responder' journalist most often may not be a domain 'specialist'. These issues, to an extent, impediment professional coverage of strategic events such as Fourth Generation Warfare.

Maintaining Balance

A great challenge that faces any human being exposed to very exciting and severely emotional situations, such as war, is to remain deeply detached, unfettered by the violence and human suffering all around. This is especially true with journalists covering insurgency and terrorist acts and report in a totally unbiased tone.

While taking a sectarian stand is one issue (perhaps the most common of all challenges to the news media) another factor is the reporter's lack of deeper understanding of issues and his/her ephemeral association in covering the conflict. Often, due to resource issues, news media organizations substitute a dedicated resource with an 'assignee'. This has a direct impact on the balance necessary when covering a conflict.

The news media and any of its platforms – print, television, radio or new-age media – needs to take a hard call on how a healthy balance should be maintained when reporting fourth generation conflicts: neutral communication as against confrontational writing, providing insight into the cause of conflict over lack of knowledge, when reporting events on conflicts. It is imperative that the news media "have their fingers on the pulse of the people," because they have "a pious obligation not to jeopardize or harm the welfare of the society." (Reddy, 2002)

The Tone of Coverage

The news media is the population's window to affairs in their neighborhoods and around the globe. Thus, the language that the news media uses – or the pitch they make – makes an impact on the perception and response of the public. The news media tones and frames the attitudes and perceptions of the public on terrorist acts. Its coverage provides a multiplier effect of a terrorist act which furthers the impact of the original act (Shankar & Verma, 2011). Popular author and journalist George Orwell says, "…if thought corrupts language, language can also corrupt thought. A bad usage can spread by tradition and imitation, even among people who should know better. (Hussain, 2008)

The News Media is a 'Mass Communication' platform. Reading, listening and – most impactful – seeing are influenced by the tone of language, sound bytes and camera work. It is through these mediums that journalists define, explain and cover this type of war – be it covering terrorist incidents or military operations. The tone of coverage depends on multiple factors. (Lockyer, 2003)

1. The definition that state and national governments give and those by international forums. Often these are not in sync making it difficult for the news media to properly align the position of non-state actors.
2. The news media, especially regional media are bound to take sides – as witnessed in every Indian insurgency/militancy infested region – either willingly or by force. Often what they witness and write are highly influential on the local population. This makes fighting militancy in the region difficult for security forces as the local populace may be hostile. This is tantamount to negative publicity to the armed forces and a major tactical impediment to their operations. A recent case in point of extreme 'biased' coverage – even going to the extent of 'fabrication of news' is the example of The Hindu's journalist Rahul Pandita. Rahul Pandita is known to be an open sympathizer of Maoists. He has written many books on the subject of insurgency in India. His books on Maoism in the country, 'Hello, Bastar: The Untold Story of India's Maoist Movement' and 'The Absent State', are well received. However, his Opinion article in The Hindu 'The Central Reserve Police Mess' dated December 13, 2014, was written in a style that was overtly considered anti-CRPF. But the question of concern here is the allegations that specific incidents were doctored (Pandita, 2014).
3. The news media may also get influenced by related events such as scams and high-level power tussles especially between the government and armed forces officials. Highlighting negativity at the high level often tends to percolate down into the psyche of the population. This also shades people's perception on the outcomes of non-traditional conflicts.
4. Lack of in-depth knowledge of the conflict, of the culture, working and ethos of the military and terrorist organizations also causes tonal issues when covering a conflict. This makes ill-informed journalists adopt either the terrorist's definition of things or the military's which, in turn, generally becomes the normative to cover the conflict for the public (Lockyer, 2003). During a conference on the media's role in the hijack of the Indian airline IC-814, the then Minister of State for Information, Arun Jaitley, stated that the news media had treated the episode just as any other media event and as such had allowed itself to be influenced by the opinion of 'self-styled experts'. He explained that the 'experts' the news media interviewed included a 'cardiologist' who was portrayed as a psychiatrist and a 'bulb manufacturer' who was shown as a civil aviation expert. News channels got carried away by such experts who expounded on issues that knew nothing about.

5. The news media is a 'business entity'. At the end of it all, their 'news' has to sell – and sell well. It thus becomes an interesting proposition for the news media to cover terrorist incidents with a mix of entertainment. Covering military operations, such as the 26/11 incident arouse empathy and thus are great sources of 'human interest' stories. The news media goes great lengths to involve the soldiers' families, especially those of 'martyred' soldiers. The national news media have been alleged to have leveraged the Mumbai terror attacks (26/11) and the Kargil War to rake up circulation and TRP ratings. This has been presented in greater detail in the following section.
6. Speed of coverage and delivery of the news story leaves little room for judicious coverage. Dinesh Kumar states in his IDSA Occasional Paper 'Soldiers & Scribblers' that "Irrespective of the type of the medium, most journalists are often in a rush and many have neither time nor the inclination to do any research or cross-checking. This could result in misinformation and inaccurate stories being filed and printed" (Kumar, 2001). In fact, the rapid enhancement of supporting technologies that enable the news media to reach out wider, faster and more impactfully (such as through videos, sound bites and imagery) in a Fourth Generation Warfare scenario has also compounded military-news media relations. For example, live coverage on television of terrorist acts with parallel commentaries and analyses do not seem to augur well as it a debatable balance "between the public's right to know and national interest thereby creating a perennial conflict between media operators and military commanders" (Saxena, 1997).

BUSINESS ISSUES FOR THE NEWS MEDIA

Financial Issues in Covering Conflicts

Another challenge that journalists face is the business viability of covering a terrorist incident or protracted militancy. The news media is predominantly a 'for-profit' industry. This makes an impact on a number of questions that the news media must ask itself – is the conflict widespread in nature, is it newsworthy and does it have potential for 'human interest' stories with dramatic effect? How long can a particular news media organization fund its resources in a war zone? The cost of conflict coverage does not only include the reporter's salary, but covers the entire gamut of operations right from the reporter's boarding and lodging, cost of technology and communication, information cost (buying information from sources), expenses incurred when accessing terrorist groups/insurgents, and so on. Long haul coverage that includes frequent long-distance travel and campaigned coverage involves a high amount of budgetary commitment – a challenge that smaller regional news media organizations may be unable to commit to and hence wouldn't be able to get involved directly into covering larger, but distant, issues of strategic significance.

Exclusivity

This is what every news media organization targets. Exclusivity assures maximum attention of the reading, viewing, and listening public. It propels the news media organization ahead of competition and gets it recognition from peer groups and associations. However, due to the drive for exclusivity journalists and sometimes news media organizations may themselves fall and adhere to unethical practices, such as doctoring information – that is cooking up information based on loosely heard third-party accounts. The drive to be the first, see it first and to report it first, though key to every news media organization, occasionally tends to be a heady exercise.

Another reason for the news media's penchant for exclusivity stems from the need to retain novelty when covering protracted conflicts. What adds spice to an otherwise widely covered conflict is the need to create a distinct tone and this is done through 'specials' such as interviews and unique coverage. As a 'for-profit' organization, it is imperative for the news media to build and retain its audience's limited public attention span.

Covering the Perspective of Fourth Generation Actors

The symbiotic relationship between the news media and terrorists/insurgents could be a major impediment in the relations between the military and the news media because unlike the armed forces that are bridled by protocol, legacy regulations, state policies of 'no communication', terrorists are largely media friendly (not to be confused with personal affinity with journalists, especially from target states). Terrorists are able to attract and retain large spans of media attention and, thus, the people's attention by directly communicating first-hand information. Also, there have been many instances of local news media organizations and reporters in regions, such as Kashmir and the Northeast, who have open affiliations with insurgents. They tend to identify and empathize with the cause. Thus, insurgents are able to effectively leverage the news media.

The news media in such a situation is in midst of two conflicting antagonists. The news media does showcase lapses of the government, national security issues that crop up due to governmental oversight (or short sight) and crisis management or mismanagement through editorials and television panel discussions (Ray, 2009).

The issue for the military is that the reports of the news media tend to make a deep impact on the audience. This, in turn, has effect on the government's response and crisis management. It must also be understood that the news media may not be an instigator, but may definitely facilitate it. It may not affect the frequency of terrorist attacks, but surely plays a strong hand in the perception of the populace and the political outcome of an incident (Abraham, 2012).

CHALLENGES FACED BY THE ARMED FORCES

Colonial Mindset of the Organization and an 'Elitist' Perception

The Ministry of Defence is a legacy of the British Raj, which has been the source for poor history of media relations. Thus, since the days of the British Indian Army, it has secluded itself from media glare, being content with an occasional brief appearance.

Post-independence, the Indian armed forces have inherited this culture. Information on defence matters have come to be treated as too sacrosanct to be divulged. For example, after the 1962 debacle the Indian bureaucracy was averse in to publish Henderson Brooks Report. The media was denied access to these documents because they 'betray national security interests'. There was a feeling that questioning defence related issues and policies, questions one's patriotism. The consequence was that till recently there was hardly any public knowledge of defence-related topics such as budget, production, technology or any other important subjects. Even though the Indian media is relatively free and unfettered by governmental draconian media laws, very little discussions take place and that too only after the government has made its decision.

Today, this perspective is changing. Considering the nature of conflicts under the Fourth Generation, which includes the winning of hearts of the population as much as exterminating insurgents, the armed forces are making a slow, but deliberate change in their perspective and strategy to interact with the news media.

Ministry–Armed Forces Divide

In India the three services of the armed forces do not form part of the government establishment and thus have no say in an decision making concerning them. The Ministry of Defence, headed by a politically elected Minister of Defence, is run by civil servants who largely do not have any deep understanding of military affairs. Also, while the three service chiefs hold the rank of cabinet secretary, it is the lower ranked defence secretary who plays a more important role. This set up in the South

Block has been a source of discontent and strategic gap in communication both within the ministry and outside.

In counter insurgency operations, the Indian Army plays the larger role compared to the other services. The Army PRO at both the field and HQ face issues in communicating information as and when required, placing army units in unsavoury moments when interacting with the news media locally and at Delhi. This is a result of the notion of army leadership of the news media and the perception of the PRO within the services as a less desirable posting compared to others.

Limiting Government Protocols

The Indian military has been hidden from public scrutiny by a 'security syndrome' – anything about defence is under wraps. Operational security is often misinterpreted as national security due to the narrow understanding of concepts and perceptions of the incumbent government. Military commanders use orders such as the Special Army Order (SAO) 15/S/81 and the Army Rule (AR) 21 to prohibit any contacts with the media (Singh, 2006). In reality, these orders are not unyielding regulations, but indicative principles laying down guidelines for the foundation of interaction. However, over and above such orders, lies the government diktat that armed forces personnel should not communicate with the media on any matter – military or otherwise without the explicit authorization of the Central Government.

In context to the armed forces' engagement with the news media in the framework of Fourth Generation Warfare, the primary agenda is public relations - the consistent projection of positive image in an activity that has high potential to generate negative sentiments on the armed forces due to the nature of warfare. More often than not, the Indian Army invests much effort in damage control and image crisis management that are result of adverse reporting (Lt. Gen.Nanavatty, 2009).

Any communication is sanctioned only under the auspices of the Directorate of Public Relations (Ministry of Defence) who mostly are not uniformed officers. Staffing of knowledgeable Defence PROs is imperative to the seamless execution of communication in complex conflict environments. The person should have deep knowledge about military matters and comprehensive understanding of the conflict. However, that is sadly to be. Lieutenant General R K Nanavatty (Retd) in his article says, "They (Defence PROs) lack aptitude, communicating skills and motivation; and their preparation and training leaves a great deal of room for improvement. At least one sub-conventional conflict ridden area – the state of Tripura – is bereft of dedicated defence public relations officer cover."

Internal organizational lacunae, especially in communication official communication channels, create communication gaps that impediment coherent, effective, and consistent communication.

This was witnessed during the opening hours of the 26/11 attacks when the news media received conflicting reports on the field on the status of the anti-terrorist operation. Ashutosh Gupta, former Managing Editor - IBN 7, stated, "The government has to prepare a proper protocol for coverage. If they had been providing us with regular briefings, our coverage would have been more cohesive. Similarly, the government should have indicated how far they wanted the TV cameras to be positioned - 500 or 1,000 metres. We would have all complied with their requirements" (Sehgal, 2009).

Tactical and Operational Issues

The media can be a double edged weapon. While one side faces the enemy, the other could inadvertently face oneself. This becomes especially a point in Information Warfare such as Psychological Operations. This is because of a clash in interests between the news media and the military. For very obvious security and operational reasons, the military requires strict control of the flow of information. However, on the other hand the news media needs complete access to information. There are two basic challenges that the military faces due to uncontrolled media coverage of a military action – emotional impact of coverage and operational security.

The first challenge affects the opinion of the audience and thus, also impacts the morale of the troops engaged in operations. Perhaps the greatest example one can see in recent times in India was the 26/11 Mumbai terror attacks. This particular incident was unprecedented and hence a novel opportunity to cover for the news media. Barkha Dutt, Consulting Editor - NDTV, states, "We are not following any foreign model, but are in the process of evolving. The BBC has its own code, CNN its own. The present broadcaster code has not been able to arrive at a consensus and so I believe our self-regulation code needs to be fleshed out more. Our own broadcasters did not anticipate this kind of attack. Justice Verma is looking at how the code should be strengthened, with the government also providing inputs. We need to flesh out the code but that does not mean that the government should mandate what the code should be because then that will be an infringement on the media" (Sehgal, 2009).

Even in countries where military-news media relations are in an advanced stage, such as the United States, the coverage of conflict has been a source of discomfort at home. For example, during the stint of President Bill Clinton, military engagement in Somalia received negative publicity in the United States. The photos of a killed US Ranger being dragged through the streets of Mogadishu, Somalia in 1993 revived fears that were initially evoked in Vietnam. Thus the news media has to be extra careful in what it covers.

The second major challenge is in the actual execution of an operation and the threat that inadvertent media coverage may cause to tactical and strategic military planning of the current operation. Steven Livingston states that "the fact remains that some operations are extremely sensitive to media disclosure," therefore, "maintaining operational security during conventional war and tactical operations…is essential." Also the "…media have the technological capacity to hinder some types of operations simply by exposing them" (Livingston, 1977).

The perception within the military command is that when covering a military operation the news media may unknowingly reveal information that may compromise the military's tactical operational advantages. Margaret Belknap, in her article 'The CNN Effect: Strategic Enabler or Operational Risk?' states that while the news media is indeed a 'force multiplier' and thus an enabler for the military, it can also be a cause for a strategic risk (Belknap, 2002). Again, this was seen in the initial phase of coverage of the 26/11 terrorist attack and the Indian Army's operations at The Taj.

Many 'prospective terrorists' such as the recruits who are joining ISIS often get indoctrinated through the Internet. Many seemingly innocuous chat rooms offer 'real-time' counseling in the philosophies and policies of terrorist groups. Indian news media is replete with stories of how recruiters plan 'online baiting' to fish for emotionally charged candidates. While such news stories do provide information on terrorist modus operandi, it also inadvertently leaks security forces' and agencies' plans to combat menace on the virtual world. A recent article titled 'Netting Jihadis Online' (published on 9 January 2015) on India Today's website throws light on Indian security agencies' plans to net terrorists online. It reveals plans of an operation called 'Operation Chakravyuh' that details plans of how "officers create accounts with assumed identities of Jihadi groups and get on Facebook, Yahoo or other chat platforms to lure youths influenced by online propaganda". Such reports can jeopardize operational plans of the government / security forces / agencies. News media organizations should understand sensitivity and not report such 'sensitive' news and hamper efforts to combat terrorist/insurgency (Tripathi, 2015).

TOWARDS POSITIVE MILITARY–NEWS MEDIA RELATIONSHIP: RECOMMENDATIONS

Change in Mindset of the Military

The military establishment in India needs to approach the news media more as a partner in its conflict against insurgency and terrorism than as a painful duty in meeting the Democratic requirements of reporting to the citizens of the country.

Also, alienating the news media leaves open the arena of public opinion more in favour of anti-national forces. Thus, in terms of operational requirements and business outcomes, it is clear that the military needs the news media more than the media the military. This makes it obvious that 8the armed forces should engage with the news media with the idea of mutual benefit. This calls for a change in mindset. Thus, it becomes imperative to be more transparent for the armed forces in their relations with the news media of the country – overcoming the colonial mindset of secrecy – and in adopting newer techniques for communication.

In today's age of cutting edge IT, it is verily impossible to preserve secrets or disinformation for sustained periods of time. The Indian military authorities must adopt the view of former Army Chief, Gen BC Joshi, who recognized and propagated that the Indian news media was a force multiplier that had to be understood and befriended. His stance towards news media relationship over two decades ago helped thaw relations after the Bofors crisis. The relations did improve later during the period of his successor Gen SR Chaudhary and during the tenure of Gen VP Malik. However, there is much to be desired for at the Directorate of Public Relations, despite the fact that there are limitations in engagement as laid down in defence information policies (Press Council, 1994).

In context of Fourth Generation Warfare it is necessary to educate citizens – those who are affected by the conflict as well as those who are not directly impinged – on the facts of the conflict. This should be viewed as a binding duty of the military to ensure that the citizenry are with the establishment. Needless to say, the news media will have to be considered as an equal playing partner.

Align the Military to the Changing Media Scenario

The days of 'news reels' and propaganda flyers are long over. So are the days of government-owned news media channels. This is the age of the Free Press, Social Media, and decentralized publishing. It is important that the military authorities are cognizant of this emerging media scenario. Ajay K Rai, Research Fellow at IDSA, states,

There are basically three elements to it. First, there is no such thing as niche information. The compartments of information into command, public or niche group information are becoming increasingly blurred. Information campaigns must be targeted at all groups. Second, in a global village, information ought to be both a principle of war and of conflict resolution. And with more information empowering the individual, power now vests with the people. Third, the new environment is engendering a new universal morality, and by implication, a new media morality which does not respect old social and professional taboos and national borders like their predecessors" (Rai, 2000).

However, Military commanders, in general continue to feel that the best way to interact with news media personnel is by conducting it through well-orchestrated and choreographed visits that include high-class hospitality, followed by handouts of what they want to convey least realizing that journalists crave for interactive sessions instead of tutored information.

Firstly, the military has to convince itself on news media-related benefits and challenges of Fourth Generation Warfare. Presently the concept and analysis thereon is largely limited on paper and academically. This largely based on operational scenario existent today. This was very categorically explained by Col. Danvir Singh (personal interview, 2016),

It would be fair to say that the Indian Army is largely infantry and is technologically backward by any global standards. They largely operate in Counter Insurgency and Line of Control / Line of Actual Control environment. Predominantly, conventional operations are based on attrition (Second Generation) rather than maneuver (Third Generation). The change of the mind set in dealing with Fourth Generation is still farfetched. As a veteran, I would rather say our military is still vintage and in the Second Generation mindset, with some capability to conduct Third Generation operations. The realisation of Fourth Generation, in which a state loses its monopoly over war, is yet to don upon us.

Thus, the news media will undoubtedly play a major role as a force multiplier in Fourth Generation Warfare, the day the military realizes that it is not at a dominant position despite all its fire power and technology. In future, Fourth Generation Warfare will force changes and there will be a paradigm shift in strategy towards engaging the news media. Internet enabled live television streaming, social media platforms and others - all on a smart phone - has revolutionized the ways of information sharing and media reporting. These have empowered every individual to seek information and carry out own analysis. It would be prudent to say that the military mind set is still fixated at times of the First Generation while the media is already playing at the levels of the Fourth Generation. Under no circumstance the media can be managed. Only solution lies in collaboration and joint-man-ship while strategizing a counterstrategy to the enemy's Fourth Generation designs.

Improve Quality of Communication

As stated earlier in the thesis, there are separate Public Relations Officers (PROs) for each of the services at the ranks of Lt. Colonel, Commander and Wing Commander. The PRO is the key link between the News Media, the Services Chiefs and their Principal Staff Officers. However, there is an issue in the existing setup. Positions such as PROs are often made on an ad hoc basis and the officers selected for these vital positions, more often than not, may not have an in-depth operational understanding of the news media and the unstated business drivers of such organizations. Also, most officers deputed as PROs may not have any training or flair for public relations. These deputations are viewed as dry and valueless in the career of the officers. This consequently leads to low quality public relations and communication output.

Another factor that needs immediate attention of the DPR is the training offered to deputed officers of the three services on public relations. While it was an established practice many years ago to familiarize officers on the intricacies of public and media relations, sadly this practice does not seem to be in vogue. It is essential to revive training in such critical matters – especially in organizations such as the Indian Institute of Mass Communication and offer certification that are of value in the career of deputed officers.

There have been thoughts on improving communication and in this regard, in 1996, the Army Liaison Cell was established. This body, headed by a Brigadier at the Army HQ, New Delhi, oversees public relations with respect to operations. This body is directly placed under the Vice Chief of Army Staff. This gives it greater admittance to information silos that are otherwise out of purview of the DPR. *This cell, due to its position, would be better placed to serve the news media.*

Devolution of News Distribution

The armed forces are widely spread across the length and breadth of the country and across its overseas assets as well. However, interaction with the news media at the regional level is almost non-existent. Any local public relation activity requires clearance at the highest level. Today, it is highly critical that information dissemination be decentralized to make any propaganda effective. While this is especially true for the news media – to have regional reach so as to seem to cater to the ‘local’ needs of the population, it is also applicable to the armed forces when interacting with the local new media. This requirement becomes especially critical when engaged in fighting insurgents or when countering terrorist incidents. At such times local authentic and authorized news sources become imperative. It makes relationship building easier and more effective if an official spokesman is designated at the levels of command, corps, division and independent brigades. Introduced to the local news media personnel, this officer will be the single-source of truth and will be a catalyst to build and improve military–news media interaction.

Sensitizing the News Media on Military Affairs

For any relationship to be successful, it has to be a two-sided affair. The same applies to military–news media relations. While the military has to be more decentralized in its outreach and must take into confidence the news media, the latter too should be sensitive to the unique culture, needs and behavior of the military.

Aspiring journalists should be provided training on national security issues including the security apparatus, force structures, organizational structure, military psychology and everything that pertains to the day-to-day tactical operations of the armed forces, not to mention strategic issues. Professional mass communication courses at the undergraduate and master's levels should cover the above mentioned topics. Faculty should also include military officers – serving or retired – to provide first-hand inputs on military matters. In fact, visits to military command centers, field installations, training centers and forward posts would help young journalist trainees to sense the life, issues and concerns of military personnel and thus, sensitize and tone the coverage of military matters.

When covering operations, the news media should be sensitive of the activity and the potential impact of their coverage of the event. Thus, they should have standards of conduct and coverage that comprise of adequate attention to serious efforts taken by the authorities and the armed forces to resolve conflicts, without obstructing or even worse, inadvertently aiding terrorists thus compromising the effort of the armed forces in dealing with an issue as was initially seen in the coverage of the Mumbai terrorist attacks in 2008. In fact, a council should be set up comprising of both military personnel and senior journalists to set standards and guidelines when covering events live from the front (van Dijk, 1992). The India Today article (Netting Jihadis Online) on 'Operation Chakravyuh' also drives home this point (Tripathi, 2015).

Need for More Specialists

Sports, business, finance and investments, science & technology… all these domains require specialization – an in-depth study of these subjects and avid interest to do justice when writing about them for the public. News media business owners and the management should enable journalists within their respective organizations to focus on military affairs as a specialist domain (beat).

The government and the Indian armed forces can allow journalists to attend select courses at the Staff College or the National Defence College.

A Commitment to Ethics: A Deeper Understanding of Responsibilities

The relations between the military and the news media takes a different tone and much more significant meaning when studied in context of Fourth Generation Warfare such as insurgency and terrorism. This is because the local populace is a direct party to the conflict and plays a major role in the course and outcome in such conflict. In such a situation it is important for the news media to understand that it plays the quintessential role of a catalyst in forming public opinion that influences the decisions of armed forces in the conduct of operations. The news media can assist in generating new idea and approaches to solutions by involving influencers and thought leaders (Chakravarti, 2009).

The best security measure against spiraling violence and human rights violations against civilians is in raising public awareness – a role that the news media has to execute effectively and with great care. This is easy to state, but in the heat of spiraling insurgent violence, aberrations by members of armed forces and misunderstanding of intentions by all conflicting and vested parties may fog ground realities. This creates opportunities for the news media to rush after 'exclusives' in the process confounding truth. When covering a conflict, additional information provided by the news media is always lapped up by the ever news hungry population. This gives opportunity for certain unscrupulous elements in the industry to 'cook up' stories – a very unethical and dangerous thing to do. The case of Rahul Pandita is a case in point. On the other hand, to 'go the extra mile' in getting information, news media personnel establish contacts with terrorist or insurgent groups. Publishing 'exclusive' information from insurgents and terrorists may actually be a ruse by the very same elements in spreading propaganda and even disinformation. This will cause incalculable damage in the victim society by creating undesirable public opinion.

Keeping Check on the Tone of Coverage

News has to sell. That is the fundamental driver of revenues for a news media organization. The more a particular news item is watched or read, the higher is its rating and viewership. The higher the rating/viewership, the more it attracts advertisers. The more the advertisements, the more profit they earn.

Zealous reporters and editors often tend to raise the tone of coverage, in the consequence creating readership excitement to the level of even creating frenzy. This is absolutely dangerous, counterproductive to coverage and absolutely against the ethics of journalism. The consequences can lead to unprecedented levels of violence – thus defeating the purpose and efforts of the armed forces. The news media should be wary of such impulses amongst its ranks. To ensure this, robust education in the ethics of the profession and complete sensitivity towards the issue in hand is sine qua non.

New Employment Techniques: Embedded Units

During the US invasion of Iraq over a decade ago (2003), members of the national and international news media organizations were 'embedded' with various units of the invading Coalition forces. This idea of embedding journalists with the military machinery was born from the public relations industry. It provided news media organizations a detailed and fascinating view of the war for their readers and audience as never seen before – riding on tanks, taking cover behind protective soldiers and covering road mine explosions – raw footages almost real time from the theater of operations. It has been said that the popularity of such coverage is akin to popular sport back home.

Back home, embedding journalists with fighting units during phases of a counter insurgency operation allows journalists to get closer to the action and – more importantly – get first-hand information of the fighting. Also, from the military's perspective, it enables to control information flow to the news media. While this may limit the freedom of the press, it helps build a bond between the 'lens man' and the 'gun man' – a bond that is built on sharing the hardships of war. Dr Tehmina Mitha states, "Engaging media people to accompany the military during operations will help provide an insight and develop a bond between the both. One must give a policy defining principles of combat coverage while giving full access to media persons, and appraisal of level of success and role of media during an operation ought to be provided for future course to be taken" (Dr Mitha, 2011).

Increased Use of New Age Media

Since the turn of the century, especially over the past decade, the phenomenon of Social Media has been increasingly attracting the attention of the public. Facebook, Youtube, Twitter, and various blogging sites – the list is actually numerous. The singular advantage of this new platform is that content creation is not limited in the hands of a limited few – consumers may generate influential content as much as parties with vested interest (the armed forces and insurgent/terrorist groups). But what makes it truly potent is that publication on these platforms are simple (can be done by almost anybody), raw and direct in impact. The military engagement between the Israeli Defence Forces and Palestinian forces in Gaza in early 2014 was captured and broadcasted on Youtube in almost real time creating world-wide ripples on the bloodiness and horrors of unscathed rocket attacks on civilian population.

Social Media platforms may not have a voice of 'authority' as do established news media organizations, but their free and easy-to-use and publish features often make them the choice of communication by Fourth Generation actors. The news media and the armed forces would do well if they leverage these platforms with equal élan as do Fourth Generation actors.

Finally, Its All Based on Cooperative Approach

The Indian armed forces and the news media are mutually dependent. During the days of the British Raj, it was beneficial to keep both the bodies away from each other as the Indian military was the iron arm of British rule. The local news media was patriotic questioning the legality of British presence in the country and raking up issues with administration and day-to-day life. Today, the picture is entirely different, but the mindset still remains.

Policies formed in those bygone days still continue to discipline relations. While the military is opening its minds today, a lot more needs to be done. Members of both the organizations should be sensitized about the professional requirements of the other. Mutual understanding in terms of personal and institutional relations needs to be increased.

Interactivity should be increased especially in the form of forums, workshops, seminars and conferences on how to further military-news media relations and thus derive mutual benefits. The Ministries of Information and Defence need to look deeper and enable stronger relationships.

CONCLUSION

Fourth Generation Warfare activities, such as counter insurgency and anti-terrorism operations, by nature hinge on the dominance (control) of information than in merely physically exterminating militants. It is a battle of both hearts and minds. This is also a responsibility of the armed forces, though it may not be fully independently capable of this. Thus, it needs the support of platforms such as the news media and social media to get its message across to the populace as well as to the adversary. In India, since its Independence, the Indian armed forces and the news media have had many opportunities – especially since the late 1990s – to develop a strategic relationship keeping in view growing instances of terrorist incidents. However, interaction was carried out only on ad hoc basis.

In the final analysis, it must be understood that the armed forces and the news media, though varying by nature, are not entirely mutually exclusive. They need to go beyond established restraining policies and take proactive steps to build a robust relationship that serves their needs. Both the institutions have very important roles to play in safeguarding and building the national fabric. Their mutual cooperation will definitely help take the country a safer and stronger place.

The media on its part should play a more expansive role. Its power to build and guide public opinion is sometimes more powerful than all the weaponry systems of the armed forces. It is advantageous for the news media – even from a business perspective – if it does not indulge in sensationalism and jingoism – as in the long run, this would dilute the brand and values that the news media organization has stood for.

Thus, the key to maintaining a robust working relationship – if not partnership – lies in compromising of a few non-imperative policies and grievances. It is but natural that natural operation-derived and cultural issues will continue to exist between the armed forces controlled by the Ministry of Defence and the Indian News Media. It will never be possible to bring a complete understanding between these two dissimilar entities. However appreciation, of each other's professions, challenges, and the immense value that they bring to the nation and its citizens will help bridge the cultural divide.

Both the organizations must learn to cooperate to protect and uphold truth. The news media must respect the armed forces' reason for existence and operational realities. Likewise, the Indian armed forces must learn to embrace the news media as a strategic enabler.

The Press Council of India states, "The media has an adversarial role to the extent that it questions authority, all authority to look at the other side. This must be understood and a relationship of creative tension accepted as a democratic necessity. For the rest, they (the military and the media) are partners in trying to build a better society, a stronger nation" (Rai, 2000).

REFERENCES

Belknap, M. (2002). The CNN Effect: Strategic Enabler or Operational Risk? *Parameters*, 100–114.

Caparini, M. (2005). *Media and the Security Sector: Oversight and Accountability*. Retrieved from www.se2.dcaf.ch

Chakravarti, R. (2009). *Media Coverage of Terrorism and Methods of Diffusion*. New Delhi: MD Publications.

Chaudhury, R. (2011). Big trouble in the left's last post. *Tehelka Magazine*. Retrieved from http://www.tehelka.com/2011/07/big-trouble-in-the-lefts-last-post/

Dr Mitha, T. (2011). *Guidelines to Media-Military relations*. Retrieved from: www.pkarticleshub.com/2011/09/09/guidelines-to-media-military-relations/

Dunne, T. (2012). Media and National Security. KW Publishers Pvt Ltd & Centre for Air Power Studies.

Gupta, A. (2010). South Asia in India's National Security Strategy. *Proceedings of the IDSA International Workshop on National Security Strategy*, 6.

Hayes, B. (2012). *The other Burma? Conflict, counter-insurgency and human rights in Northeast India, Transnational Institute*. Amsterdam, The Netherlands: TNI. Retrieved from https://www.tni.org/files/download/theotherburma-webspreads.pdf

Hussain, N. (2008). The Role of Media in National Security: A Case Study of 1998 Nuclear Explosions by Pakistan. SASSI Research Report, 13(20), 5.

Jeffrey, R. I. (2007). Deconstructing the Terrorism-News Media Relationship, Crime Media Culture. *Sge Publication, USA*, *3*(2), 218.

Kumar, D. (2001). *Soldiers and Scribblers – Media in Information Warfare: A Case Study of India*. Occasional Paper, Institute of Defence Studies and Analyses.

Lind, S. (2004). Article. *Military Review*, *84*(5), 13.

Livingston, S. (1977). *Clarifying the CNN Effect: An Examination of Media Effects According to Type of Military Intervention*. Research Paper R-18. The Joan Shorenstein Center, Harvard University.

Lockyer, A. (2003). The Relationship between the Media and Terrorism. Strategic and Defence Studies Center.

Nanavatty, R. K. (2009). Army-Media Relations in Sub-conventional Conflict. *Centre for Land Warfare Studies Journal*, 136. Retrieved from: http://www.claws.in/images/journals_doc/1400825447R%20K%20Nanavatty%20CJ%20SSummer%202009.pdf

Pandita, R. (2014). *The Central Reserve Police Mess*. Retrieved from http://www.thehindu.com/opinion/op-ed/the-central-reserve-police-mess/article6686784.ece

Press Council. (1994). *Pen and Sword - Towards More Openness*. Retrieved from: http://presscouncil.nic.in/OldWebsite/history.htm

Press Council of India. (n.d.). *Military-Media Interface: Changing Paradigms New Challenges*. IDSA. Retrieved from: http://www.idsa-india.org/an-aug-400.html

Rai, A. K. (2000). *Military-Media Interface: Changing Paradigms New Challenges*. IDSA. Retrieved from: http://www.idsa-india.org/an-aug-400.html

Ray, G. N. (2009). *Terrorism-New Challenges and Media*. Press Academy of Andhra Pradesh.

Reddy, K.J. (2002). *Present Turmoil Godhra and After: Role of Media*. Inaugural function of Indian First Foundation.

Report of UN Special Rapporteur on Extrajudicial Execution to the UN Human Rights Council A/HRC/4/20/Add.1 (Para. 18), Asian Centre for Human Rights. (2010). India Human Rights Report 2009.

Saxena, S. (1997). *Defence Journalism in India*. New Delhi: Manas Publication.

Sehgal, R. (2009). Terror on TV, or by TV? *InfoChange News & Features*. Retrieved from: http://infochangeindia.org/agenda/reporting-conflict/terror-on-tv-or-by-tv.html

Shankar, A., & Verma, J. P. (2002). Role of Media in War and Terrorism. New Delhi: Sunrise Publications.

Toffler, A., & Toffler, H. (2006). *War and Anti-War*. New Delhi: Natraj Publishers.

Tripathi, R. (2015). Netting Jihadis Online. *India Today*. Retrieved from: http://indiatoday.intoday.in/story/jihadi-group-intelligence-agencies-islamic-state-chakravyuh/1/412233.html van Dijk, T. A. (1992). *Power and the News Media. In Program of Discourse Studies* (p. 9). University of Amsterdam.

Vohra, N.N. (2008). National Governance and Internal Security. *Journal of Defence Studies, 2*(1), 7.

Wilson, G.I., Sullivan, P., & Kempfer. (2003). *4GW: Tactics of the Weak Confound the Strong*. Retrieved from www.Military.com

Chapter 2
Indian Approaches to E-Diplomacy:
An Overview

Sree Krishna Bharadwaj Hotur
National Law School of India University (NLSIU), India

ABSTRACT

Diplomacy refers to the professional activity or skills that are used to manage and strengthen the relations on international or global level. E-diplomacy can be termed as the new mode of conducting diplomacy acts with the help of internet and information and communication technologies (ICTs). In general, we often say that diplomacy is maintained of relations through communication. It is the art of conducting negotiations, forming alliances, discussing treaties, and reaching agreements. This can be done with proper communication which helps maintain a social image. Moreover, communication in diplomacy is that tactful move that ensures that the diplomat smoothly handles the relations with the other parties and makes them do what is needed without harming the interests and profits of either of two or more parties. This ensures peace and eliminates the feeling of ill-will. The chapter sheds light on the emergence of e-diplomacy in India, its advantages, use, and the future uses as well.

DOI: 10.4018/978-1-5225-3859-2.ch002

INTRODUCTION

Former French President and General Charles de Gaulle (1890 – 1970) had said, "Diplomacy is the art of letting someone have it, your way." India is country that is globalizing and growing at a very fast pace. With the emergence of various new ideas and technologies, the government is now taking measures to strengthen the country's position at world level. One of the major and all time important resource to achieve this is diplomacy. As mentioned, emergence of new technologies has influenced the government to enter into e- diplomacy. E- diplomacy is a more convenient form of maintaining a healthy relation both within the country and at world level. Its use would help in making the country more versatile and hence more globally renowned and recognized (Elassar, 2014).

EVOLUTION OF DIGITAL DIPLOMACY

Our country is recently ranked among the top 10 nations in terms of its digital or e- diplomacy. The contribution of India towards digital diplomacy is commendable and worth a praise. The Diplomacy Live, a global research, advocacy, consulting and training platform has mentioned the country's name in the list based on the diplomacy performance of India over the past years. Apart from India, Mexico is the only developing country who made it in the list. India has been ranked number 7 according to Diplomacy Live. This surely is a fantastic start for the country.

What is a surprise here that our country doesn't maintain a high budget for public diplomacy. The official Facebook page of Ministry of External Affairs has more than 1.2 million followers. This excludes its companion page 'Indian Diplomacy' which itself has around 850,000 followers. On Twitter, the combined presence of Ministry of External Affairs Official Spokesperson's account plus the Public Diplomacy account has crossed 1.2million followers. There around 40,000 subscribers of Ministry of External Affairs on YouTube. Ministry of External Affairs has an official Instagram, G+, Soundcloud account/page. All these various social media page or account of Ministry of External Affairs has a following that ranges between 4 million to 20 million and is increasing day by day. The unique Mobile App of Ministry of External Affairs has bagged more than 150,000 downloads on both Android and IOS platforms. Encouraged by the success, the App is now being launched with updated technologies. One of the officials of Ministry of External Affairs said, "Online presence plays a critical role in many crisis situations and was instrumental during recent evacuation effort from Yemen, Libya and during the earthquake in Nepal."

THE APPROACHES TOWARDS DIGITAL DIPLOMACY

Digital Diplomacy is new in our country. It's commendable that the government and the society had adapted and utilized this boon of technology in a good sense. As already acknowledged, India has ranked seventh among various countries on the platform of digital diplomacy. But what is the approach of the government towards E- Diplomacy? How the BJP government look at the idea of using social media for maintaining its foreign relations. Below are 25 points which will give a clear picture of the mindset and approach of India towards Digital or E- Diplomacy (Kurbalija, 2016).

Organisation and Management

Sushma Swaraj, the honorable Minster of India's External Affairs and Foreign Relations is a powerful force and support behind the emergence of digital diplomacy in the country. Many a times, she has been witnessed answering queries and questions on social media by herself and taking prompt actions. Leaderships like her are a reason behind India to rank 7TH in the list of global digital diplomacy countries. The government holds a forward-looking vision towards electronic diplomacy. As an essential element, some basic guidelines must be implied so that the act of diplomacy via internet does not end up in mess. Surely, the government is working on implementing the basic guidelines for its diplomats.

One positive attitude which the country has maintained that it has not refined the diplomacy via internet to social media and public diplomacy only. India has an approach which covers public diplomacy with social media activities of presidents or ministers and hence is sometimes denoted as 'twiplomacy'. But this is not the end; the government has used digital diplomacy as a tool in various diplomatic negotiations, policy initiatives, management actions etc. For example, Ministry of External Affairs took the help of social media during the crisis of Libya and Iraq. Social media was used as a mode of communications with the two countries and the result was that the matter was very well managed. Moreover, the BJP government has made a smart move. The basic tradition followed in our country was 'higher the budget, higher the result.' But the current central government has done smart work. Knowing that their barriers of diplomacy via internet cannot be solved by high budget, they kept the expenditure to modest level. Instead, they used their mind. Sites like Wikipedia are used by the Ministry of External Affairs to action out their planned diplomacy. Wikipedia is regarded to be cheap and inexpensive and easy to work on. It becomes simple and handy for diplomats to shape and transform their ideas into words on Wikipedia which is easy and widely approachable by the public.

It's not that the government is only stuck with Wikipedia. Its smart work doesn't end here. The government has opted for some of the best and highly approachable sites and methods that made them connected with the public. We can find Ministry of External Affairs Facebook fan page, YouTube channel, Twitter and Instagram accounts and some very well working out blogs. Obviously, the country is new in the modern digital diplomacy stuff so the government learned and adapted from other nations who are very well aware about diplomacy via internet. This approach of learning that the government showed is progressive in itself. As a developing country, India took a positive foot ahead in this field. The government is encouraged to interact with a bigger mass in general. They are constantly making their digital availability highlighted which encourages the public to be a part of this globalizing new India. For this work, young diplomats are hired. This is because they are much more versatile and flexible on World Wide Web as they belong to the generation that is very much active on social media. Secondly, they act as a youth icon and the majority of the population in India falls under the youth and teenage category.

Security

Cyber world is regarded as unsafe and open. It is a firm belief that once a thing gets on the cyber platform, it's not 100% safe and secure. Keeping in mind the disadvantages this boon to human race brings, the government is taking all necessary steps. The government has taken the initiative to train their cyber workers in the best possible manner. The staff of the cyber cells is trained at an advance level and digital hygiene and smart cyber using is being ensured. The government is highly motivated towards the idea of digital diplomacy and hence is not demotivated and morally broken down by the trolls and failures they sometimes had to encounter on this non-real world. The diplomats are taking the act of digital diplomacy quite seriously and are devoting proper time towards it. They are keeping themselves aware and updated. New and useful technologies are utilized so as to maximize the output from the internet and to enhance the effectiveness of digital diplomacy.

Content

Content always matters. When you are saying something through articles, blogs and site, then you miss the chance to use of your tone and facial expressions which are vital in making your ideas clear. On sites and blogs you cannot use your voice or facial gestures. Your only tool is the words that you type. So, the content that you choose to show to the world and decide to use as a tool to express your thoughts must be very well jotted down and cleverly crafted. The content is the only weapon on such platforms. The content must be clear, friendly, just and away from controversies. It should be simple but effective. What a diplomat tweets on twitter, writes on a blog and comments on an instagram picture is what is going to tell the general public about the ideology of the government and the kind of work they are doing. Effective content not only highlights the ultimate objective of the message but also attracts a large mass. Another key factor of a great content is to keep in mind the audience you are about to interact. The content at different sites should vary according to the mass that use it. While LinkedIn is used by professionals, the content there posted should be formal, high in vocabulary and straightforward. Similarly, Facebook and Instagram are mostly used by youth and teens so to interact with them the content should be a much more audience friendly with an informal outlook. Much like a general conversation.

The government has done another positive work by separating its official and informal communication channels. This avoids miscommunication and confusion to a great extend. The Ministry of External Affairs has a separate platform for official diplomatic communication and an informal communication platform to perform public diplomacy. The official page of the Ministry of External Affairs is @MEAIndia. It is the platform where the official announcements and final decisions are declared. For having a discussion with people and to connect to them at a more personal and grounded level, @IndianDiplomacy is the tool of the Ministry of External Affairs.

Knowledge

The Indian diplomats are working with the idea of learning. They are not of the viewpoint that their current information and skills are enough for the process of digital diplomacy. They indeed believe that they should learn and gain more knowledge from different resources and even from other countries. They are learning new ways of expressing themselves and making themselves much more flexible with writing as diplomats are now more or less writers as they have entered into digital diplomacy. Now why I said writers? It's because digital diplomacy revolves around social media and social media is about writing. It is nothing but expressing through words. No denial of the fact that diplomacy is a broader topic. It deals with UN meetings, discussions, arguments, settlements but then what it ends up to? Signing of treaties and agreements that are written on paper. A diplomat is believed to be able to express the interest of the party he/she represents in a concise and informative manner through mostly written content. Thought the approach of diplomacy has changed to a digital one, but the work here also is the same for our dear diplomats. Here also they have to write and tweet and comment in a courtly and sophisticated manner (Jelena, 2010).

Our Indian diplomats are very successful in these fields. One outstanding example is Ambassador Vikas Swarup, the current spokesperson of the Ministry of External Affairs and a very concise digital diplomat as well. His novel 'Q&A' was transformed into a movie which was the talk of the 2005 Oscar Awards. Didn't get it? Well, it's 'Slumdog Millionaire'.

Support

India is getting a huge support from its public and diplomats over the idea of spreading digital diplomacy. The government is keen and strict is picking up its digital diplomats. Candidates are screened based on the UK guidelines of an ideal e- diplomat. But this is where it doesn't end. The Ministry of External Affairs is taking measures to train their digital diplomats in the best possible manner so that they have the knowledge as what to write? When to write? How to write?

A very good step taken by the Ministry here is to bridge the gap between the senior digital diplomats and junior digital diplomats. The senior diplomats are experienced people with a lot of knowledge and an understanding that how the words are used so as to put forward some effective message without any controversial statements. On the other hand, the junior diplomats belong from the era where the virtual world is much more active and alive than the real world. They are very well aware about the pros and corns of diplomacy through web. Using social media as medium of public diplomacy needs a much more social and casual approach. This is something junior digital diplomats are expert in. they know the potential audience at different networking sites and are aware what dynamics will suit well in delivering a meaningful message. As the numbers of social diplomats are reduced by the government, the process has become much more convenient and energized.

The job doesn't end here. Thought these digital diplomats are knowledgeable and help each other learn the different tactics of e- diplomacy but then to they require training so that web world can become a much stronger weapon for the government. The Ministry of External Affairs has taken a number of measures which would increase the skills of social diplomats and would make them flexible with new technologies.

The government is moving forward towards progress, modernization and globalization. The positive and learning approach of the government towards digital diplomacy is worth praise. Digital diplomacy is a revolution and a need of time. Digitalization is strengthening its roots in international diplomacy and public diplomacy is making the work for the government much more fast and convenient. If the government and its leaders maintain the same level of energy and zeal, soon India will rank above 7th position on the Diplomacy Live list (The Pioneer, 2016).

Criticisms

There are many drawbacks of the E-Diplomacy in India. As Elizabeth Hanson notes, "Public diplomacy should emphasize India's diversity, secular orientation, and vibrant democracy, she continued, while negative information and stereotypes must be countered effectively. The work of projecting a positive image overlaps with cultural diplomacy, as well as the efforts of business and industry to promote brand India. India's efforts to promote socio-economic development abroad should be made more visible."

Another major criticism is that the Government uses the diplomacy for its own purposes. Mukhopdhyay notes, "Prime Minister Modi sees the media as an "adversary and this establishes that he does not appreciate scrutiny of his actions." (Heng, 2016) Thus questions of transparency and competency in political level are another set of drawbacks faced by the e-diplomacy stand taken by the Government.

SOLUTIONS AND RECOMMENDATIONS

A major policy change is required to solve the abovementioned issues. India's public image can be boosted to much greater length with the use of e-diplomacy. With the current problems at international borders, e-diplomacy can be challenging but a new approach is necessary for the country. The Department of External Affairs can be strengthened and be made to promote India at global level.

FUTURE RESEARCH DIRECTIONS

With the present social media, there is always a challenge what comes next or what should be the future step. Role of youngsters and their involvement in international relations can be considered as a further step in this research. Also, impact of the citizen journalism on diplomacy can be another area for exploration.

CONCLUSION

India is a friendly country. The country doesn't want war or tension. The country supports peace and security of people wherever they go. India has a progressive and friendly attitude in the form of Prime Minister Narendra Modi. The basic reason the government is planning out various diplomacy acts with or without the involvement of digitalization is to grow and stand strong at the global platform. This is modern era. Its 21st century. India is now emerging as a new claimant of a place on world platform. India is now taking the help of internet and social media for its various diplomacy acts. Be it its International Diplomacy or Public Diplomacy, India is seen using web and social media as its powerful weapons. India first entered into the world of digital diplomacy properly in the year 2010. It was when the Ministry of External Affairs made its twitter account and tweeted about its policy and working. Soon after that we found Ministry of External Affairs on Facebook, Instagram, Snapchat, G+, Souncloud, YouTube and what not. Leaderships like Prime Minister Narendra Modi, Sushma Swaraj, Minster of External Affairs etc. used twitter and other social networking sites to interact with the public and to strengthen their bond with them. This is what name of digital public diplomacy. Digitalization and diplomacy via internet has helped India take quick actions during Nepal Earthquake, Libya and Yemen case etc. Moreover, digitalization and entering of the government into diplomacy through web has created a more direct and strong communication chain between the government and the people. People can now tweet the leaders of the central government on twitter and give their views or ask for help. Various apps and digital platforms launched by the Modi government are working as a boon for society. One thing that is to be liked of the government is that they focused both Public Diplomacy and International Diplomacy through digitalization. The work of the government is good and worth to mention and praise. If the government and the Ministry of External Affairs continue to work at such a fast pace, that day is not far when the 'Digital India' theme of PM Modi will become a reality and that India will become a power diplomat country on global platform through its effective digital diplomacy acts and schemes.

REFERENCES

Elassar, N. (2014). *What is Diplomacy?* Retrieved from http://bestdelegate.com/what-is-diplomacy/

Heng, S. M. L. (2016). *Diplomacy and Image-Building: India Rides on Its Soft Power.* Retrieved from http://www.orfonline.org/research/diplomacy-and-image-building/

Jelena. (2010, January 16). *What is e-diplomacy anyway?* Retrieved from https://www.diplomacy.edu/blog/what-e-diplomacy-anyway

Kurbalija, J. (2016, November 7). *25 points for digital diplomacy.* Retrieved from https://www.huffingtonpost.com/entry/25-points-for-digital-diplomacy_us_581c78bae4b0334571e099ec

The Pioneer. (2016). *Digital Diplomacy: India Ranked Seventh by Diplomacy.* Retrieved from http://www.dailypioneer.com/nation/digital-diplomacy-india-ranked-seventh-by-diplomacy-live.html

Chapter 3
New Media and Its Role in Stabilizing Nepal:
A Geopolitical Context

Umesh K. Bhattarai
Independent Researcher, Nepal

ABSTRACT

Most scholars advocate that the people are seeking identity, and for this purpose, they are reinventing ethnicity to establish their ideology. So, they need opponents and create enmities. Among the civilizations, the sectorial powers that represent common ideology within the geography provoke extremism, and through religious and cultural pundits, the extremists are radicalized to disturb the entire world through terrorism.

DOI: 10.4018/978-1-5225-3859-2.ch003

Modern technology is revolutionizing how people receive information. Satellite technology is doing to television what the short-wave did to radio. The trans-national media is helping to shape public opinion and is influencing the decision making of public, business and military leaders in an unprecedented fashion. - Edmund Ghareeb

INTRODUCTION

In recent years, the innovation of social media like Facebook, Twitter, LinkedIn and many more other channels like YouTube, Google, Wikipedia and blog have changed our life styles and capacity to communicate each other. Now we can make our own websites and advertise in the cyber world where anybody can reach anytime and from anyplace. The limited sharing of information just a decade ago has now enabled us to communicate a large segment of society with minimum effort and less amount of expenditure. We can just recall the time of Gulf war, as what Edmund Ghareeb[1], during 1998-99 when Americans and British attacked Iraq, Saddam Husayn opted two influential but relatively new measures to counter them as pan-Arab satellite television networks—the Qatar based al-Jazeera and the London based Arab News Networks—to broadcast messages to the outside world. The other televisions used the footage as a part of al-Jazeera's feed from Bagdad to their audience.

Accordingly, the situation in Nepal during Maoist rebellion was the same up to 2000 when most of the televisions were not satellite connected and internet was limited among the elites in Kathmandu. The situation has dramatically changed after the evolution of social media where people not only share but also post their views and make messages. In one side it has made us vibrant but other side we are becoming more arrogant to each other's. In absence of sufficient laws and bylaws, and low will power to implement existing laws have deteriorated social tolerance against corruption, intimidation and malpractices. New media has empowered people in terms of transparency- at the other it has encouraged youths to become more violent.

At present, the popular predictions, assumptions, assertions are failing. Sometimes, we tend to forget that all the extremists are radicalized but not all the radicals are extremists. Why the society is becoming more radical? It is a matter of empirical research. But now, we will talk about information technology that has enabled us to reach to mass easily but the way we make messages that are not only leading us to become more radical and faulty but also dragging us into the controversy. Mostly the media messages of public concern are made and disseminated by power centers. The power centers run the media houses for their easy reach to the people. And, these media houses not only carry the commentary part of the incident but also they collate, integrate and synthesize the available information as an intelligence agency to accomplish their mission. Although we claim the present media as it is voice of the voiceless but in reality it is controlled and directed by those who control regime or who has enough finance to influence it.

The case is not only plagued in Nepal, but it is worldwide concerned. When we talk eastern powers, it is democratic India and undemocratic China- who are both suffering from institutionalized corruption. And it is not just potential source of internal strife but it points to wider problems creating trustworthy institutions that are acting as a brake on both Chinese and Indian power, in a globalized economic system (Rachman, 2016., p. 15). The demonetization of 500 and 1000 rupee currency notes by Prime Minister Narendra Modi in effort to fight against the black money and Xi Zingping's endeavor to balance on cleansing high level corruption with undemocratic Communist Party strengthen needs to be seen from neutral prism as a whole.

New Media and Geopolitical Relevancy

Politics is the study of society, so it is related to human development. Stability and development are synonym, cannot flourish without each other. At times, politicians claim for credit to those developments that take place with change of time and continue even during war and crisis. Hence, Harvey Starr truly writes as the study of international relations sits at the convergence of human inquiry that cross both time and space (Starr, 2016, p. 1). When we talk about international relations- it is dictated by geopolitics. In one side, we agree as politics is an art as well as science because it deals with that knowledge related to governing the society- on the other, geography is also a study of earth, its features and live on it. There is no doubt that politics has become complicated due to the complexities on our relations- but it remains an overriding to settle our disputes. And, by geopolitics- it is a relative analysis of influencing forces/powers in society and geographical relevancy to it that can accelerate its potentiality to others.

To define geopolitics, according to Shafick Osman[2], it is not a science but it is a discipline that analyses various forces on a given territory in a specific space. Perhaps he may be true as science deals with knowledge and to understand geopolitics- knowledge is not only sufficient. Of course, geopolitics is a branch of knowledge which one has to be expert upon to become master on it. If geopolitics is discipline, we need to have a training that makes us willing to follow certain rules otherwise to bear punishment if we break the rule. In other words, it is also an ability to control ourselves even at the time of crisis. Such professional ethics do not have on our politicians, academia, and journalists- so our positions in international relations are weak.

Nepal is surrounded by three nuclear powers of Asia- needs to adopt a careful policy as to whom to be aligned with. The policy of 'non-alignment' has no value now- so, where Nepal wants to incline for its betterment is a burning question (Bhattarai, 2016, p. 6). The Tibet factor for Nepal is hard nut to crack. Tibet was the protectorate state of China from 1720 which was annexed fully into it since 1949-50. USA envisioned China as a strong rivalry when it turned to communism by Mao Zedong in 1949 and the way it was involved in Korean War. Due to this, President John F. Kennedy's tenure was fully engaged to manage Soviet's Inter-Continental Ballistic Missile threat from Cuba and free Tibet movement against China. The Nepali land had been used by CIA to air drop of 29,000 pounds of equipment- enough arms and ammunition for 400 Tibetan rebels and ample number of graduates from the Colorado base into Mustang of Nepal (Riedel, 2015, p. 61).

The Nepali world view in the modern period appears to be primarily a reflection and extension of its perception of the countries' two enormous neighbors, India and China (Rose, 2071, p. 15). We need to trace history for this. During the British rule in India– Nepal's feudal rulers managed to stay relatively independent by offering diplomatic and military support to the British. Due to various reasons– British did not conquer Nepal; though it trapped it by supporting autocratic rulers to prolong their regime. The British philosophy was guided to keep Nepal under de-facto control through autocratic ruler.

Nepal's perception of its huge neighbors is influenced by its history of total war in ancient and medieval era in which Lichchhbi, Malla and lately Shah Rulers were engaged with imperial China in the north and initially with Gupta dynasty and later British East-India Company in the south. Although rulers of Nepal were concerned to safeguard its sovereignty, independence and freedom—they agreed to invaders demand to secure their regime. Nepal was aggressive itself to expand its territory up to 1816 when it was stopped by British and compelled to sign a treaty. With prolong denial by its palace and the court—Nepal had to accept British representative in 1840- from then onwards, it is embroiled with foreign powers in its internal matters.

At times when Nepal was in dire need of Chinese support during war with East-India Company, the Qing dynasty declined—similarly when it needed British help during Sino-Nepal War 1792, the British declined. In such a milieu, Leo E. Rose writes in 1971 in his book "Nepal: Strategy for Survival" as the imbalance in Nepal's perception has definitely influenced its relations from its inception. Perhaps, inspired by history—King Mahendra on his special interpretation to nonalignment cited as Nepal must treat China and India on the basis of absolute equality, at least superficially (Rose, 1971, p. 17). Further to his note, Nepal although aims to prove that cultural and intellectual influences from China and India have been equally important in shaping Nepali social value and culture is factually nonsense, but psychologically it makes very good sense. Unless we understand this, our media messages will not help to consolidate Nepali nationhood in particular.

Media does not only mean to write a commentary but also to form an opinion and help the policy makers to formulate the plans. Nepali media failed to generate such energy from the past and the policy makers also did not pay enough attention to groom them appropriately. That is why- the public opinion remained bifurcated and aloof to support the regime. The case of 'free Tibet' is much sensitive than what is apparently seen. The asylum of Dalai Lama in India, radicalization of Tibetan diaspora and international campaign of the westerns to free Tibet are bound to keep the Himalayan dispute on the world's front pages as the Tibetans and Chinese each seek to determine a successor they consider legitimate (Upadhya, 2016, p. 1).

And, in consideration to legitimacy- British and China had huge trust deficit that was surfaced from the time of Opium War in 1839-42 when British used India as launching pad for an assault on the Chinese market to sell opium produced in India (Rachman, 2016, p. 23). From then onwards, it had an eye on Tibet as a commercial prize and, later, a back door to more lucrative opportunities in the western Chinese market, went on to consider the region a critical part of the imperial chessboard (Upadhya, 2016, p. 1). Basically, the British Empire in India preferred a weak Tibet as a useful buffer on the Raj's northern border and treated Tibet as an all but independent country while acknowledging ultimate Chinese sovereignty (Riedel, 2016, p. 21).

The British legacy remained in the Indian philosophy to counterpoise Afghanistan and China to protect South Asia. Hence, as British envisioned- India too wanted Tibet as buffer not Nepal to safeguard its territory (Bhattarai, 2014, p. 206). For strategic and logistic reason- British did not conquer Nepal; though it conferred on Nepal all the trappings of an independent country- it treated Nepal as any princely state in India (Mehta, 2006, p. 2). Nepal's sovereignty and independence is intact and reasons could be any- but tussle between China and India has brewed since long over Tibet issue. It will be relevant to quote Neville Maxwell- an Australian journalist, responsible to look after South Asia for the *Times* magazine of London from 1959 until after the 1962 Sino-India War writes in his book, *India's China War* as squarely blame for the war goes to Jawahar Lal Nehru and India (Reidel, 2016, p. 93). The reason mentioned as Nehru's refusal to negotiate a compromise territorial deal that would give China what it wanted in the west (Aksai Chin) and India what it wanted in the east (the McMohan Line).

Of course, there are many ups and downs in the history of South Asia and mostly they underpin through Indo-China relations. According to Anand Giridharadas, in his article "JFK Faced India China Dilemma" in New York Times, August 26, 2005- Mao Zedong told a visiting delegation from Nepal in 1964 that the issue of war was not the border in Kashmir or the McMohan Line but Nehru and Indian

Government believed that Tibet belong to India. He also revealed that Mao made the same argument to the Soviets before and after the 1962 war. Those legacies do still perceive in both ends that is why Himalayan states' independence and sovereignty are always in question.

Nepali establishment whenever slips to follow 'one China policy'-on single buzz, China sees conspiracy in its unity. There are more than 20,000 Tibetan refugees sheltering in a country which is in dire need of international support itself. Dalai Lama and his exile government want to open contact office in Kathmandu- which is opposed by China. Westerns want Nepal to have more liberal policy towards Tibetans and let them fight for 'free Tibet' against China. The geopolitics of Nepal does not allow it to go against Chinese interest in Nepal. Likewise, it has religious, cultural and traditional relations with India. The established communication networks with Indian cities enable Nepal to trade and easy access to sea as well. Being India locked from three sides- it has to bear big brother bully at times whenever former's interest overlooked.

Nevertheless, new media has definitely enhanced connectivity among as well as outside the Nepali society even though they are diverged ethnically, lingual as well as culturally to understand that unity strengthens nationalism to counter common threat. The way Nepali society reacted against five months economic blockade of India through social networks is a burning example of its kind and to generate the opinion for trade diversification having vast deficit on it. To boost up the mutual understanding, the new media played important role not only to generate opinion but also to garner consensus on national unity and pride. In addition, it has also helped in controlling corruption, enabling transparency and buffeting such information that weakens national sovereignty, independence and freedom of action.

As new media has no boundary unless it is retrieved by the state policy to block for some reason. The commonalties and cultural affiliation in Indo-Nepal relations have unique value. In its long history, it has witnessed many ups and downs. The vested interest of the leaders and the political parties has undermined its uniqueness as well. Nepal has been a victim many times due to over-dominating 'China factor' syndrome in Indian politics. At times, pro-nationalist approach of Nepali leadership to remain in power by radicalizing the youths has also victimized Nepal at large.

The quality of making media messages and its literacy in social media counts important value. The pre-conceived idea and knowledge about Nepal's history and its relations with two huge neighbors in our social domain depicts how we have understood as well as want to develop it in future. At times, the generalized opinion helps the leadership at the top to decide overall relations of the nation. In such a milieu, the role of new media is extremely important to track the trend of the popular wish to find out a bottom line conducive to stability.

Role of New Media in Geo-Strategy

Before understanding new media and its role on geo-strategy we must understand the geopolitics of that area first. By geopolitics as what we have discussed earlier- it is simply a study of the political and strategic relevance of geography in a pursuit to national and international power (Khanal, 2011). So, the location and the physical environment are important factors to decide international power structure of a nation in the global as well as in regional context. And, geo-strategy is a branch of geo-politics that deals with strategy. It characterizes a certain geographic area that affects the analysis of a region (Dahal, 2009).

When we talk about geo-strategy, we seldom mix that geopolitics fully dictates our strategic autonomy that we enjoy within the region. But it is not so- it is also influenced by situation and time that makes some nations powerful. In order to understand the importance of geo-strategy of Nepal, we need to understand geographical context of the Indian subcontinent and the changing dynamics of the situation around the world. Of Course, it is a self-contained region that includes India, Pakistan, Bangladesh, Nepal and Bhutan. We may call the subcontinent "self-contained" because it is a region that is isolated on all sides by difficult terrain or by ocean. In geopolitical terms it is– an island (Friedman, 2008). In this subcontinent, all the counties connect with India but no countries other than India connect to each other. So, from socio-politics and economic perspective- it is India influenced sub-region who follow common media culture. Hence, to study new media and its role in geo-strategy of Nepal—we must understand sub continental media behavior specially India in particular.

New media in 21st Century meant all that activities related to internet and the interplay between technology, images and sound. It is felt to be evolved with changes continuously. So, what is today cannot be expected tomorrow. The technology is changing so rapidly that nobody can pace with it. And, it has a profound effect on three of the most important sector of society that is economics, politics, and the exchange of ideas. Economically, new media has global reach. The Fiber optic wiring networks connected to major world's cities enables corporate world easy to render service and simplify global finance and trade a physical reality, since data networks between firms and investors are universally accessible (Socha & Schmid, 2014). In the political and other fields, it can do lot to restructuring of research, social interaction, and dissemination of information that have direct bearing to national development and stabilization.

In the pace of changing world which is hyper now; the clash of civilization is turning to much critical state compared to cold war era. Most scholars advocate that the people are seeking identity and for this purpose they are reinventing ethnicity to establish their ideology. So they need opponent and create enmities as what Samuel

P. Huntington advocates like it occurs across the fault lines between the world's major civilizations. Among the civilizations, the sectorial powers that represent common ideology within the geography provoke extremism – and through religious and cultural pundits, the extremists are radicalized to disturb the entire world through terrorism. Nepal is also not exceptional to this threat in another form. The indigenous and minority groups are over demanding to federate a moderate sized nation with limited resources into pieces where more than 125 such groups shelter.

Media has also provoked this issue knowingly or unknowingly by raising the expectation of normal citizen to drag into new vicious circle of revolution which has no end. The cognitive approach from a broader perspective by the state is only the option to make citizens positive towards the system. And for this, a responsible media should also be developed and groomed faithful towards the nation. Nepal being Hindu dominated multi-ethnic; multi-lingual country needs to adopt a balanced policy to maintain social harmony. The agenda of secularism and federalism was highly vocalized by the European Union and the west to divide Nepali nationalism basically to weaken both India and China in the long run. Most intellectuals view this as a grand design to infiltrate culturally and spoil the eastern civilization globally (Bhattarai, 2015). It is not beyond the thinking of Samuel P. Huntington what he has envisaged in his book, "Clash of Civilization".

Provoked by like-minded elements, the world powers are also divided on issues and principles, having hate and love relations with each other supporting sectarian powers accordingly. In such a milieu, the analysis of geopolitical situation of Nepal will be quite interesting as it being unique on its location between two emerging global powers India and China. The west has its own stake because China is next on line in power after the United States of America. The geopolitical location of Nepal has encouraged the major powers to show their presence due to following reasons-

- China and India are growing powers- hence other global powers trying to destabilize them through their strong presence in Nepal.
- As China is using North Korea as proxy power to entire world- other global powers suspect India might use Nepal in the similar line or vice versa by China.
- Inspired by fragile politics in Nepal, westerns are spreading Christianity to influence eastern civilization to escalate religious and cultural conflict in Asia.

If we see China, its huge population comprises of recognized 56 ethnic groups dominated by Han identity with distinct linguistic and regional culture. In religion-Confucianism, Taoism, and later Buddhism constitute three teachings in China. Similarly, Indian civilization is blended with Indus Valley civilization and Indo-

Aryan culture influenced by Vedic civilization. Nepal is influenced by both the civilizations having diverged ideology and philosophy. It is comprised of more than 125 tribes with above 100 languages spoken.

As education as well as exposure has increased over a period of time due to democratization and liberalization of the society- the people are much aware of their rights and duties. But the political leaders are not serious to discharge their duties. Why nations plunge to be in the verge of failure is due to its lacking on commitment to Rule of law, control over the corruption and commitment to development. For this, nation should have inclusive policy- friendly investment environment and successful foreign policy as a tool for public diplomacy. As we all are aware that foreign policy is the extension of internal policy- Nepal lacks to formulate sound internal policy to empowering the people and advocate its position in the international forum.

The effect of globalization has enriched Nepal in communication and information technology to grow at the par with other regional countries in Asia although the speed of the internet is poor compared to others. The growth of cellular phone network and internet connectivity- the reach and role of the new media has increased considerably. The people share and show their likes and dislikes in the social media openly and sometimes go beyond to their limit above the electronic laws and bylaws of the country. But the dilemma is the political leaders never bother to such feedbacks as Oligarchy prevails in the system. It may also be called as rogue state as the leaders with poor popular base form the coalition government because of faulty mechanism.

How Media Destabilize a Nation?

Media needs to map the mind of the people and make news based on reality. Fabrication of the incident and 'yellow journalism' generally discredit it and damage the image of media house it represents. Performing governments are the choice of the people that help stabilizing the system whereas oligarchical regime frustrates people leading to revolutions. Generally, such regimes capture the media to fulfill their selfish desires. Hence, at times people, people desire radical change due to frustration as well as humiliation from the prevailing system.

The burning example is Donald Trump's victory as new president in USA. As most of us agree to the fact that there is no alternate to democracy, but not necessarily everybody must understand as we do. Hillary Clinton's victory could have been a follow-up of Obama's legacy which most Americans did not like. The media's prediction of Clinton's victory was failed as it could not read the minds of the American people accurately.

Let us examine a case of Nepal how a barbaric killing of 12 Nepalis by a militant faction 'Army of Ansar al-Sunna' in Iraq in the year 2004 took a serious incident of vandalism and chaos in Nepal. Footage of that killing was shown by BBC[3] and that was carried by some of the media houses in Nepal to make the news sensational. The like-minded political parties escalated the issue and blame the government as why it did not stop working people in war torn Iraq. Irrespective of whether government was wrong or right or was that under its control or not, country has to bear a huge loss from that vandalism because of provocative news disseminated by the media.

This is an example of media insensitivity and irresponsible political institutions. Democracy has been misinterpreted in Nepali society. Access to information plays a significant role in the success of participatory democracy (Brand, 2009) and press freedom is the key to transparency that helps to lead a state to 'good governance'. But it cannot be applied when democracy has itself driven against social justice. Ian Shapiro[4] argues as democratic values come primarily from its potential to limit domination rather than operation as a system of participation, representation and preference aggregation. In gist, he describes as how democracy and social justice clash to each other. To match his philosophy with ongoing Nepali democratic culture, Sten T. Brand[5] writes the democratic process in Nepal was fueled by injustice and belief in that democratic change would end autocratic rule that is viewed as the reason for injustice. He also argues as the way to counter the interference between democracy and social justice is to place democracy in the center of social relations so that distribution of authority becomes the focal point and not distribution of assets. In short, it is related to delegation of authority and decentralization of power. The people who make media need to understand what Ian Sapiro wants to convey and Sten T. Brand argues upon. Notwithstanding the underpinning phenomena of democracy—people ruined its entire ethics blindly supporting incompetent, shortsighted and selfish leaders.

After the end of absolute monarchy in 1990, the main concerns of the people were to restore democratic practices. The political parties having been suppressed for years were not sure how to institutionalize the democracy. Managing the power centers and meeting the aspiration of the people was a big challenge. Although Krishna Prasad Bhattarai's interim government not only concluded the parliamentary election successfully but also promulgated a new constitution in 1991-92. The newly adopted multi-party parliamentarian system with constitutional monarchy declined its popularity in 4-5 years duration when Maoist party declared rebellion in 1996. It was failure of the establishment to delegate the authority and decentralize the power at the outset.

Media messengers have failed in Nepal to understand that amalgamation of democracy and social justice is one way or other to strengthen nationhood. Mapping up the standard of a nation depends on how its statehood has been developed. The ongoing political system and economic governance are the backbone to stabilize it. For this, we must understand the relationship among authoritarianism, patrimonialism and de-concentration of power before molding a state into an ideal nation (Koirala,

2011, p. 2). If the regime is authoritarian type with patrimonial base and has no de-concentration of power within it, then it is authoritarian corporatism. Likewise, if it has all the character as above but some degree of de-concentration of power is there then it will be oligarchic or fragile government. If the regime has authoritarian nature with less patrimony and de-concentration of power can be categorized as delivering dictatorial government. Similarly, having democracy with patrimonial character and less de-concentration of power is considered poor governance. Lastly, fool democracy with no patrimonialism, with de-concentration of power are taken as good governing state. The table below describes with example of such states in detail. Before we make media messages—we must understand where we are and what should our endeavors be to stabilize our nations.

Is Media Conducive to Empower People in Nepal?

As in most countries, Nepali media also can be divided into print, broadcast and internet. The development of ARPANET through Advanced Research Project Agency (ARPA) was said to be inspired by the success of Soviet satellite sputnik in 1957[6]. Later, US Department of Defense developed it for defense as well as under research domain. It was officially started from 1969 for limited use which later took up with advancement in world- wide wave (www) in 1990 (Acharya, 2012, p. 47).

Internet could enter into Nepali communication sector only after 2000. Although it was getting pace with elites in Kathmandu quite early, there were only 23 percent of total population who had access to internet up to 2010. This report also seems fabricated as National Census Report 2012 indicates that households reach to internet

Table 1. Type of regime

Authoritarian Rule	Patrimonialism	Democracy	De-concentration of Power	Type of Regime	Example
Yes	Yes	No	No	Authoritarian Corporatism	North Korea
Yes	Yes	No	Yes-Little	Fragile Government	Syria, Yeman
Yes	No-Little	No	Yes	Delivery Dictatorial	China, Russia
No	Yes	Yes	No	Poor Governance	Nepal, Myanmar
No	No	Yes	Yes	Good Goverance	USA, Western Countries

(Source: Koirala, 2010)

that time was 3.3 percent of total population- telephone access was 7.37 percent and cellular phone in households at 64.63 percent.

To trace the development in communication sector, 1985 is the turning point when Nepal entered into electronic media introducing Nepal Television to telecast news, other entertainment and informative programs. Before to that in 1984, Nepal's entire district headquarters were connected by STD network. As media development shapes with literacy standard, Nepal's literacy rate in 1990 was just 39 per cent and television could reach only a small proportion of the population (Whelpton, 2005, p. 170).

In a short span of time, around 4000 Village Development Committees were connected with VSAT[7] in 1996. The cellular phone was introduced in 1999. Of course, its role was definitely supplemented with increase in literacy rate of Nepal that had reached to more than 65.9 percent as per 2011 nationwide census by Central Bureau of Statistics. Despite of early introduction of internet service, access to public in the form of social media was comparatively late.

In the latest report of National Tele-Communication Authority, it has revealed that data/ internet penetration rate, the telephone (wired and WLL) penetration and the mobile penetration to be around 20 percent, 3.5 percent and 59 percent respectively (Nepali Telecom, 2012). As per the data of Central Bureau of Statistics (CBS) census which is based in per household, it is not easy to compare. Although the internet reach in household is low- as per Nepal Telecom report, it is expected to increase in coming days with it having Wi Max extending to whole of Nepal. Also the fast roll out of Wi-Fi (most easily accessible internet) from private ISPS, fierce competition between mobile operators NTC and NCell are expected to boost the internet to rural areas.

With this hope, it will be relevant to review the media development in general and internet in particular to map the overall empowerment process in Nepal. There was the system of *'Katuwal karaune'* (a person designated by the community to disseminate information verbally), *'Damaha bajaune'* (use of drum to gather mass), *'Sankha fukne'* (buzz the bugle) to aware the community about state policy and warnings if necessary. From the time of Lichchhbi era in medieval period- this system is still continued in rural area. King Prithvi Narayan Shah had first introduced postal system in Nepal (Acharya, 2012, p. 82). Due to poor literacy rate, postal facility could not gear-up and traditional system continued long specially in the backward area. With rises in literacy rate- the situation has quite improved.

The history of print media started from 1851 by Prime Minister Jung Bahadur Rana after his state visit to Great Britain and France. He was much impressed with printing press as well as circulation of newspapers in Europe. Hence, he brought a mini press along with him in Nepal. Initially it was nick named as *'Type chhapakhana'* as well as it had a trade mark of vulture on it so in typical Nepali name it was known as *'Giddhe press'* (Acharya, 2012, p. 85).

The development of social media has empowered the people from transparency point of view but the way the messages are made against the women are not only vulgar it is indicating the real picture of our male dominating society. A reporter of BBC Nepali Service Ms. Brikuti Rai has covered a report about few remarks made against Government of Nepal's decision to support Nepali Congress Leader Sujata Koirala financially for her treatment to breast cancer. Similarly, the reporter also revealed as the media persons ask questions to female like 'how you manage being a lady?' or 'why you are unmarried till now?' or 'how you are managing time for your profession and household?" (BBC News, 2016).

Such questions embarrass not only a lady- but we tend to forget that more than half of the population belongs to female. With such a philosophy about the female- how we can think of maintaining stability and development of our society? The questions above degrade the professional achievements of the female. Our media is not only biased—it is seldom criticized for reporting lightly in public about domestic violence, sexual harassment against women.

Similarly, Nepali society has not learnt so far how to make media messages and understand its literature; perhaps it is much important for them now to use social media to enhance their nationalism. The way media houses provoke anti-national elements and their advocacy in ignorance unknowingly help growing anti- national feeling in the country. In their wish to promote nationalism- are not they becoming ultra- nationalist hurting the sentiments of those who migrated to this country in different time-frame? Hence, national integration is much sensitive issue now than ever in Nepal[8].

From the ethnical point of view, Nepal has more than 125 tribes. There are almost 100 languages spoken nation-wide. Nepal was integrated by King Prithvi Narayan Shah from more than 53 principalities in 1767. There was Shah monarchical rule up to 2005 which was converted into 'federal democratic republic' whose new constitution was just promulgated by constituent assembly in 2015. The provincial governments are still not in existence due to prolong mistrust among the political parties. The implementation of the new constitution is in limbo due to parties' mistrust to each other. As the politics is severely divided, the social media could not fully be utilized to form strong opinion as such.

Although social media is used by all the power centers to advocate position for own benefit- no one is fully successful on it. The coalition government has no control over the media; any national as well as anti-national elements make messages and float into the floor. The people are misguided as well as misled by the power centers. If the present situation remains status-quo, conflict may reverse from different dynamics in Nepal. The only major lag on it is the absence of dynamic leader to lead the people and structure to support.

New Media's Role in Nation- Building

In post conflict societies, nation building is not only a priority but also a challenge to all its stakeholders. Failing to understand the adversaries affecting the challenges may revert the conflict anytime. So everybody must understand the geopolitical constraints of the country, lapses on geo-strategy it has opted and socio-economic limitations before making any media messages in this regard. We must understand that the citizens of most countries are seeking new nationalist values, life-styles, communication and positive sprits for both adaptations and process (Dahal, 2014). They are not only trying to retain Nepali identity but also asserting determined and diligent efforts to strengthen its literary foundations. Dev Raj Dahal, a renowned scholar shared along with Nanda R. Shrestha as such narrative of Nepali nationalism to find a wider voice and appeal in the form of its national identity and a common effort to garner its historical heritage on global values through cross-cultural communication are not an easy task.

Nepal's stability has been achieved by its citizen's constant endeavor to maintain communication and interaction from one generation to another for improved political system, economic upliftment and social reconciliation. Its stability, as what Leo E. Rose has evaluated is influenced by two enormous neighbors' perception about its democratic practices to fulfill their aspirations. The lay of the land facilitates better communication with its southern neighbor compared to the north, so the cultural affiliation exits accordingly. India locked geopolitical constraints handicap at times to it whenever the regime fails to satisfy its establishment. The Tibet factor is crucial in Sino-India relations from the time of British East-India Company. The British Empire in India preferred a weak Tibet as a useful buffer on the Raj's northern border and treated Tibet as an all but independent country while acknowledging ultimate Chinese sovereignty (Riedel, 2016, p. 21).

The British Empire followed a dual policy acknowledging Chinese sovereignty in one side, signing a treaty with Tibet in 1914 that gave their border line which London wanted. Bruce Reidel also reveals in his book as Chinese were invited to sign the treaty which they refused. On the similar line British followed with Nepal by trapping its autocratic rulers signing a treaty in 1816 which not only capsized Nepal's desire to expand but also controlled entire its resources for imperial India. The case of Tibet changed once the communists won the Chinese civil war in 1949, they accepted neither the semi-independence of Tibet nor the boundary lines drawn by British imperialism between Tibet and India (Riedel, 2016, p. 22). But the case of Nepal remained status quo with independent India replaced by old treaty of

1816 by new Peace and Friendship Treaty in 1950. In almost seven decades- no amendments on the treaty have taken place. So far, the Eminent Persons Group by both the countries has been formed to look after entire relationship.

Nepal is independent from the date of its evolution. During the British rule in India– its feudal rulers managed to stay relatively independent by offering diplomatic and military support to the British. Due to various reasons– British could not conquer Nepal; though it trapped it by supporting autocratic rulers to prolong their regime. The British philosophy was guided to keep Nepal under de-facto control through autocratic ruler. The Nehru doctrine was the continuation of the British philosophy (Bhattarai, 2014). The history has always a relevancy with the present. The legacy of Nehru doctrine so embedded in Indian establishment that it does not want to set it aside and apply Gujral doctrine of reciprocity that has been propounded and even applied to improve its neighborhood policy in 1997. But the hardliners have different view in India.

Immediately after its independence in 1947, the Indian regime supported the democratic alliance under the Nepali Congress to abolish Rana autocracy at one side and in a chronicling deal forced Rana ruler to sign the Peace and Friendship Treaty in 1950. Most Nepali think they are deprived of their rights due to this unequal treaty—it is said unequal because there cannot be an equality which is not only landlocked—it is India locked by three sides. Besides to this, there is no comparison on power balance. The privilege and facilities provided by international conventions are also deprived at times due to this treaty. Unless the people and our respective regimes do not understand the change of time, the relations remain strain at both ends.

The power of new media has enabled all the citizens reach to each other then and there. The dissemination of information at times credits our leaders and vice-versa. The social media spreads bad news faster and becomes viral compared to good news. As we agree that bad news is always good news for the media persons. Fabrication of news is common in our society. In the lapse of sufficient laws and bylaws—the media persons manipulate the news and accordingly distort to fulfill their vested interest. Notwithstanding as news can be manipulated, Nepali state allowed a single media house to run print, electronic and frequency modulated (FM) radio at the same time. The situation was much critical for the establishment at the time of Maoist insurgency to control such media houses in the lapse of appropriate laws and bylaws. The situation is still similar to control them in the transitional set-up because of diverged interest of the power centers with which the media centers are align to.

In consideration to Nepal's geopolitics, the diverged world civilizations are exploring own values to dilute others. As what Samuel P. Huntington envisaged the nation states are formed based on religion and language which at times contradicted by scholars like Dev Raj Dahal who questions that western political forms and ideals are really appropriate or even relevant for nation-building in developing countries including Nepal with different values, cultures, language? (Dahal, 2014). He argues as inducing people of different culture a vision to create a nation-state on own values by advance countries which are not owned by the people invites confrontation. Perhaps it could be the reason that people in Nepal are reverting back from federalism, Hindu religion based instead of secular state and directly elected executive head. These issues are highly circulated in social media that are not only creating an opinion but also exerting pressure to the power centers to oblige to popular wish of the people.

In other context, why globalization is gradually declining its popularity? And rise of organizations like BRICS, AIIB coming up to counter institutions like World Bank, International Monetary Fund (IMF) and Asian Development Bank (ADB). These are the results of western hegemony loaded to most developing countries of the world; and their impression as of being deprived of own values. Demand of restoring own values and promoting own culture cannot be unjustifiable to any nation-state in their development models. Imposition of western values has invariably invited clash of civilization and consequently leading to destabilized world. Nepal is also deprived of such clash and in consideration to its geopolitical location—volatility is much high. If we fail to stabilize it, the repercussion will be much devastating to both the neighbors as it being buffer to them who are enormous, rising as well as rival powers of the world.

If we see the present world order, most countries are advancing towards populist regimes. The people are much radicalized leading the whole world into the turbulence. Decline of internationalism and rise of national as well as sectarian powers inevitably create terror to entire human society. The world leaders have not understood the radicalized nationalism which at times may follow extreme line as of the case in Middle-east destabilize the whole world order. Nepali nation-state is not exception to this and has been much critical due to its geopolitical locations. We, who make 'media messages' must understand that Indian establishment playing 'Madhes Card' so as Chinese to 'One Belt One Road' and Nepali radical leaders playing both 'India and China Cards' one to another to sensitize the situation will ultimately destabilize the nation.

CONCLUSION

Stabilizing a nation is an endeavor to peace and development. Information technology is developed to enhance power to disseminate information so as to make public opinion for decision making. The innovation of social media has drastically changed our capacity to communicate each other. Nepal passed through a decade long violent insurgency to restore popular rights from prolong autocratic rule. And in this effort, media played a significant role to succeed it. Though its role was crucial—it could not remain unbiased as well as uncontroversial.

Due to populist approach all over the world, our regimes have failed to maintain rationality over popular predictions, assumptions and assertions; continue to follow extremist line to fulfill their vested interest. Consequently, such efforts make us fail to follow democratic path as what has been defined—for the people, of the people and by the people. New media always and every time aware us whenever we derail from the track to real democracy.

Geopolitical relevancy to new media and stabilization of a nation is a great concern for the social scientists to know about the popular choice of development in general. Nepal's geopolitics being buffer in between two huge global powers and its limitations to development enable a greater scope to study in this field. The struggle for Nepal to survive as an independent sovereign state can be a unique example for social scientists as well.

In such a milieu, it remained a compulsion for Nepal to manage high level of diplomacy with both the neighbors and coinciding geo-strategy accordingly. Media, being a modern de-facto power needs to be understood by all the citizens to facilitate leaders to make viable public decisions. We have different types of regime who deliver public goods based on their foundations. Unless we have good governance—we can never expect public goods reaching to people effectively.

Nation-building is a challenge for every welfare state in modern world. The clash in our civilizations is common. Our endeavor should be to avoid it and flourish own values and culture. Such values can only be promoted through citizenry effort to communicate and interact from one generation to another to improve political system, thrive for economic development and social transformation. In failing to do so, the spillover effects of destabilized Nepal may also affect neighboring China to some extent with more to India as it is becoming closer from religious, cultural as well as economic perspectives.

REFERENCES

Acharya, B. (2012). *Mass Communication & Journalism Study*. Kathmandu: Pradhan Book House.

BBC News. (25 November 2016). *Are you a woman too?* Retrieved from http://www.bbc.com/nepali/news-38104211

Bhattarai, U. K. (2014). *Conflict to Peace Transition in Nepal*. New Delhi: Adarsh Books.

Bhattarai, U. K. (2014). *Responses on India-Nepal Relations*. Journal 19 of Foreign Policy Research Centre, New Delhi, India. http://www.fprc.in/Pragya NEPAL 19.pdf

Bhattarai, U. K. (2015). *Madhesi Agitation: Comprehending Consequences on Indo-Nepal Relations*. Retrieved from http://diplomatist.com/dipo201511/article001.html

Bhattarai, U. K. (2016, September 28). *US-India-Nepal Alliance: Countering China*. Retrieved from https://thehimalayantimes.com/opinion/us-india-nepal-alliance-countering-china/

Brand, S. T. (2009). *Thought on news media's role in Nepal's democratic process*. Kathmandu: Bodhi. http://www.nepjol.info/index.php/BOHDI/article/view/2810/2494

Dahal, D. R. (2014). *Media's Role in Nation-Building in Nepal*. Retrieved from http://www.spotlightnepal.com/News/Article/Dev-Raj-Dahal-Nation-Building-Nepal

Dahal, R. K. (2009). *Emerging role of Nepalese diplomacy in regional and global politics*. The Weekly Mirror.

Friedman, G. (2008). *The Geo-politics of India: A Shifting, Self-Contained World*. The Himalayan Times of Nepal.

Ghareeb, E. (2000). The New Media and the Information Revolution in the Arab World: An Assessment. *The Middle East Journal, 54*(3).

Khanal, R. (2011). *Geo-Politics and Socio-Political Development in Nepal.* The Shivapuri Journal.

Koirala, B. (2011). *Economic Management: Fault lines and ways to Resolve. A panel discussion held by Nepal Administrative Staff College.* Kathmandu: Jawalakhel.

Mehta, A. K. (2006). *The Royal Nepal Army: Meeting the Maoist Challenges.* New Delhi: Rupa. Co.

Nepali Telecom. (2012). *Only 3 Percent Household Have Internet Access in Nepal.* Retrieved from http://www.nepalitelecom.com/2012/11/only-3-percent-household-have-internet-access-in-nepal.html

New Media Institute. (2014). Bailey Socha, Barbara Eber-Schmid. *Defining New Media Isn't Easy.* Retrieved from https://www.facebook.com/permalink.php?story_fb id=200470393410745&id=200469916744126

Rachman, G. (2016). *Easternisation.* London: The Bodley Head.

Riedel, B. (2015). *JFK's Forgotten Crisis.* Washington, DC: The Brookings Institution Press.

Rose, L. E. (1971). *Nepal: Strategy for Survival.* London: University of California Press.

Starr, H. (2016). *On Geopolitics.* New York: Routledge.

Upadhya, S. (2016). *Nepal and the Geo-Strategic Rivalry between China and India.* New York: Routledge.

Whelpton, J. (2005). *A History of Nepal.* London: Cambridge University Press. doi:10.1017/CBO9781107050860

ENDNOTES

1 An Adjunct Professor at the American University and a specialist on media issues and Middle Eastern Affairs.

2 A Mauritius based professor specialized on geopolitics of Indian Ocean revealed in a talk program at Institute for Defense Studies and Analyses, New Delhi, India.

3 See http://news.bbc.co.uk/2/hi/south_asia/3614866.stm

4 A renowned professor of political science at Yale University.

5 In *Bodhi:* An Interdisciplinary Journal is an annual publication of the Department of Languages and Mass Communication, School of Arts, Kathmandu University.

6 See http://history.nasa.gov/sputnic/

7 Very Small Aperture Terminal- It provides high speed, broadband satellite communications for Internet or private network communications.

8 Based on a post made by the author in 'facebook' on February 6, 2017.

Chapter 4
Print Media's Role in Securitization:
National Security and Diplomacy Discourses in Nepal

Sudeep Uprety
Tribhuvan University, Nepal

ABSTRACT

This chapter attempts to understand the inter-relationship between the media and the national security/foreign affairs sector in Nepal, particularly unfolding the perceptions between each other and the resultant impression in the print media – thereby carrying forward the "securitization" discourse. Through the process of content analysis and expert opinions, this chapter advocates for the "desecuritization" of sensitive issues such as national security and diplomacy, promoting peace and cooperation rather than polarization of ideas and perspectives.

DOI: 10.4018/978-1-5225-3859-2.ch004

INTRODUCTION

In Nepal, national security became a national political agenda, particularly since the 'People's War[1]' commencing from mid-1990s. On the diplomatic forefront, the transformation was also huge in terms of Nepal's internal political change affecting the regional geo-politics. There were polarized notions of the rise of the Maoists with regards to their political gain within Nepal and the message that would spread.

At the national level, with the roots of the conflict going back to the early democratic era where the seeds of the dissatisfaction were laid with the 'discriminatory' attitude and behaviour towards the marginalized sections of the society, the voices for political and social change gradually became strong. The civil war that the country went through, apart from the political dimension also had a 'media' angle. Local media was extensively used by the Maoists to spread their word to securitize that the oppressed and the marginalized are under existential threat. On the other hand, there was extensive use of national and international media by the state and other power centres highlighting and in some cases, exaggerating the extent of bloodbath that took place in Nepal. Particularly after the end of the civil war ending and the formalization of the peace process with the signing of the Comprehensive Peace Accord in 2006 by the two conflicting groups, the agenda of peace building was established.

It is therefore, a matter of significance to understand the interrelationship between media and national security and diplomacy issues that led to the development of public and intellectual discourses. For a nation-state to ensure that people's perception regarding national security and its diplomatic relations, especially at the South Asian region is a positive one, it should see to it that the discourses carried out within its territory give a positive indication so that it is disseminated in the same manner as government's 'diplomatic duty'. It is also imperative to understand the duality whether print media in Nepal is securitizing issues or just reacting to the discourses carried out by NGOs/INGOs and academicians in various public forums. Hypothetically, there could be a range of factors determining this such as the establishment motive, ideological affiliation, funding or donation, agenda preference and interest of the leadership.

Although Nepal hasn't remained aloof in the technological advancements in the media sector, print media is still the dominant force in carrying out the security discourse in Nepal. The readership culture of print media is quite encouraging. Newspapers are popular amongst office workers and the educated elite in Nepal's towns and cities and in nearby rural areas (Internews, 2011). The daily newspapers and the magazines published on a weekly and fortnightly basis are the most preferred sources for news. Latest annual report of Press Council Nepal (2016) shows that there are 3795 registered print media sources in Nepal with 644 dailies, 2749 weeklies and 402 fortnightlies. It's a common sight to find people gathered in the local stationery shops and debating on news items printed. Nowadays, with newspapers available in online editions, there are lots of debates and discussions on various socio-political issues through social media such as Facebook and Twitter.

Henceforth, the analysis of role played by print media in the development of national security and diplomacy discourses is very important in Nepal, especially considering the threat that could be posed by media securitizing various contentious issues through the stories published.

Through this chapter, the author seeks to understand three pertinent issues surrounding national security and diplomacy discourses in Nepal:

1. Nature of messages print media are carrying to the intellectual circles/academia and general public in terms of building a discourse about national security and diplomacy issues
2. Level of prioritization/importance given by the print media in its coverage of those national security and diplomacy related issues
3. Extent of securitization by print media whether stories are blown out of proportion and building a case of an existential threat or has it just been a factual reporting – without elements of any exaggeration

BACKGROUND

It is believed that the theory of securitization, which rests on the principle of media manipulation was conceptualized by Ole Waever (1997) in the mid-1990s and later developed in his co-authored book *Security: A New Framework of Analysis* in 1998. Guzzini (2011) defines securitization as "the positioning through speech acts (usually by a political leader) of a particular issue as a threat to survival, which in turn (with the consent of the relevant constituency) enables emergency measures and the suspension of 'normal politics' in dealing with that issue." The notion of securitization has also been closely linked with linguistics through scholars like Jacques Derrida. Derrida's theory of deconstruction, where his famous quote that "a text matters more for what it does than for what it says" was inspirational for the securitization theory's fundamental premise - *security is what it does*. Recent contributions of scholars like Lene Hansen (2013) have been instrumental in developing the notion of "security as a discourse".

Vladimir Sulovic (2010) discusses the contribution of the Copenhagen School of Security Studies in conceptualizing security as a process of social construction of threats which includes securitizing actor (mostly political elite), who declares certain matter as urgent and a posing threat for the survival of the referent object, that, once accepted with the audience, legitimizes the use of extraordinary measures for neutralization of the threat. Thus, the issue is securitized and removed outside the normal bounds of democratic political procedure and put on the "panic politics" agenda.

Media Inter Linkages in Securitization and Desecuritization

Several studies have also highlighted the role of the media in securitization. In his theory of securitization titled *The Three Faces of Securitization: Political Agency, Audience and Context*, Balzacq (2005) takes the association of securitization with linguistics forward by his claim that theory of securitization is that the articulation of security produces a specific threatening state of affairs. He further explains that within this theory, power is derived from the use of 'appropriate' words in conformity with established rules governing speech acts. Balzacq (2005) puts forward three basic assumptions — (i) that an effective securitization is audience-centered; (ii) that securitization is context-dependent; (iii) that an effective securitization is power-laden.

Christina Uhlig (2015) in *Moving towards Securitization* shows how French and German media reported on the terrorist attacks and how terrorism and Islam were portrayed as a threat to the referent objects of the West, its citizens and values, fostering an essentialist and dichotomist understanding of the West and Islam. Likewise, Ciaran O' Reilly (2008) in *Primetime Patriotism: News Media and the Securitization of Iraq*, examines the role of the US news media in supporting the government's push for war in the context of heightened national feeling and patriotism after the events of 9/11. O' Reilly talks of direct correlation between levels of nationalism and patriotism and the ease by which a securitization actor can successfully legitimize something or someone as a threat to national security. Building this case, he argues that the media can play an instrumental role in playing the agent that carries that message. He adds that news media exists in a specific and trusted position within our society, in order that accountability and truth may be presented against the sometimes self-serving political motives of government and military powers.

Vultee (2007) in *Securitization As A Theory of War Effects: The Contest Over the Framing of Political Violence* cites the example of "war on terror" as a securitization frame. He opines that the degree to which the frame is contested suggests the value it appears to hold for political elites and others who want to control the lens through which framing magnifies or shrinks the different elements of a news account. Based on the experimental evidence, he adds that securitization –when successfully invoked, creates a shared understanding of an existential threat that admits to any means necessary in solving it. Therefor securitization could be an effective and powerful way of inducing news audiences to organize their thoughts in a particular way.

Nico Carpentier (2005) in a workshop report *Media Representations of War and Conflict* discusses a range of issues from war coverage to the historical pattern of military – media relationship. He breaks the news media representation into three facets: narrative, representational portrayal and advocacy. Dusan Reljic (2004) in *The News Media and the Transformation of Ethnopolitical Conflicts* talks of political context, economic conditions, quality of journalism and public attitudes as the four elements influencing the direction of the media.

In South Asian context, Navneeta Chadha Behera (2002) in *State, People and Security: The South Asian Context* touches upon the notion that a large proportion of the South Asian national security and diplomacy discourse is not produced by South Asians themselves, but is borrowed and adapted from the West. There are specific South Asian perspectives of state's role, modernist development leading to security/insecurity, feminist interventions, military matters, environmental debate and securitization that makes this article a relevant South Asian reading on security discourses.

National Security, Diplomacy and Media

Cristina Archetti (2012) views that effective communication strategy in diplomacy is a social product that is shaped by the contingent interplay of macro structural factors (international relations) and the local initiatives of social agents. Therefore, better understanding of international relations, politics, communication and the micro-interactions of the social actors—the diplomats, officials, journalists and audiences with whom embassies and governments aim to communicate is required.

It is widely noticeable that despite the obvious significance of the role of current or future diplomacy, research on this topic is still scarce or underdeveloped (Gilboa, 2001). The interwoven relationship of media being used by diplomats as agents of communication and negotiation also extends the argument of need to study media's role in national security and diplomacy affairs.

In this light, Hacker and Mendez (2016) discuss the role of the current communication ecology in understanding not just the global communication system but also trying to understand how national influence (including public diplomacy) serves national interests and national security concerns. Likewise, Mary Murphy (2013) in her blog post opines that the information age has also brought the media and national security/diplomacy sectors closer with the advancement in public diplomacy through the use of micro-blogging sites such as Twitter.

In a similar vein, Archetti (2010) argues that the technological advancement in the field of media and communications has increasingly 'blurred' the distinction between international and national politics. He also discusses about the 3 different ways in which media are used as a tool of foreign policy and international exchange: public diplomacy (where state and non-state actors use the media to influence public opinion abroad); media diplomacy (where officials use the media to communicate with actors and promote conflict resolution); and media-broker diplomacy (where journalists serve as temporary mediators in international negotiations).

Theoretical Framework

The theoretical ground for this chapter is based on the main argument of the securitization theory which says that security is a speech act (illocutionary) performed solely by uttering 'security' something is being done. 'It is by labelling something a security issue that it becomes one' (Waever, 2004; as cited in Taureck, 2006). By stating that a particular referent object is threatened in its existence, a securitizing actor claims a right to extraordinary measures to ensure the referent object's survival. The issue is then moved out of the sphere of normal politics into the realm of emergency politics, where it can be dealt with swiftly and without the normal (democratic) rules and regulations of policy-making.

Another important component of this theoretical ground of security as conceived by Ole Waever (Taureck, 2006) is the act of desecuritization whereby the security issues are moved out of threat and defense sequence into the 'ordinary public sphere' where they can be dealt with in accordance of the (democratic) political system.

In a figurative presentation, the theoretical analysis of this chapter rests on analyzing the elements of securitization and desecuritization prevalent in national security and diplomacy discourses carried out by Nepali print media.

Nepal's Context

Talking about media and national security/diplomacy relationship in Nepal, Sudheer Sharma (2009) in an article, *Media and the Security Sector: Shifting Relations* talks of multifarious relations of Nepali media with security actors. In this article, Sharma talks of relations between the police and the media, Maoists' fascination with media, early relations with the army, army in public role, the pitfall of emergency, army in the media house, resistance by the media and appointment of new army chief and cozying up with media.

Figure 1. Principles of securitization and desecuritization, adapted from Waever (2004)

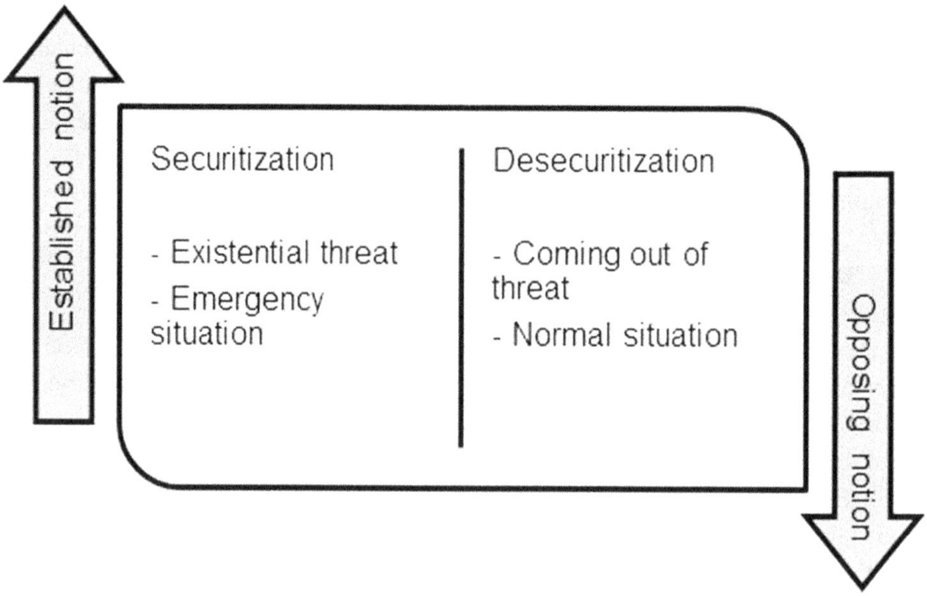

Rabindra Gurung (2011) in an International Alert report, *Journalism in Transition: Media, Information Flows and Conflict in Nepal* gives a fascinating account of the SMS survey conducted in sample districts where out of 3031 SMSs received, 47.2 percent agreed that media play a very important role in maintaining peace and security in the community while 21.5 percent of respondents believed that media play a negative role and 31.3 percent believing media play both the roles. Gurung, in the same report gives examples of media aggravating conflict citing the Hrithik Roshan scandal[2] and a student union clash between Nepal Student Union and All Nepal Free Student Union as news reports of the clash caused confrontation between student unions in Liwang due to under reporting by the media.

A noted Nepali media scholar Dharma Adhikari (2016) in his article, 'Art of the Conscious' discusses about the political, socio-cultural context that shapes the media prioritization of issues as he opines:

The deeper contours of press performance are invariably shaped by the type of society we live in, and more importantly, by the type of politics we practice. Democracy, despite its classic meaning emphasizing direct public participation (people rule) in politics, has today degenerated into political cartels orchestrated by a few leaders. Their contestations form the mainstay of news coverage.

Adhikari touches upon how the relationship between the media and the public has been a distant one with limited effort made by the media in terms of educating the public in the right manner, thereby the understanding being somewhat 'distorted':

Public perceptions of press performance without their knowledge of media's values and professional routines run the risk of painting a distorted picture of the role of press in a democracy. Unfortunately, the media do little in explaining their workings to the public. We can most definitely liken them to a lamp. But the lamp exudes light in all directions except on its own foundation. (Adhikari, 2016)

This 'over-indulgence' on politics has been affecting reporting on other crucial areas comments Adhikari as he highlights that Nepali 'elitist' press covers competitive politics more often than other substantive issues and therefore public centric debates on media are silent in Nepal. An empirical study conducted by a Nepali journalist Bhuwan KC (2014) related to political inclination of journalists showed that 72 percent of the journalists in Nepal maintained that political faith influences writing and presentation of news. However, it was also encouraging to see that 80 percent of the journalists did not filter news and maintained their journalistic professionalism while writing the news. A noted Nepali media scholar Adhikari (2017) comments, "lack of sociological grounding in media writing, dearth of research and current information on media, a poor reading and writing culture, inadequate investment and lack of appreciation for criticism are cited as some key impediments in writing about media in Nepal".

The unprecedented growth of social media use worldwide and in Nepal also contributes to the securitization of sensitive issues such as national security and diplomacy. The 'share syndrome' among social media users helps to maximize the reach as well as influence of media stories. Statistics of January 2017 show that Nepal – a country of 29.02 million population has internet penetration among 14.12 million out of which 7.10 million people are active social media users (We Are Social, 2017).

IMPRESSIONS FROM EDITORIALS AND KEY INFORMANTS ON NATIONAL SECURITY AND DIPLOMACY ISSUES

The author used both primary and secondary data as basis of analysis for this chapter. Primary data was collected through key informant interviews (KIIs) with media researchers, security experts and foreign policy experts to understand the broader context. Secondary data was collected from the editorials published by *Kantipur* daily (the largest selling vernacular daily in Nepal) published during the first three years after the People's Movement II[3] (2007 to 2010), looking into editorials that concern about foreign affairs, diplomacy and border issues. The theoretical ground for the analysis of editorials is based on the main argument of the securitization theory which says that security is a speech act (illocutionary) performed solely by uttering 'security' something is being done. Other relevant readings were also gathered as part of secondary data for more theoretical and contextual understanding.

Through this exercise, 17 editorials concerning national security and diplomacy issues were included as part of in-depth content analysis. The editorials were categorised into 5 themes depending upon their tone of argument whether they were declarative, directive, expressive, assertive or commissive. Out of the 17 articles, mostly the editorials were declarative (5 of them), directive (4 of them) and expressive (4 of them) in nature as compared to being assertive (3 of them) or commissive (1 of them).

The editorials that were declarative were related to news about the process of investigation by the People's Movement II Investigation Committee and declaring that heads of security heads to resign from their posts to support the investigation; 3 day visit of UNHCR official to advocate for third country resettlement of Bhutanese refugees; extension of service period of police officers who have completed 30 years of service; resumption of recruitment process by both Nepal Army and Maoists and breaching the peace agreement; and 'attempted coup' by Chief of Army Staff of Nepal Army.

The editorials that carried the directive discourse concerned with the Indian government restrict Bhutanese refugees to return back to Bhutan; Prime Minister Prachanda visiting for the first time to India; officers of Armed Police Force involved in mutiny; and Nepal Police creating hassles to the public in the streets.

Likewise, the editorials that carried the expressive security discourse were related to series of criminal incidents that took place in the space of 3 days and rising insecurity concerns among the public; rise of armed groups and increasing communal tension in the Madhes region; government decision to allow Bhutanese refugees to go for third country settlement; and Maoist head claiming that he had a talk with Nepal Army officials regarding the integration of PLA soldiers.

The assertive editorials were about protection and security of diplomatic officials, citing an incident of US ambassador's vehicle being attacked; violent clash between cadres of Maoists and Madhesi Janadhikar Forum; and Nepal Army giving a royal salute of 21 canons to the ex-king even after political change.

There was only one editorial which was commissive in nature which dealt with the issue of high level experts' committee giving recommendations to the government for improvement of foreign policy making practice in Nepal.

Content Analysis of these 17 editorials provide an impression that there is wider securitization of security discourses in Nepal with most articles being declarative or directive in nature rather than being commissive or assertive. Though the context in which these editorials were written could have affected the 'tone' of the articles, *Kantipur* daily has been more straightforward in terms of putting forwards its arguments in declarative and directive fashion.

Apart from the in-depth content analysis, various themes were also drawn as findings from the key informant interviews with media researchers, security experts and foreign affairs/diplomacy affairs as discussed below:

Negative News "Sells"

Majority of the key informants had a view that for media agencies to sustain themselves for a prolonged period of time, they need to look out for stories that can make headlines for better circulation. In that advent, given that the readers are more interested in reading stories of war, conflict and crime related news, such stories are included as cover stories or prioritized often.

Over these years, I have not found any drastic change the way Nepali media has covered news related to war, conflicts or crimes. As there is a greater 'interest factor' in such stories, they make the front page or become cover stories. I think that is the general trend globally as well. - Media Expert

As an editor of a responsible publication, when my team needs to select stories from a range of stories that are reported to us on a daily basis, we do not deliberately look forward only to negative stories with our interest that those stories could make our circulation of that day more. However, we do acknowledge that there has been better circulations of such stories due to greater interest of the readers. – Editor of a national daily

I don't know how do I evaluate my journalistic practice but it is reality that the highest attention readers give to my stories on national security and foreign affairs as compared to other issues. For that matter, my editorial manager as well as my publication also encourages me to search/investigate on such matters as they regard it as something 'sellable. – Journalist reporting on national security and foreign affairs

These negative stories seem to have a better scope for securitization whereby the securitizing actor can possess a 'threat' to its audience about a certain issue. During interviews with key instances, some of the instances of the languages of threat in direct or indirect fashion have been reflected in the news stories:

A media outlet extensively covered the incident of Chief of Army Staff Rookmangud Katuwal's 'attempted coup'. Coming from a security background, I could envisage that things were not heading in the right direction but the way that media portrayed the incident something as a 'national threat' – with series of cover stories day after day, I think created a lot of panic in the public domain. So, that way, I think there was a threat but not such an 'existential threat' how it was portrayed in the media. – Security Expert, Retired Brigadier General, Nepal Army

There are incidents where as a media insider, I can gauge whether the issue has been securitized with certain elements of threat involved in it. Language plays a big part in framing the issue as a threat. The way the headlines and the quotes are highlighted in large size to gather people's attention and provoke the readers of the threat, I consider that negative stories have a great prospect of securitizing the security discourses forward – Media Researcher

Security Sensitivity: Sometimes Overstretched, Sometimes Undermined

There are various underlying factors that determine the level of sensitivity the media agencies need to possess while covering the security issues. At times it is also dependent upon how media and security sector look upon each other or have an impression about each other. The impression that these two sectors have about each other, over a period of time, tends to shape the nature of security discourses in the media. Journalists deny this though as they claim that the basis of their structuring of stories on security issues is through the evidences and facts collected about the story. However, they also agree that a certain level of unintended subjectivity might have been reflected based on the relationships between the two sectors and how the security sector might have dealt with media personnel in the past.

As a government bureaucrat, while I had to work as an intermediary between both these two sectors, I have found their relationships quite tricky. There were phases where the two sectors were openly antagonistic about each other – which also greatly affected the negative media reporting and at times it was quite neutral. Often the personalities of the chief of security forces as well as the effectiveness of the spokespersons in handling the media played a pivotal role in shaping their relationships. – Retired Bureaucrat, Ministry of Home Affairs

In my defense upon accusations that our stories have been biased in terms of being subjective to the content, we have been very true to our profession and maintained professional integrity at all levels possible. Yes, reflecting back, at a personal level,

I might have brought in some of our previous relationships with the security sector unconsciously, but that hasn't been a deliberate attempt. – Journalist reporting on security issues

Therefore, the relationships between the two sectors did play an instrumental role in understanding the level of sensitivity of the issue and taking those security discourses forward. The key informants have also highlighted in their interviews that while there have been too much of discussion and discourse around the over-reporting and sensationalization in the media, there have equally been instances where the media has failed in reporting some important national security and foreign affairs related matters. So that way, there have also been 'under-securitization' as well:

I completely understand that there are various political-economic and other 'influential' factors surrounding the under reporting of certain issues. However, it does not negate the fact that there is a greater need for the media professionals to be 'adequately aware' of various dimensions of national security and foreign affairs. As for instance, climate change could just be understood as an environmental or social issue but with the evolving concept of human security and environmental threats, probably issues such as environmental security have been overlooked or undermined so far in the media. On the other hand, issues such as border encroachment and threat to national sovereignty remain 'dumped' in a small, unnoticeable segment of the newspaper instead of being a cover story with series of follow up stories. – Media Researcher

Capacity and Competency of Reporting on Sensitive Issues Such as Security

One of the major accusations posed forward by the security agencies as highlighted through the key informant interviews as well as observed in various speeches and anecdotal accounts of the security personnel's perceptions is the capacity and competency of journalists to report on sensitive issues. A key informant highlights an instance how lack of understanding about the security complexities have resulted in inaccurate reporting about security issues.

I remember once when a media reporter came to me for an interview when there was the buzz regarding Security Sector Reform (SSR) and the implications of introducing SSR in the current structure of Nepal Police. He was thinking that SSR is about completely dismantling the existing structure and developing a new one, which is entirely wrong. It is more about bringing reforms to the current structure. This sort of misunderstanding could be considered as a 'capacity crunch' to understand the changing dynamics of security. This has huge implications upon what the journalists report and how it is perceived by the lay reader. – Retired Senior Superintendent of Police

Media researchers who have been closely observing the media reporting trends also acknowledge the lack of capacity and competency of journalists to report about national security and foreign affairs matters primarily because a larger section of the journalists who enter the media field.

I have closely observed the journalists over two decades now and the sad reality is that journalism field is considered a 'miscellaneous' field where anyone can join without proper education and expertise. This tradition has evolved with some senior journalists holding powerful position and authority without having a strong technical know-how. This is a sad reality of the journalism field which doesn't support its development in a proper manner. – Media Researcher

Professionalism of Media and Security/ Foreign Affairs Agencies

Some key informants also viewed that level of professionalism that the two sectors maintained was crucial in securitizing security discourses:

While it is also true that media agencies – given their role as a medium to communicate and not directly influencing role in any affairs of the security/foreign affairs agencies, the level of professionalism that they maintained while covering the stories, keeping aside all other political-economic factors was also instrumental in their nature of reporting and their attempt in securitizing the security discourses. On the other hand, it was also important for the security/foreign affairs agencies to maintain the same degree of professionalism dealing with the media to make them aware of the sensitiveness of the issues and possible implications of being misreported in the media. – Media Researcher

The question of professionalism of the media agencies of maintaining neutrality did come up strongly in some of their coverage of controversial security discourses such as that of Rookmangud Katuwal incident of the 'attempted coup' or that of the corruption case of Armed Police Force in the Peace Mission. According to a key informant, the question of professionalism was also relative based on their own stances and positions:

Professionalism is also defined and interpreted differently. I completely understand that the accusation of the security agencies towards the media agencies being unprofessional that they just read the surface of the story and 'blow stories out of proportion' for their own advantages. – Retired Bureaucrat, Ministry of Home Affairs

Interestingly, the media professionals and diplomatic officials also defend their professionalism in handling security discourses in this manner:

Security officials blame us we are not professional, but it is clearly evident from the level of reluctance that they have in admitting their wrongdoings whenever they are revealed in the media. Sometimes they go to the extent of threatening us, which is completely unprofessional of them and their institution. – Editor of a national weekly

It is high time that the media agencies reflect their own reporting pattern and maintenance of media ethics. The way they are handled by various interest groups and the nature through which they reflect the negative image of the high-profile security officials for their own benefit does not go by their claims of professionalism. – Retired Bureaucrat, Ministry of Foreign Affairs

These instances reflect that the professionalism – being relatively defined and interpreted and own relative positions of the two sectors has influenced in shaping the securitization of security discourses in different ways and patterns.

"Threat Framing" and Its Political Economy

Threats are not always actual. Threats can also be framed and there have been studies by securitization theorists and media researchers about how threats can also be framed to create fear about things or situations that are non-existent. Various political and socio-economic factors also come into play behind the act of "threat-framing".

Some of the key informants reveal that despite the claims by media agencies that they are 'neutral' and do not have any political standpoints, there is always a political perspective or voice that the media agencies carry, which the influencing actors easily exploit.

I do not think that Nepali media has reached to that level that any media agencies claim to be completely unbiased towards any political influences. Even in developed societies, where media has evolved into a highly professional sector, there are political perspectives or voices they carry. For a country like Nepal, the political intervention is much easier. – Retired Bureaucrat, Ministry of Home Affairs

I have noticed on several occasions such as during the 'Tibet uprising' incidents in Kathmandu, some media agencies have covered the issue as a national threat giving it a more 'nationalist' colour while some have gone soft on the issue. Likewise, issues related to border encroachment, Madhesi issues, Army issues and other security concerns, the discourses that are carried by the media agencies are not on the same line due to various political preferences and thereby varying political interventions. – Media Researcher

Economy also plays a major role in the 'interest' of media agencies to securitize any national security and foreign affairs discourses and engage in threat framing. Economic power-play is closely embedded with political power-play in terms of sensationalizing or keeping quiet on certain issues. Key informants regard this as an interesting and sometimes 'obvious' phenomenon:

I sometimes regards this as an obvious phenomenon. For example, if a media house is politically aligned with the centre-rightist ideology, that agency is likely to be backed by foreign political power houses politically and economically. So, any news about Indian border encroachment could be hidden or could be covered very scarcely in a small section in the middle pages rather than on the first page itself for everyone's attention. – Media Researcher

I don't deny that reporting on security, international relations, diplomacy and politics is one of the interest factors for the journalists as there is an economic incentive attached to it. If the journalists would like to prefer remaining within their comfort zones, they report on some 'soft' issues such as education and health and if the journalists would like to take up some challenges for their career advancement, they go for 'hard' issues such as security, politics, international relations, diplomacy. As the hard issues are more prioritized by the media agencies based on audience interest, there is also better financial incentive for journalists to report on such issues. – Journalist, reporting on security issues

Advertisements are other aspects closely linked with the income sources of media agencies and they also consider this while securitizing any security discourses that have political colour. Advertisement companies are also part of the political interest groups and there have been previous instances where media agencies have gone out of advertisements or been temporarily closed down due to their 'over-reporting' or sensationalizing incidents that defame or criticize such ideologies of such interest groups.

I recall an incident when the issue of border encroachment by neigbbouring country was covered extensively by a Nepali daily that resulted in no advertisement by any foreign commercial companies and close down of the daily within few days due to the political and economic pressure. – Retired Bureaucrat, Home Ministry

Despite our efforts to maintain high degree of neutrality and ethical values of journalism, I do not deny that we live in a very fragile political and economic context that sometimes we are succumbed to such pressures to keep our work alive. We have witnessed incidents of our fellow colleagues falling prey to such pressures and we are sometimes in no position but to accept this fact. – Editor of a Nepali daily

Situation of Fragility: Changing Actors and Agents of Securitization

Frequent changes in political landscape in Nepal has created a situation of fragility, not only in terms of good governance but also for the media agencies with the fear of being victims of frequent political power-plays. Media management also becomes one of the core agendas of any new political force that makes media more vulnerable to various political pressures due to the frequent change in actors and agents of securitization.

I do not deny the fact that after every change in government or new political force coming into power, one of their major strategies is about media management and public relations. So, this adds pressure to the media agencies about the way they need to respond to the interests of these political groups. Despite the claims that the media agencies are watchdogs and they report/write based on factual evidence, the political-economy context also plays a pivotal role in what and how they report/ write. – Media Researcher

As a journalist, we bear the brunt the most. As we would be regularly reporting about a political leader or a political party as they would be in power and their thoughts about security, international relations and diplomacy issues, we are most of the times labeled as lobbyists of a political party or a leader's agenda. This is particularly difficult when the regime changes and the new leaders in power are reluctant to talk to us given the backdrop of the labeling we have had. – Journalist, reporting on national security and diplomacy issues

The changes in political forces also bring about the changes in personalities and changes in perspectives. A prime minister could be 'media-friendly' and willing to share his insights about the national security and diplomacy issues more openly as compared to the previous prime ministers. The media friendliness could then add to extensive reporting and securitization of any national security agenda. Whereas, with the change in political force, another prime minister could be 'media-shy' and there could be hardly any interviews about him being reported in the media. This could subside the securitization of the security discourses that he/she wants to carry due to lack of national debates on the agenda.

Personalities of the political forces do matter. Some come out in the media and are willing to share their ideas while some are not. We report based on what they share and we do not have our own preferences. It keeps us in a difficult position when we are analyzed externally without analyzing the context properly and just in terms of what we report and what we don't. – Editor of a national daily

The fragility also extends to the frequent changes of editorial positions of the media agencies that also plays a major role in securitization of the security discourses. The editors, given their long years of expertise and experience also bring along with them certain ideologies which is well reflected in their media outlets.

There has been hardly any critical analysis done in terms of changes in perspectives and 'voices' of the media outlets towards their securitization of the national security and diplomacy discourses with the changes in editors. But I see that as an existing phenomenon and a good topic for media researchers to understand critically and reflect upon it as to how a change in agent can also affect the course of securitization. – Media Researcher

Therefore, the fragility of a certain security discourse is also conditional to the changes in agents (media editors) along with the actors (political and economic power holders).

Lack of Uniform Standards: Varying Perceptions and Understanding

As discussed in earlier sections, due to the fragile political and socio-economic context of both the actors and the agents, there are no uniform standards about media reporting on security issues. There are some ethical provisions in place such as having spokespersons and guidelines from the security forces to disseminate any information publicly through media. Likewise, media agencies also have journalism ethics and protocols about publishing any 'sensitive' information. However, the key informants view that in practice, ethnical principles by both security and media agencies do not seem to be practiced in a highly professional manner.

I think we could have done better, in terms of providing information to the media agencies in a more crystal clear manner. Many a times, reflecting our own practice, I feel that as security agencies, we wear a different hat and that sometimes the pride of being a senior security personnel comes along while we express our opinions as well. We think from our own perspective and sometimes that do not translate well with media agencies and ultimately the public are not fed with the right information. It is not entirely the fault of media agencies to 'mold' the news in that fashion. We do have ourselves to blame as well to some extent as well. – Retired Brigadier General, Nepal Army

'Our journalism practice has not yet been so matured for us to apply high journalism standards. Having said that we are not hiding our pitfalls. We have various weaknesses, one of them is to abide by globally accepted standards such as Conflict Sensitive Journalism which we have applied to some extent, but not in uniform practice. Moreover, over the years, in the name of fragile political and socio-economic context, we may have not well reflected back on ourselves about how we report on security issues and the impact our reporting would have on the public developing an opinion based on our reports. – Editor of a national daily

Findings from both the content analysis and the key informant interviews therefore give a picture of the nature of securitization of national security and diplomacy discourses in Nepal in terms of how various contexts play a role in shaping up the perceptions and perspectives of the media in understanding the issues and then later on shape that understanding of various securitization elements into the tone of the articles/stories written about them.

"Speech Acts" and Resulting Public Perceptions

Media has been an integral part of shaping public perceptions and henceforth national security and diplomacy discourses in Nepal have also been securitized through the "speech acts" in different ways and forms. As illustrated by the study findings, while most of the editorial articles were declarative and directive in Nepal, the probability of public perceptions being shaped accordingly would be higher. While the print media – provides its voice through editorial and has a position about the process of investigation by the People's Movement II Investigation Committee and declares that heads of security heads to resign from their posts to support the investigation, the readers or the public automatically sets an impression about the need for the resignation of the security heads. There could have a very good rationale behind the editorial's stance on that, however, such securitization "speech acts" have direct influence upon public perception that have equal pros and cons at the same time.

On the other hand, the media "playing safe" on issues by just being expressive and condemning the act, than being directive and hitting nail on the head, results in public perceptions even for heinous acts being "soft". To cite an example, the editorial on the rise of the armed groups and the increasing communal tension in Madhes region was not declarative or directive enough to condemn such act but was playing safe on just being expressive. When the "speech act" was moulded in such a way to avoid any conflict later on, it did not have a good impact upon shaping the public perception as the public also perceived that the event/incident was not that worse, while it actually was.

While it is true that media is followed by the public and the educated mass who do have ability to decide what is right and what is wrong, it would be unfair to put forward that all the general public would have the same level of critical understanding. Henceforth, while the speech acts may not influence decisions of the critical mass, they would definitely shape the perceptions of the less aware public who would make their perception about any matter by following the media.

Contextual Factors Resulting in Securitization of National Security and Diplomacy Discourses

It was also well learnt through various instances that the media agencies also decide their stance about national security and diplomacy issues based on the political and socio-economic context and then decide the level and extent of securitization required. As opined by the key informants that the negative news sell more, media agencies are compelled to securitize a certain security discourse to create that "newsworthiness" in order to make them sellable.

Likewise, the way the media and security agencies perceived each other was also an important determinant about how the stories would be presented. As one of the key informants viewed that the personalities of the heads of the security agencies and the way the spokespersons handled the media also affected how the media carried the security discourses forward.

The level of professionalism that the two sectors maintained was also a determining factor in shaping the security discourses. As informed by the key informants, relative positions of the two sectors influenced in shaping the securitization of national security and diplomacy discourses in different ways and patterns. Capacity is also an important component when we talk about the professionalism as the narrow understanding of media just as the "mouthpieces" of the influential interest groups by the security agencies and not understanding of the wider ability of the media to shape the public perception on one hand while lack of capacity of media professionals to comprehend and analyze the complex political-security contexts on the other hand also led to misleading those discourses through media.

Lack of Interactions Between Media and Security/Foreign Affairs Agencies: Resulting Unhealthy Relationships

As demonstrated through the content analysis and also perceived by the key informants, there has hardly been any joint interactions between the media, security and policy makers in order to bridge this existing gap. While there are no serious interactions, the current trend of blame game and narrowed and pre-determined perception about each other would continue resulting in unhealthy relationships.

SOLUTIONS AND RECOMMENDATIONS

The study has derived the answers to the research questions that were formed during the inception phase of the study:

1. On the messages carried forward by the print media to the intellectual circles/academia and general public in terms of building a security discourse surrounding national security issues: Messages were mostly declarative and directive in nature which was a good thing rather than being expressive and suggestive; however the tone that the messages carried was determined by various socio-political contexts that also hindered the media to be explicit in certain situations about the message it wanted to convey.
2. On prioritization/importance given by the print media in its coverage of those security issues: Print media was found to give adequate prioritization/ importance in terms of covering the security issues. Sometimes it was also found over-prioritizing stories – subject to securitization of the issues while on some occasions, playing it safe and leaving the stories go uncovered. Various socio-political contexts, capacity of the media professionals to comprehend and interpret complex issues critically and the existing relations with security agencies also played a part in the level of prioritization/importance provided to the coverage of security issues.

3. Nature of coverage of security issues: During the interactions with key informants and also illustrated by our analysis of editorials, the securitization elements has come out strongly in the media coverage. Moreover, there were instances that issues that were 'securitized' were actually not required and the issues that had to be 'securitized' were given a 'mild' touch.

Considering the sensationalism that securitization creates, this study advocates for desecuritization whereby the security issues are moved out of threat and defense sequence into the 'ordinary public sphere' where they can be dealt with in accordance of the (democratic) political system.

Therefore, the following recommendations are made moving towards desecuritization of security discourses in Nepal through media by mitigating the current loopholes that led to the securitization:

1. Guiding policies should be in place for both security/foreign affairs and media agencies in order to ensure that there all activities carried out by security and media agencies are implemented through common understanding. Guidelines and policies also limit subjective interpretations and any wrong doings by the actors.
2. The policy makers – especially the law makers in the parliament dealing with security and defense committees; officials at Ministry of Home Affairs, Ministry of Defense and other line agencies need to need to play an intermediary role between media and security agencies and act as a 'desecuritizing' agency to avoid any security sensitive issues to be used as a tool for threat framing by the media.
3. There needs to be regular discourses through public debates and interactions by security and media experts identifying the trends of media reporting on security issues and how the sectoral experts can work together for better understanding of both the sectors for improved relationships and coordinated efforts of bringing the security/diplomacy sensitive issues in the media for public sensitization.

Figure 2. Process of securitization of security and diplomacy discourses using media

Figure 3. Process of desecuritization of security and diplomacy discourses using media

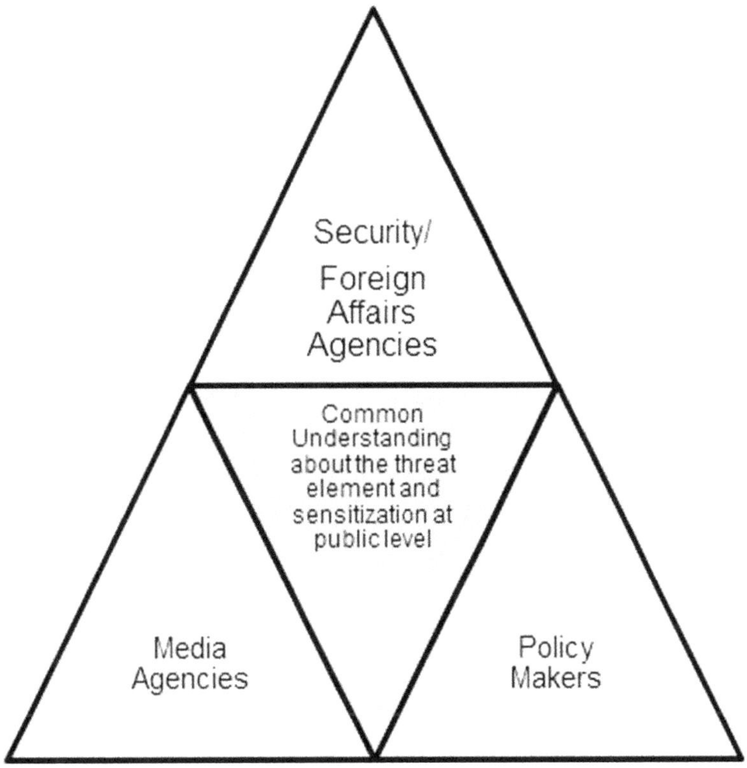

FUTURE RESEARCH DIRECTIONS

The importance of desecuritization in taking forward the security and diplomacy discourses using media in the right manner as compared to securitization can be better explained in the following figures.

Securitization of Security Discourses: A Linear and Isolated Approach

See Figure 2.

Desecuritization of Security Discourses: A Non-Linear and Integrated Approach

See Figure 3.

CONCLUSION

National Security and diplomacy issues – given their sensitivity could be misinterpreted or manipulated easily by powerful agents such as media given their reach and ability to influence mass audience within no time with the evolution and unprecedented growth of social media. Particularly, in the context of Nepal, where media is gradually expanding its network, there is a need for desecuritization of security discourses to sensitize the right information about security matters to the public through media, promoting peace and cooperation rather than polarization of ideas and perspectives.

REFERENCES

Adhikari, D. (2016, September 13). Art of the Conscious. *Republica*. Retrieved December 19, 2016, from http://www.myrepublica.com/news/author/1221

Adhikari, D. (2017, January 17). On Media Writing – III. *Republica*. Retrieved January 20, 2017, from http://www.myrepublica.com/news/13197

Archetti, C. (2010, September). *Media Impact on Diplomatic Practice: An Evolutionary Model of Change*. Paper presented at American Political Science Association (APSA) Annual Convention, Washington, DC. Retrieved November 17, 2016, from https://www.academia.edu/378891/_Media_Impact_on_Diplomatic_Practice_An_Evolutionary_Model_of_Change_

Archetti, C. (2012). *Why Diplomacy in a Global World is Shaped by Local Media*. Retrieved December 27, 2016, from http://www.e-ir.info/2012/11/02/why-diplomacy-in-a-global-world-is-shaped-by-local-media/

Austin, J. L. (1962). *How to do things with words*. London: Oxford University Press. Retrieved October 23, 2016, from http://pubman.mpdl.mpg.de/pubman/item/escidoc:2271128:3/component/escidoc:2271430/austin_1962_how-to-do-things-with-words.pdf

Baldwin, D. (1997). The Concept of Security. *Review of International Studies*, *23*(1), 5–26. doi:10.1017/S0260210597000053 PMID:10164688

Balzacq, T. (2005). The Three Faces of Securitization: Political Agency, Audience and Context. *European Journal of International Relations*, *11*(2), 171–201. doi:10.1177/1354066105052960

Basnyat, P. S. (2009). *Military Media Relation and Security*. Retrieved 13 December, 2016, from http://www.premsinghbasnyat.com.np/topics-details.php?articleid=12&type=0

Behera, N. C. (2002). *State, People and Security: The South Asian Context*. New Delhi: Har-Anand Publications Pvt. Ltd.

Booth, K. (2007). *Theory of World Security*. New York: Cambridge University Press. doi:10.1017/CBO9780511840210

Buzan, B., & Hansen, L. (2009). *The Evolution of International Security Studies*. New York: Cambridge University Press. doi:10.1017/CBO9780511817762

Buzan, B., Waever, O., & Wilde, J. (1997). *Security: A New Framework for Analysis*. London: Lynne Rienner Publishers.

Carpentier, N., (2005). *Media Representations of War and Conflict*. KUB Center Communication for Social Change, the Communications Department of the Vesalius College (VUB) and the Pascal Decroos Fund for Investigative Journalism.

Floyd, R. (2011). Can securitization theory be used in normative analysis? Towards a just securitization theory. *Security Dialogue*, *42*(4-5), 427–439. doi:10.1177/0967010611418712

Gilboa, E. (2001). Diplomacy in the media age: Three models of uses and effects. *Diplomacy and Statecraft*, *12*(2), 1–28. doi:10.1080/09592290108406201

Gurung, R. (2011). *Journalism in Transition: Media, Information Flows and Conflict in Nepal*. International Alert. Retrieved 18 December, 2016, from http://www.ifp-ew.eu/pdf/201110IfPEWJournTransMediaInfoConflict.Nepal.pdf

Guzzini, S. (2011). Securitization as a Causal Mechanism. *Security Dialogue*, *42*(4-5), 329–341. doi:10.1177/0967010611419000

Hacker, K. L., & Mendez, V. R. (2016). Toward a Model of Strategic Influence, International Broadcasting, and Global Engagement. *Media and Communication*, *4*(2), 69-91 Retrieved January 05, 2017, from http://www.cogitatiopress.com/ojs/index.php/mediaandcommunication/article/view/355

Hansen, L. (2013). *Security as Practice: Discourse Analysis and the Bosnian War*. New York: Routledge.

Internews. (2011). *Media and Telecoms Landscape Guide*. Retrieved December 3, 2016, from https://www.internews.org/sites/default/files/resources/nepal_media_landscape_guide_final_011011_19.12.12.pdf

KC, B. (2014). *Political Inclination of Journalists and Its Influence on News*. Kathmandu: Centre for Media Research (CMR) - Nepal. Retrieved November 23, 2016, from http://research.butmedia.org/wp-content/uploads/2014/10/PoliticalInclination.pdf

McDonald, M. (2008). Securitization and the Construction of Security. *European Journal of International Relations*, *13*(4), 563–587. doi:10.1177/1354066108097553

Murphy, M. (2013, July 3). *How has social media affected diplomatic reporting?* Retrieved November 26, 2016, from https://www.diplomacy.edu/blog/how-has-social-media-affected-diplomatic-reporting

Press Council Nepal. (2016). *41st Annual Report*. Kathmandu. Retrieved 25 December, 2016, from http://www.presscouncilnepal.org/np/wp-content/uploads/2016/10/Final-Yearly-Report.pdf

Reljic, D. (2004). *News Media and the Transformation of Ethnopolitical Conflicts*. Berghof Research Centre for Constructive Conflict Management. Retrieved 15 November, 2016, from http://www.berghof-foundation.org/fileadmin/redaktion/Publications/Handbook/Articles/reljic_handbook.pdf

Sharma, S. (2009). Media and the Security Sector: Shifting Relations. In B. Sapkota (Ed.), *The Nepali Security Sector: An Almanac*. Geneva Centre for the Democratic Control of Armed Forces and the Centre for European Studies.

Sulovic, V. (2010). *Meaning of Security and the Theory of Securitization*. Belgrade Centre for Security Policy. Retrieved 19 December, 2016, from http://www.bezbednost.org/upload/document/sulovic_(2010)_meaning_of_secu.pdf

Taureck, R. (2006). Securitization Theory and Securitization Studies. *Journal of International Relations and Development*, *9*(9), 53–61. doi:10.1057/palgrave.jird.1800072

Uhlig, C. (2015). *Moving towards Securitization. How the Paris Attacks were Used to Justify Extraordinary Measures*. Linnaeus University. Retrieved 19 December, 2016, from http://lnu.diva-portal.org/smash/get/diva2:824877/FULLTEXT01.pdf

Vultee, F. (2007). *Securitization as a Theory of Media Effects: The Contest Over the Framing of Political Violence*. Retrieved 22 November, 2016, from https://mospace.umsystem.edu/xmlui/bitstream/handle/10355/4792/research.pdf?sequence=3&isAllowed=y

We Are Social. (2017). *Digital in 2017: South East Asia*. Retrieved 20 February, 2017, from https://www.slideshare.net/wearesocialsg/digital-in-2017-southeast-asia

KEY TERMS AND DEFINITIONS

Desecuritization: The process of nullifying an issue, particularly related to politics or national affairs, that was securitized or considered a threat to human survival.

Diplomacy: Overall matters of a conduct of a country towards another country.

Discourse: Interchange, discussion, and conversation over an idea or topic.

National Security: A broad concept encompassing a country's protection particularly related to territory and defense, internal and external politics, and economics.

Print Media: Paper publications of circulations such as newspapers, weekly and monthly magazines.

Securitization: The process whereby an issue, particularly related to politics or national affairs, is considered a threat to human survival and therefore requires emergency actions or coercive means.

Speech Act: The process of analyzing the meaning behind the use of words in a particular manner.

ENDNOTES

1. People's War was a decade long armed struggle against the government by the revolutionary force labelled as Communist Party of Nepal (CPN) – Maoist.
2. Indian movie star Hrithik Roshan's allegedly anti-Nepal comments sparked huge protests in Nepal in December 2000, leaving 4 Nepalis dead in the riot.
3. People's Movement II is the name given to the democratic movement in Nepal that happened in April 2007 to mark the movement against 'autocratic' and 'undemocratic' rule of the then King Gyanendra Bir Bikram Shah Dev which ultimately dethroned him and Nepal became a republican state.

Chapter 5
Role of E-Diplomacy in Maintaining India's Diplomatic Relations and in Shaping Foreign Policy With South Asian Countries and With International Community

Swati Jaywant Rao Bute
Jagran Lakecity University, India

ABSTRACT

In a globalized world when countries are working together in different areas such as economic, political, geopolitical, defense, security, and science and technology, media plays an important role in keeping them updated about the actual and ground level realities about different countries. This chapter examines how new media is important in international relations and diplomatic affairs, what role new media is playing in international relations, India's relations with South Asian countries and role of media diplomacy, India's relations with international community and role of e-diplomacy, people's participation in discussion and dialogue in international relations and its impact in diplomatic policies, relation between people's participation and deciding policies and national level, increasing role of new media and changing practice of international diplomacy, and foreign policy adopted by governments.

DOI: 10.4018/978-1-5225-3859-2.ch005

INTRODUCTION

In last few years we are observing change in media practices and reporting patterns in contemporary and digital media. Politicians and government officers who are involved in shaping, drafting and making foreign policies have realised that in the changing scenario using different media to get connected with common people and to get their involvement in making people centric policies is very important . In last few years due to technology upgradation and change in media business models and media practices we are observing changes in the way media produces stories and do their businesses. Media policies and practices adopted at global level also affecting the domestic and local media practices and business patterns. History tells us that Media always played an important role in international, bilateral and diplomatic relations. In this age of information technology both contemporary and new media are playing important role in informing and keeping people update about international happenings and affairs. Now diplomats are using different media platforms, they have adopted new policies, practices and working style to adjust and adopt the changing working environment which is more technology oriented, dependent on technology, more transparent and people centric.

Now the strategic and diplomatic relations between the countries are based on public image, by getting reflection through different media outlets, public opinion, information available on digital media platforms in the form of public opinion and views and news which comes from different National and International media channels. In a globalized world when countries are working together in multiple areas like economy, politics, geopolitics, strategic relations, defense, security and science and technology, diplomatic relations between the countries are also shaped on the basis their relation and mutual understanding in all these areas. This chapter examines what role new media is playing in shaping international relations and diplomatic and multilateral relations. What foreign policy is adopted by the present government in India to strengthen its relations with the South Asian countries and with international community. What changes we are observing in diplomatic practices in the age of public and e-diplomacy. People's participation in discussions on global affairs and its impact on government decision and in policy making.

What Role Is New Media Playing in Shaping International Relations, Diplomatic and Multilateral Relations?

Shaping the perceptions of opponents, supporters and neutral groups influences whether they will become involved and how they will participate. "Over the past century politics has increasingly come to be played out through the media. This is not a narrow claim about internet or satellite television but rather a claim about the way that modern society has been transformed (and indeed constituted) by changing forms of mediation (Innis, 1951; McLuhan, 1964)" (as cited in Thusssu & Freedman, 2003, p. 88). "Over the course of twentieth century, politics has been transformed by the increasing involvement of the public and of interest groups linked, informed and mobilised by the media of communication" (Brown, 2003)

India is observing positive impact of use of new media and internet in diplomatic affairs. The Extreme Affairs Ministry of India is using new media and internet to make their job easy and reachable to everyone at home as well as abroad. External Affairs Minister Sushma Swaraj, who ushered in a new style of diplomacy through dynamic engagement on Twitter, "was named in the Global Thinkers List of 2016 compiled by Foreign Policy magazine. Swaraj was included in the 'Decision-makers' category alongside former US secretary of state Hillary Clinton, German Chancellor Angela Merkel, UN Secretary General Bank ki-Moon and Canadian prime minister Justin Trudeau. She was cited in the list 'for fashioning a novel brand of Twitter diplomacy.' The minister, who has 6.8 million followers on Twitter, has resolved issues ranging from passport problems to rescuing overseas Indians trapped in conflict-prone conditions. Her popular perception was so positive that many came ahead to donate their kidneys for her transplant surgery. "From evacuating Indians from Yemen to helping replace lost passports, Swaraj has earned the nickname "the common tweeple's leader" for her aggressive use of Twitter" (Express Web Desk, 2016)

In his recent visit to US, Prime Minister of India Mr. Narendra Modi once again appreciated the way External Affairs Ministry of India is interacting with common people in solving their problems and said that the External Affairs Minister, Mrs. Sushma Swaraj has converted diplomacy into human diplomacy.

The past decade has also witnessed increased global migration and the globalisation of media, with new satellite technologies and the internet making McLuhan's 'global village' truly global. These trends have impacted on the choices available to governments in dealing with national and international issues and bilateral, regional and multilateral relations. This has had its inevitable impact on India, which has been transformed this past decade by its increased economic openness. This in turn has shaped India's relations with the world economy and global communities (Baru, 2009).

The Internet has emerged as an essential worldwide medium.

The net's future is impossible to predict, since it has such flexibility to develop in so many different ways. The Internet operates as a hub for the development of a variety of services that are easily shared within or across ethnic, national, linguistic and cultural boundaries. Its influence is increasingly reinforced by a growing range of new software and hardware allowing internet based content to be more easily created, accessed, and stored and shared by individuals and groups located anywhere in the world (Baran & Davis, 2015).

As Hillary Clinton once said during her tenure as Secretary of State: "Just as the internet has changed virtually every aspect of how people worldwide live, learn, consume and communicate, connection technologies are changing the strategic context for diplomacy in the 21st century" (Kluz & Mikilas, 2015).

The audience members are

no longer really part of a mass but is either a member of self-chosen network or special public or individual. In addition the balance of audiences activity shifts from reception to searching, consulting and interacting more personally. Medium is just not an applied technology for transmitting certain symbolic content or linking participants in some exchange, It also embodies a set of social relations that interact with features of the new technology. The most fundamental aspects of a information and communication technology is probably the fact of digitalization the process by which all text (symbolic meaning of all encoded and recorded items) can be reduced to a binary code and can share the same process of production, distribution and storages (McQuail, 2005).

Foreign policy of India - What foreign policy is adopted by the present government in India to strengthen its relations with with South Asian countries and with international community

The foreign policy adopted by Prime Minister, Narendra Modi's government is proactive in nature and has changed many set rules by taking some revolutionary decisions in the process of policy making which is more transparent and people centric in nature. After three years of Modi government we can see many positive changes directly but at the same time we can also see many positive changes which is effective indirectly. Modi governments foreign policy focuses more on expanding geographical and technological zone for boosting economy of the country and to build up or create and domestic market system for indigenous technology and on locally manufactured products. Through his foreign and economic policies he wants to create a foundation for new economic revolution in which India with a 1.2

billion population is just not a country which is a big open market for the sell and consumption of foreign products but also a country which is capable in fulfilling its domestic needs and requirements and also capable in providing/ selling its technology and products globally in International market. Somewhere the Modi government has realised and feeling very strong and deeply that due to policy paralysis in past government, unstable political scenarios during the era of coalition governments in India and due to lack of political will India has remained far behind in South Asian region in the economic development and in establishing itself as a country who is capable not only in consumption of technology and products and also self-sufficient in manufacturing technology and products. This delay in the economic growth is not only affecting India in establishing itself as a strong geopolitical partner domestically and internationally.

Even having all the potential, resources, market and talent India is not able to establish itself as a leader at economic and strategic front. The present government has also realised that domestic political, economic and security related affairs are keeping us so busy that we are not able to see our strength areas, our political-cultural linkages with international community, existing resources and talent, strengthening our relations with old reliable friends and making new friends globally for economic development and strategic partnership, rebooting dying relations with neighbouring countries and getting maximum benefit through all which is with us in establishing a new image of India. And that is why when Prime Minister of India Mr. Narendra Modi travels to different countries he focuses more on getting economic-strategic partnership, technology exchange, collaboration, cultural exchange and bonding, finding diplomatic solutions for strategic, geopolitical and security related long existing problems with neighbouring countries. During his swearing in ceremony PM Narendra Modi had invited Prime Ministers of all South Asian Countries which was a signal of improving and strengthening regional relations. But soon through his visits to different countries he indicated that India is open in building and strengthening relations at Global level. He initiated this idea that cultural bonding can also play important role in improving relations and building trust and mutual understanding. In this pro-active approach they are using media in the promotion and projection of new image of India. This approach is helping government in getting positive response in political, economic and strategic negotiation.

The Narendra Modi government in the last three years has successfully transformed India's foreign policy. There has been a major shift in India's external affairs. India has successfully shifted its gear from role taker to rule maker. The Modi governments foreign policy in the last three years has ticked all the important silos - counter terrorism, climate change, trade and technological cooperation and energy security.

According to Amarendra Khatua, Director of Indian Council for Cultural Relations, "India first, India aggressive is the theme song of this governments foreign policy," engaging with the foreign diaspora is yet another key features of Modi government, PM Modi is involving Indian diaspora which contributes significantly towards India's foreign exchange reserves in India's development agenda.

Another important feature in India's external affairs under Modi is adding cultural symbolism to the foreign policy diplomacy, during his visits to China, Japan, Sri Lanka, Nepal and Mangolia, PM Modi have successfully revived the thousands of years of civilizational connect of these countries with India.

India has launched GSAT-9 satellite to provide communication and help in disaster management to South Asian countries. Modi's foreign policy is also packed with economic diplomacy never before any Indian Prime Minister visited so many countries as Modi did (Panigrahi, 2017).

We can say that e-diplomacy for improving regional and international relations and in shaping foreign policy is helping to the present government a lot but we have to understand that strong and sustainable relations also needs execution of strong and prompt actions and decisions and attitude of maturity in implementation of all planned goals and visions. Foreign policy also needs reflection of execution of strong decisions and policies to show a strong hold and implementation of taken decisions.

We are at the threshold of year four of Prime Minister Modi's regime and it is measure of the unpredictability and rapidly shifting nature of international political and economic currents that the foreign policy outlook for India at this juncture looks decidedly different from the heady days of his first year in power. In reaching out to the large Indian diaspora spread across the globe Modi created an influential global constituency of support for India.

India's engagement with its neighbours continues to be episodic, driven by events such as high level visits or by political crisis which erupts in one country or another. We have not created a capacity to engage with our neighbours on a sustained basis and at multiple levels. The failure to deliver on time, the commitments made to neighbouring countries erodes India's credibility is one of the most important components of a successful foreign policy (Saran, 2017).

The Modi team has dismantled the older policies towards Pakistan and China but nothing new seems to be on the horizons. The one dimensional policy is not yielding any results (Joshi, 2016).

What Changes Are We Observing in Diplomatic Practices in the Age of Public and E-Diplomacy?

This mediatization reflects politics changes in the media sphere. At a political level, International governance is changing.

A growing range of issues are subject to 'International regimes', agreements that regulate aspects of international affairs, transnational relationships and domestic society even in the absence of formal international organisations. There has been growth in multilateralism as a mode of governance, addressing international problems through action by groups of states. In the twenty first century politics is conducted via the mass media (Brown, 2003).

Diplomacy is a hard subject but in a globalised world its nature is changing. Now it is just not limited to country to country relations for geopolitical, security and economic related issues but is also influenced by many other elements. In a globalised world countries all over the world has realised that they cannot live in isolation or in a group of selected few countries, which has forced them to break boundaries and work with different countries in multiple areas to fulfil various needs and secure different interests and that is how diplomacy is involving different areas to make fundamental areas of diplomacy such as geopolitical relation, security and economic relations more strong, sustainable and result oriented.

Media was always a integrated part of diplomacy and international relations, with changing technology new platforms for information are emerging. Mass involvement is a new trend in open economy. Information creation, distribution and consumption is not blocked, closed and centrally oriented but is more decentralised, liberal and democratic. In a commercial media environment, audiences are now consumers, information is not freely available, but it is a paid commodity. Media consumers are paying money not only for the information but also for channels. They are now more selective, wanting more involvement and hold. International media business practices and patterns are not only allowing audience centric approaches but media houses and organisations are inventing new business patterns to give guarantee of audiences and consumers more share and hold in the business of information creation, sharing and distribution. In a changed information creation, distribution and consumption practices and media business patterns we are also observing change in creation, presentation, distribution and consumption practices of diplomacy and international relations related news and information.

India is not the only country which has involved digital media for the promotion and projection of policies and for reaching to the people nationally, internationally specifically the internet community. There are many other countries who have involved new media in States affairs and have seen positive results not only in building people friendly and an open image amongst the international community but also in changing the working patterns of diplomatic affairs of their country and in establishing new Diploma practices.

People's Participation in Discussions on Global Affairs and Its Impact on Government Decision and in Policy Making

People participation in discussion related to diplomatic relations has increased in last few years. During many international and national events, movements and during agitation it has been observed that people are very quick in responding on social media and if some news or event is related to country, many groups get activated on social media, some who are appreciating government, some who are against governments decision. These groups on social media get converted into aggressive mob and can create any situation in the society and any type perception in the mind of people active on social media. Normally people easily get influenced by anything which is coming from their close circles on social media and easily believe and get motivated through that. In such cases if anything is related to government or system and if no one is available from governments side on social media to clear their side, it misleads people more. To solve this problem and to avoid any such situation where government feel helpless, when situation is out of control, when people are in attacking mode and speaking against government. Government of India has taken all these challenge seriously and have started taking part in online discussions and views coming from different sides on any issue or event to read people's mood on that. During UPA government, politicians and government officials had realised this need to remain connected with people on media, understand public mood and nature of information spreading on digital platforms, get an idea flow of information and discussions, identify and differentiate true and false news coming on online media and take steps accordingly to counter and solve the problem. Since online media is a open media, many people react on it, many open and hidden actors take part in discussions, each topic or group is a bucket of diverse actors, views, opinions and intentions and to deal it in a professional way is not only necessary but required for the government.

Since the beginning of its tenure Modi Government has realised this need and have set up a proper system to keep people update about government policies, change people's perception in their favour, respond quickly and be available on social media 24/7. All major Ministries are working on this agenda and have adopted this strategy for social media handling. Apart from this defensive approach which government have adopted to curb any criticism against government on social media, this government has also realised the potential of medium in directly connecting with the people and diluting the power, authority, single ownership and dominance of mainstream Indian and foreign private media in India.

During the initial growth phase of electronic media in India when apart from newspapers and radio, television was most popular media in India and only government run public broadcasting service Doordarshan was available and was the only channel for Information and entertainment. Many media pundits used to criticise government run media because of governments control and hold on that. And it was considered as a mouthpiece of government. When economic liberalisation was happened in India during Nineties, private media came into existence and it was thought that it will bring revolutionary change in the political, government and in social system. But with privatisation foreign media also came to India with the primary intention of business. Before privatisation mostly Indian media was under government, few newspaper were working for the welfare and with a mission of social upliftment and service that time media was not commercialised in India. But in new set up the entire system was changed now the intention was making more money and profit in such situation idea of free press get totally lost as in new set up old and established Indian media organisations and houses quickly adopted new business models, patterns and technology to compete with foreign media and to maintain and sustain their hold in the market. At the same time emerging Indian and foreign media organisation were coming with new strategies to capture the vivid, diverse and big market of consumers in India. In such condition the entire focus was on to expand the business and make more and more profit by experimenting with new media and Journalism practices, formats, with political and corporate setup and negotiation, diverse audiences and needs and by providing exposure of foreign culture and products to the Indian audiences. In such scenario media organisations were doing lot of adjustments and experiments and the real focus of providing more information and making or building a more informed, alert and aware society was totally lost from the agenda. There was a period when private 24/7 News channels were giving a large percentage broadcast time to entertainment and soft news. Corporate houses and political parties were entering into media business and a different kind of culture was developing when media, politics and corporate was more powerful and were making good money by fulfilling each other's interests and agendas. In India, media is a fourth pillar of democracy which plays important role in strengthening democratic establishment and practices but due to closeness with political parties and corporate houses for making money, fulfilling each other's interests and achieving more power and dominance in political decisions making, influencing political decisions and setup, influencing audiences with a purpose and agenda and changing public opinion in the favour of favourite political party, running a parallel judiciary and political system, getting authoritative power, local and foreign media was almost working like a parallel government. There was a time when due to corruption and political interest government was working under the monopoly and pressure of Indian and foreign media and corporate houses. This practice is still in use but now with the entry of social media, people's more presence on digital media, relying more on information coming from ground zero, close circles, friends and relatives, use of digital media by politicians, direct interaction with politicians and public somewhere mainstream Indian and foreign private media has changed their media practices and focusing more on serious journalism rather focusing on political and corporate settings and business.

Then time came when through news coverage, media scams and wrong media practices audiences getting realised that media, politicians and corporate are working together for their own interest and agendas and not serious towards providing true information and focusing on public issues. They got a new or social media as a alternative or substitute of mainstream media to raise their voice and opinion on issues of their interests and needs. In the beginning we have seen people used social media during natural catastrophe people used social media. And this is how they got a parallel media where they can write what they feel, reveal real facts and can mobilise people to take action if required. With increasing crowd of users on social media, social media mobilised mob was able in creating pressure not only on government but also on mainstream media channels. To keep the vote bank with them and maintain, capture and hold the viewers and audiences politicians and mainstream media started taking social media and users seriously. Government have adopted a special and proactive strategy to remain more visible on social media, handle social media campaigns successfully, satisfy social media users by providing timely information, promotion of government work, policies and decisions, involving diverse people in online discussion by poles and voting, take their views in policy and decision making, make themselves popular among social media users to maintain positive and healthy relations as well as to reduce the distance and break the wall between people and politicians. Mainstream media is using social media news, updates, campaigns, videos and views as a source for their news stories, sometimes as a primary source of the news.

This entire development and change came with positive response and results, today politicians, bureaucrats, government officials are working closely with social media users, solving their problems online, providing 24/7 help online regularly and at the time of international-national crisis, listening their complains, requests seriously and providing timely solution. This clean and transparent work style not only making politicians and decision makers popular amongst social media users but also giving positive message to international community and in getting international communities positive and timely response at the time of crisis. This activity not only helping in expanding bilateral relations and mutual understanding between countries but also international community showing positive response in expanding relations in other areas such as business and technology development and transfer. With huge presence of Indian users and media consumption international community sometimes use India centric media platforms to send positive message and building their positive image in the international circle.

Social media users' presence, involvement, participation in discussions, sending their views, opinion across the table, raising questions, objecting, agitating on issues is not directly affecting the government system and decision, but yes it is playing important role in shaping the blueprint for policies and programs, decision making.

Role of E-Diplomacy in Improving and Strengthening India's Relations With South Asian Countries

The present government in India is working on "Neighbourhood First" policy, and trying its level best to improve relations in the area of political, economic, cultural and security related issues.

In the 21st century there has been more of a need for states to use soft power so as to enhance one's attractiveness in international arena and to show one's better side in order to stimulate cooperation and dampen resistance, particularly concerning security policies. In this context, public diplomacy has become a very important instrument of soft power, as well as being a vital tool of Indian foreign policy (Ritambhara, 2013).

Soft power, the term coined by Joseph Nye, has become a portent measure of a country's power and influence in the world today. Soft power is the ability to get what one wants through attraction rather than coercion or payments (Nye, 2004). Soft power largely emanates from a country's culture, its political values and institutions and its foreign policy (Nye, 1990).

India finds itself well-placed in possessing soft power resources because of its rich culture and history, its democratic credentials, its technological advancement, its large and influential diaspora and the leadership India wields among the developing nations through multilateral institutions like Non-Alignment movement. Thus, what distinguishes India's claim to global leadership is its unique, unobtrusive, persuasive "soft power" or what South Asia expert Steven Cohen calls "India's Repetitional Power" (Moharir, 2009).

Prime Minister Narendra Modi's foreign policy is currently focused on improving relations with the neighbouring countries in South Asia; engaging extended neighbourhood in the Southeast Asian region and other major global powers. However, the main objective of its foreign policy has been promotion of trade; maintaining security; promoting transit facility among member states; sprucing infrastructure and enabling connectivity etc. Through 'neighbourhood first' policy, more emphasis has been given to our immediate neighbors (Kaur & Kumar, 2017).

Role of E-Diplomacy in Building a New Image of India at a Global Platform

Various analysts have observed that the success of Prime Minister Modi's strategy relies especially on his charisma, a powerful use of the media (social media in particular), an effective media management strategy, and the capacity to avoid the mistakes made by past governments. Managing the media allows for better management of public perception. The Prime Minister relies on relationships, and the Indian business community—which supports Mr Modi—has heavily invested in the Indian media.

Prime Minister Modi is also one of the first political leaders to have recognised the immense power of the fairly recent trend of 'selfies', which he uses for promotion: "selfies and other social media tactics can help shape the image of the BJP leader" (Taylor, 2015).

Selfies are featured prominently on Modi's widely followed Twitter account, and such clever use of social media contributes to his popularity among the youth (Heng, 2016).

Social media have also become one of Modi's instruments of choice for conveying his messages to the countries he visits. He would even communicate to people in other countries in their own language. Social media is one way (not the only way) of telling the better story about India and the policies of its government. As such, it remains a valuable arrow in the Indian diplomatic quiver (Tharoor, 2016).

Prior to his visit to China around mid-May 2015, for example, Modi joined the Chinese social media platform Weibo to connect with Chinese citizens: Public diplomacy through social media is an emerging modern day foreign policy tool, largely influenced and guided as means of projecting soft power (Mallapur, 2015).

CONCLUSION

E-diplomacy is playing important role in shaping or building good relations with regional powers as well as with international community. The focus of present government is on boosting economy by making good relations not only with regional alliances but also with international community and that is also a core point of India's foreign policy. E-diplomacy is helping in getting connected with foreign diaspora which reflects in the form of crowd which gathers and the enthusiasm which they show during Prime Minister Narendra Modi's foreign visits and it definitely creates a very positive impression and supportive environment globally towards India. Use of e-diplomacy in the promotion of major programs started by the present government works as a window for foreign investor to assess the areas and opportunity to work with the government, and for investment and cooperation. Use of e-diplomacy in promotions of major amendments done by present government not only in the economic sector but in other areas gives a confidence to foreign investors to initiate new projects in India as the market system and overall working system is improving under the present leadership.

E-diplomacy is helping in showcasing the soft power of India and in trust building at both regional and International level. We can see a kind of trust deficit in South Asian region where countries are working individually though many areas and channels are available to work together with neighbouring countries but we can see a kind of unawareness about the scope and potential of the region. In recent time some initiatives are taken to come closer, work together and to identify the potential exist in the subcontinent by working together for each other's interest and development rather moving alone in different directions. And we have seen good response for all initiatives taken in the direction of working together. Sometimes media messages and signals plays important role in removing illusion and in providing clear picture, e-diplomacy is doing the same job which is helping in a positive direction, though we have not seen any direct impact of e-diplomacy but we can see the support which we have received from South Asian countries at the time of boycott of SAARC summit and standing together against the terrorism exist in the region. Same support we got at the time of doclam standoff with China, when not only regional countries but also the international community is supporting stand taken by India, which is a great diplomatic support.

E-diplomacy is helping in strengthening cultural relations and bondages. we cannot use it directly for maintaining diplomatic relations but definitely it helps in maintaining good harmony in relations, in avoiding technicalities involved in bilateral and multilateral relations, the dryness and hardness which exist in the very serious area of diplomacy, e-diplomacy, cultural diplomacy and public and media diplomacy somewhere help in promoting things in a right and positive direction, finding scope for improvement and providing a productive environment.

REFERENCES

Baran, S.J., & Davis, D.K. (n.d.). *Trends in mass communication theory: Seeking consensus, facing challenges, Mass Communication Chronology - Foundation, ferment and future* (4th ed.). Academic Press.

Baru, S. (2009, February 5). *The growing influence of business and media on Indian Foreign Policy*. Institute of South Asian Studies Insights. No. 49. Retrieved from http://www.isas.nus.edu.sg

Brown, R. (2003). Spinning the war: Political communications, information operations and public diplomacy in the war on terrorism. In D. K. Thussu & D. Freedman (Eds.), *War and the media-reporting conflict 24/7* (pp. 87–88). Sage Publications. doi:10.4135/9781446215579.n7

Brown, R. (2003). Spinning the war: Political communications, information operations and public diplomacy in the war on terrorism. In D. K. Thussu & D. Freedman (Eds.), *War and the media-reporting conflict 24/7* (pp. 87–88). Sage Publications. doi:10.4135/9781446215579.n7

Express Web Desk. (2016, December 14). Sushma Swaraj named in FP's global thinkers 2016 list, PM Modi says 'very proud'. *The Indian Express*. Retrieved from http://www.Indian express.com

Heng, S. M. L. (2016). Diplomacy and image building: India rides on its soft power. *Observer Research Foundation, Issue Brief, November 2016,* (163). Retrieved from http://cf.orfonline.org/wp-content/uploads/2016/11/IB-163.pdf

Joshi, M. (2016, December 23). The Modi government has dismantled India's Foreign Policy [Weblog comment]. Retrieved from http://www.thewire.com

Kaur, H., & Kumar, A. (2017a). *A paradigm shift in foreign policy*. Retrieved from http://www.dailypioneer.com/columnists/oped/a-paradigm-shift-in-foreign-policy.html

Kaur, H., & Kumar, A. (2017b, August 10). A Paradigm Shift in Foreign Policy [Weblog comment]. Retrieved from http://www.dailypioneer.com

Kluz, A., & Firlej, M. (2015, December 22). The Impact of Technology on Foreign Affairs - Five Challenges [Weblog comment]. Retrieved from http://www.foreignpolicyblogs.com

Kluz, A., & Mikolas, F. (2015). *The impact of technology on foreign affairs - Five challenges*. Foreign Policy Association. Retrieved from www.foreignpolicyblog.com

Mallapur, C. (2015). PM Narendra Modi wields soft power to befriend Chinese. *Business Standard*. Retrieved from http://business-standard.com/article/current-affairs/pm-narendra-modi-wields-soft-power-to-befriend-chinese-115050500321_1.html

Massolin, P. (1996). Context and content: Harrold innins, Marshal macluhan, and George grant and the role of technology in modern society. *Past Imperfect (Edmonton, Alta.)*, *5*, 81–118. Retrieved from http://www.journals.library.ualberta.ca

McQuails, D. (2015). *Mass communication theory, New media - new theory* (5th ed.). New Delhi: Vistar Publication.

Moharir, V. (2009). *India Rising: The Role of Indian Diaspora in Accelerating India's Transition as a Global Power*. The Hague, The Netherlands: Foundation for Critical Choice for India, Pravasiya Bhartiya Divas. Retrieved from https://www.indiawijzer.nl/indian_diaspora/indian_diaspora_nl/pbde_paper_dr_vasant_moharir.pdf

Nye, J. (1990). Soft Power. *Foreign Policy*, *80*(80), 153–171. doi:10.2307/1148580

Nye, J. Jr. (2004). Soft Power and American Foreign Policy. *Political Science Quarterly*, *119*(2), 256. doi:10.2307/20202345

Panigrahi, S. (2017, May 26). Three years of Modi government, what India has achieved on foreign policy front [Weblog comment]. Retrieved from http://www.opindia.com

Ritambhara. (2013, April 30). On Indian Public Diplomacy, E-International Relations [Weblog comment]. Retrieved on September 18, 2017 from http://www.e-ir.info

Saran, S. (2017, May 29). In year four, Modi's foreign policy needs some course corrections [Weblog comment]. Retrieved from http://www.thewire.com

Chapter 6
Role of E-Diplomacy at the Time of International Crisis and Evacuation of Indians

Swati Jaywant Rao Bute
Jagran Lakecity University, India

ABSTRACT

The digital media has made communication between state and citizens very easy, removing all limitations and barriers between the government, service providers, and citizens. This new age media's omnipresence gets diverse attention generating multiple responses. Each era appears to have its own set of ritualized phrases that enable diplomatic agents to communicate even unpleasant things with an amount of tact and courtesy. This chapter explores e-diplomacy.

DOI: 10.4018/978-1-5225-3859-2.ch006

INTRODUCTION

Nations are built by the imagination and untiring enthusiastic efforts of generations - APJ Abdul Kalam

The principle of non-redundancy means "a diplomatic communication should say neither too much nor too little because every word, nuance of omission will be meticulously studied for any shade of meaning" (Spencer, 2005).

Earlier, common people had to go through a long process to send their requests and share their problems with the government. Therefore, the response from government also used to be late, triggering anger and dissatisfaction among people.

The situation has changed now with social media tools like Facebook and twitter bringing in a paradigm shift in the communication process.

Timely communication with the people captured in a conflict or difficult situation and constant counselling of their relatives and family members at home is very important at the time of crisis. Specifically, in a situation when government is at the end of providing all required information and support. The e-diplomacy has thus given a new dimension to handle crisis. This chapter evaluates India's thrust on using this new age media in its diplomacy at the time of international crisis drawing positive as well as negative impacts.

Timely help during any crisis can be counted among the biggest benefits of social media. Things go fast viral on social media prompting the government to take action quickly. "Today 72 percent of global migrants are of working age, reflecting the economic motives of their displacement. Their rising assets and wealth makes these migrants vital to their home economies, whether in terms of deposits, trade, or the transfer of skills and know how" (Xavier, 2016). The percentage of Indian moving to foreign countries has increased in last few years, we can see the impact of Indians contribution not only in job sector where they are using their expertise and knowledge but also in other areas such as politics and cultural togetherness, Indian contributions has been recognized all over. Therefore, "beyond such periodic measures to secure their diaspora as a prized asset, home states are also more inclined to protect migrants in extraordinary times of crisis. As a vulnerable and dislocated population, migrants are particularly exposed to various risks abroad, including natural disasters, political unrest, and violent conflict in their host country or region" (Xavier, 2016).

Social media is a new and highly effective mode of interaction and influence, which the present government acknowledges. It requires constant engagement and adequate resources to be effective and needs to go beyond being a one-way street. Citizens would recognize good and inclusive governance only when their insights are invited, responded to, and included in policy promptly and effectively (Arora, 2016).

Communication patterns are therefore more integrated as they are focused on multi-actor networks rather than separated state and non-state diplomatic structures. This is reflected in the preoccupation with defining and operationalizing public diplomacy strategies that have tended to be seen as separate from rather than integrated into broad diplomatic strategies (Hocking, Melissen, Riordan, & Sharp, 2012).

Far from being rendered irrelevant by technological progress, where governments can communicate with one another directly on a need-to basis, diplomacy has become an increasingly critical instrument in an age of interdependence and globalization. Responding to the ever-changing world around it, diplomacy has evolved and adopted new tools and techniques to respond to the new demands and expectations (Thakur, 2012).

"The levels at which diplomatic discourse takes place, and does so simultaneously, range from the local to the national, bilateral, regional and global" (Thakur, 2012).

"Network diplomacy" is based on a much larger number of players (particularly of civil society), a flatter structure, a more significant oral component, and greater transparency. One of the most powerful tools of networked diplomacy in turn is the existence of strong, vibrant and successful diaspora communities spread across the influential countries of the world today (Thakur, 2012).

Use of E-Diplomacy by Indian External Affairs Ministry of India to Connect With Indian Diaspora

In July 2010, MEA became India's first government department to start using Twitter as part of its communications strategy. In February 2011, its head, Foreign Secretary Nirupama Rao became the first senior diplomat in India to begin using Twitter for official use The utility of social media tools in connecting the government with people who are normally well outside their range, but who can be a useful channel to send out time-urgent critical information and to receive equally valuable information from sources on the ground (Thakur, 2012).

Indian External Affairs Minister Sushma Swaraj has often made headlines in the recent past. The way she uses social media as a tool for public accessibility and quick governance sets a precedent for other politicians. Swaraj is the rare politician who displays affection, warmth and swift decision-making even while tweeting. She has about 6.28 million followers, all of whom wait eagerly for her next "saved the day" story (Vijaykumar, 2016). One of the most important tasks that come under the purview of an external affairs minister is to rescue Indians stranded or taken hostage anywhere in the world. Swaraj's ability to take swift action on multiple such instances has boosted her popularity. Between all the hateful clatter and insensitive trolls on Twitter, Swaraj spreads a sense of positivity, care and hope to Indian citizens across the world (Vijaykumar, 2016).

Swaraj's presence online is also a good example of how citizens and the government can directly connect with each other. From reuniting families to helping citizens recover their passport and travel home safe, every request for help, whether small or big, gets the minister's attention (YKA Staff, 2016).

"Politicians and journalists have suggested that the convergence of revolutionary changes in politics and communication has created a new media-dominated governing system" (Ben-Zvi & Klieman, 2016, p. 22).

These revolutionary changes have altered the meaning of power in contemporary world politics. It is nations or leader's image and ability to control information flow, not just their military and economic power that helps determine status in the international community (Rai, 2003).

The ability to respond speedily to the ever-quickening flow of events is reflected in the organization and operation of national diplomatic systems. 'Virtual diplomacy' has become a buzzword within diplomatic circles like globalization itself-and is used with commensurate imprecision. At its most general level, it relates to the application of communication and information technologies (CIT) to diplomacy (Rai, 2003).

Diplomacy is not about states talking to States. "With public diplomacy coming more and more to the forefront as an international tool of engagements social media has a huge part to play in diplomatic reporting"(Murphy, 2013).

The diplomat's prime objective is to promote and to pursue their country's interest. "The core of International relations is to promise states economic, political and cultural interests. The main actors of international relations are states, international and non-governmental organizations and individuals" (Gieboa, 2007). World economists are saying the expenditure of war is much not the budget cost of the war but it also includes human cost and that is why they suggest that it is better to promote the states interest using more peaceful means such as diplomacy and mass media (Gieboa, 2007).

Diplomacy is a peaceful method to solve conflict, maintain good relations and advance interests of the state through conducting negotiations between representatives of states. Diplomacy is a very good means to reach peaceful solutions of problem. "Mass media is a very powerful tool because it can cover big amount of people during a short period. Furthermore, very often point of view that represented by media of any country is perceived as opinion of the state" (Gieboa, 2007). It makes pressure on government and compels it to do immediate decision that can be spontaneous. Mass media is a very powerful weapon that can very easily influence on decision makers and the people of the world. Media influence diplomatic practice - an evolutionary model of change (Gieboa, 2007).

In last few years, we have seen revolutionary change in working style adopted by present government to deal all issues related to diaspora living different countries facing altogether different problems. Specifically at the time of crisis, Government of India has provided timely help to all its citizens facing critical problems in the war affected and in conflict areas. "India has extensive experience conducting evacuation operations, but given the rising economic contributions and political influence of Indian citizens abroad and the increasing complexity of these operation the incentives to insure the success of future ones are now even greater" (Xavier, 2016).

Communication (together with its twin information) is perhaps one of the most hyped words in contemporary culture. It encompasses a multitude of experience, actions, and events as well as whole variety of happenings and meanings, and technologies too (Kumar, 2012).

Today we are living in the age of information; the parameter of growth is knowledge and information. Advancement in technology not only providing new tools of communication it is also connecting us with each other. Communication, in its simplest sense, is a human relationship, involving two or more people who come together to share, to dialogue and to communicate (Kumar, 2012).

A human being's need for communication is as strong as basic as the need to eat and love. It is both an individual and a social need. It is both a natural individual demand and a requirement of social existence to use communication resources in order to engage in the sharing of experiences, through "symbol mediated interaction" (Kumar, 2012).

The Changed Scenario

In changed scenario, we are observing change in the use of media and media practices; channels of communication are also changing for interpersonal, group and mass communication. Traditional media and new media are in equally use but time is not very far when web will capture the entire market of communication and information.

Indian public diplomacy goes back to the days of Chankya who advocated the quality of listening as one of the most important attributes of an ideal king. Listening to the people on a day-to-day basis is a very important part of public diplomacy in the 21 century (Indian Public Diplomacy, n.d.). Ministry of external affairs of India set up its public diplomacy division in 2006 to advance India's conversation with the world. The key goal of Indian public diplomacy is to explain on a day-to-day basis. The background of policy decisions in Indian foreign policy to promote a positive image of India, it was merged with the external publicity division of the ministry of external affairs of India in January 2014 (Indian Public Diplomacy, n.d.).

On 8 July 2010, public diplomacy division of the ministry of external affairs set up the official twitter account of the public diplomacy division of ministry of external affairs. The opening of official accounts of the public diplomacy division followed this on Facebook, youtube, scribed, issue and blogger. Proactive adoption of social media by the public diplomacy division acted as a catalyst for other division of the ministry of external affairs (Indian Public Diplomacy, n.d.).

Diplomacy Live, a global research, advocacy, and consulting and training platform have ranked India in the top 10 nations in terms of its digital diplomacy performance over the last year.

India and Mexico are the only two countries from the developing world in this list. India's high ranking is despite a relatively modest budget for public diplomacy. The MEA's Official Facebook page, with more than 1.2 million followers is second only to that of the US State Department amongst Foreign Ministries (Chaudhary, 2016).

On Twitter, the Indian Foreign Ministry's combined presence - the Official Spokesperson's account plus the Public Diplomacy account - has crossed 1.2 million. On YouTube, with 40,000 subscribers and 30 million minutes viewed, the Ministry's video content has truly gone viral. MEA is also available on G+, Flickr, Instagram, and Sound-cloud platforms. These combined platforms have a follower-ship in excess of 4 million and an average monthly reach in excess of 20 million. The MEA also has a unique Mobile App, which has garnered more than a 150,000 downloads on Android and iOS platforms, and which is now being revamped to accommodate new technologies (Chaudhary, 2016).

Indian diplomacy is more people-centric; India's Ministry of External Affairs (MEA) has launched a smartphone mobile app to become the first foreign office in the world to integrate all its public services are on one digital platform (Chand, 2013). It is a watershed moment in India's diplomacy, which was once known to be preternaturally secretive, but has now agilely adapted to relentless demands of the 24×7 news chatter and the brave new world of social media (Chand, 2013).

Since communication is the name of the game, the external affairs ministry has also moved beyond its image as English-fixated to reach out to the proliferating media in Indian languages. In an innovative step, the ministry recently backed "Foreign Policy Classroom" broadcast on CNBC Awaaz, which aimed at taking Indian foreign policy beyond the English-speaking elite to a Hindi-speaking audience. In a wired world, as Harvard guru and the progenitor of soft power Joseph Nye says, it is not just hard power that matters. In this new-age communication war, the victory belongs to those who tell the story best (Chand, 2013).

Earlier, mass media of press and broadcasting were widely seen as beneficial (even necessary) for the conduct of democratic politics. The benefit stemmed from the flow of information about public events of information to all citizens and the exposure of politicians and governments to the public gaze and critique. However, negative effects were also perceived because of the dominance of channels by a few voices the predominance of a vertical flow and then heightened commercialization of the media market leading to neglect of democratic communication roles. The typical organizations and forms of mass communication limit access and discourage active participation and dialogue (McQuail, 2005).

New technology has freed us from many constraints. New media is interactive. It provides social presence, it has media richness which involves more personal autonomy which gives the degree to which a user feels in control of content and use, playfulness of media provides entertainment to the users it provides privacy and personalization (McQuail, 2005). New Media have been greeted with intense interest, positive and even euphoric expectations and prediction and a general overestimation of their significance (McQuail, 2005).

Medium is just not an applied technology for transmitting certain symbolic content or linking participants in some exchange. It also embodies a set of social relations that interact with features of the new technology. Information society theories indicate the rise of new kind of society, quite distinctive from mass society. The new media in fact a desperate set of Communication technology that share certain features apart from being new, made possible by digitalization and being widely available personal use as communication devices (McQuail, 2005).

E-Diplomacy in Improving International, Multilateral and Bilateral Relations

The government is using online/digital media for different purposes with a lot of precautions. Social media keep users updated about happenings all around the world. The number of people using social media to keep themselves updated about news and current affairs is increasing at a very fast pace. The easy availability of Internet, especially in urban areas, has accelerated the shift of audience from television, newspaper and radio to online media. The changing social scenario, family structures, living standards, media habits, availability of internet and increase in smartphone usage are only aiding to this trend.

Now, Indian audiences have become more individualistic and consume information and entertainment according to their personal taste. The fact is Internet has penetrated into second and third tier cities. Even in big cities, the availability of fast Internet services on smartphones has increased the number of online media users multifold. There is no specific digital divide among people from different strata. In such scenario, a casual comment is enough to raise the storm on social media. That is why knowing its importance and understanding its potential for promotion and publicity, the government is using online media with a lot of care and precaution.

The government is using online media for public diplomacy and mainstream and traditional media for media diplomacy. It uses English as well as Hindi and regional languages for its online messages. These days, politicians and government officials also conduct live press conference and provide briefings of prime minister visits to foreign countries on Facebook and twitter. In June, a video was uploaded on YouTube to provide information about achievements of government in last three years and external affairs minister of India Mrs. Sushma Swaraj briefed about India's Foreign Policy-2017.

With over eight million followers, external affairs minister Sushma Swaraj is among the most followed world leader on Twitter. According to the global public relations and communications firm Burson Marsettler, she is the only woman among the 10 most followed world leaders and yet she manages to respond to the SOS tweets on the micro–blogging site. From Indians stranded in conflict zone to visa or passport issues she often tweets back to people offering to help in any way she can (Bagchi, 2015).

Indian Evacuation During Yemen Crisis and Role of Social Media

Saudi Arabia and its aliases had started a military intervention against Shiite Haiti Rebels and this internal crisis of Yemen is known as Yemen crisis. Indian government had started operation Rahat for the evacuation of Indian citizens from Yemen in 2015. During Yemen crisis, India had started "Operation Rahat" to rescue the Indian's living in Yemen, this was a very complex operation and the Indian Armed forces worked collaboratively for the success of the mission. "Government rescued around 3, 500 Indians and around 225 foreign citizens belonging to 25 different countries from war zone Yemen. External affairs ministry of India, used social media "Twitter" to post evacuation plan details, "Social media helped connect those awaiting evacuation in Yemen with relatives, authorities and Foreign Minister Sushma Swaraj" (Gupta, 2015).

They shared information about flight timings, availability of flights, in case if flights are not available arrangements of ships and departure timing of ships all these points were shared and discussed on the twitter during entire evacuation process. "External affairs minister was closely monitoring the operation and responding to queries. Social media gave immediacy to the operation; we were constantly tweeting to our MEA Spokesperson on the latest happenings. The External Affairs minister, herself would get direct queries and reply to them. There was little lag when a demand/ query was raised. Social Media disseminated information real time" (Basu, 2015).

About 1,947 foreign nationals from 48 countries have been rescued from Yemen by India, external affairs minister Sushma Swaraj said at Lok Sabha. "I am glad to inform this August House that operation 'Raahat' conducted for the evacuation of Indian nationals from war-torn Yemen has been a resounding success, well-acknowledged by the international community," she said. "We not only managed to safely evacuate 4,741 Indians but also 1,947 foreign nationals from 48 countries till April 18 under most difficult circumstances" (Basu, 2015).

Externan Affairs Minister, Mrs. Sushma Swaraj said that following India's success with the quick evacuation of its nationals from Yemen, 33 countries reached out to India requesting assistance in evacuation of their own nationals. These countries include both neighboring nations as well as their western counterparts. "We responded positively to these requests to the extent possible based on ground realities and helped nationals of 48 countries in evacuation," Swaraj said" (Nandu, 2014).

Indian Evacuation During Iraq Crisis in 2014

During 2014,

the political instability in Iraq directly threatened the lives of the Indians trapped in different parts of the civil war-ravaged country. As fighting between government troops and the ISIS spread, several Indians were caught up in wartime privations. But the ministry of external affairs' cautious approach to the crisis and the government's evacuation efforts, which involved knocking all diplomatic doors in West Asia, focusing especially on discussions with Saudi Arabia, Syria, Jordan and Turkey. The dramatic developments leading to the release of about 175 Indians, including 46 nurses, in civil war-torn Iraq and their subsequent air-lifting marks a significant diplomatic achievement of the government (Shukla, 2014).

"According to Syed Akbaruddin spokesperson of Ministry of External Affairs in 2014, special mobile teams were sent to residences of Indians in Najaf, Karbala, Basra and Baghdad, advising them to leave the country. "They (mobile teams) were authorized by the external affairs minister to contact Indian nationals in their places of residence to advise them that in accordance with two advisories we have sent, it is best that they leave places of work and return to India" (Issac & Balan, 2017).

On 5th July 2014 forty-six Malayali nurses returned from war -torn Iraq, escaping from the jaws of death after being held captive by ISIS (Islamic State of Iraq and Syria) for 23days. It was one of the rare instances when the Islamic State Militants had freed their abductees. Their safe passage home was made possible by the concerned efforts of the Ministry of External Affairs, the Indian Mission in Iraq (Basu, 2015). The dynamic developments leading to the release and subsequent airlifting marks a significant diplomatic achievement of the Narendra Modi government (Nandy, 2014).

The smooth efficiency of operating Rahat, once it got under way, is the latest example of how India's response systems are at their best when they are put to the test. In a matter of days, the Navy, the Air Force, and Air India were able to rescue thousands Indians from the heart of Yemen's war zone, in an effort coordinated by the Ministry of External Affairs (Editorial, 2015).

Operation Rahat, the name given to the evacuation process in Yemen, was orchestrated from the tiny African nation of Djibouti, which lies on the other side of the Gulf of Aden from Yemen, and houses foreign militaries taking part in anti-piracy operations off the African coast. The success of Operation Rahat in trying conditions is an outcome of nearly two decades' worth of experience of trying to protect a small country-sized population of Indian citizens outside of India's borders (Juneja, 2015).

Indian Evacuation During Sudan Crisis and Role of E-Diplomacy

In a series of tweets on the micro-blogging site, the External affairs minister Sushma Swaraj gave updates on Sankat Mochan - the evacuation operation. Clashes broke out in South Sudan "between troops loyal to President Salva Kiir and vice-president Riek Machar after reports on social media suggested that Machar had been detained at the presidential palace" (HT Correspondent). The two have been locked in a power struggle since 2013, a struggle that has killed more than 50,000 people since. The foreign ministry earlier announced that more than 140 Indians had been airlifted from South Sudan, the world's youngest nation where more than 150 people were killed in the last week amid fighting between rival political factions (HT Correspondent, 2016).

The present government has fuelled a spike in social media

with a robust foreign policy agenda and some well-publicized diplomatic engagements, the Twitter handle and Facebook page of the Ministry of External Affairs (MEA) has seen a quantum jump of 400 percent since the Modi government, while its website has more than doubled its viewership. It was named among the 40 best government websites in the world for Design Inspiration, along with websites of the US House of Representatives and Japan's Ministry of Foreign Affairs (Indo Asian News Service, 2014).

According to Syed Akbaruddin the ex-spokesperson of Ministry of External Affairs, "Social media has added to the conventional utility of the website, the links posted on Twitter and Facebook have expanded our outreach". "Whenever we cover the prime minister's events on social media, we get a huge number of hits, including from people not interested in foreign policy" (Indo Asian News Service, 2014).

CONCLUSION

In the tweets, MEA (Ministry of External Affairs) mainly focuses on boosting ties with countries and tries to present a positive picture of the government. The Indian government is using social media as a window to display India's achievements, collaboration, political and economic ties with different countries, and for boosting multilateral, bilateral and diplomatic relations with countries all over the world. The common narrative of all tweets, which External Affairs Ministry posts on regular basis majorly focus on close partnership with countries, strengthening, securing and promoting regional cooperation, multilateral and bilateral engagements. Release advisory for Indians living abroad, to congratulate world leaders on their achievements and on victory in elections, visit of international leaders and delegations. Address global challenges and multilateralism, bilateral diplomacy at multilateral forums, strengthening bonds for cross border problems and terrorism which India is facing, strength in different areas where investments or negotiation can be done, memorandum can be signed, specifically in areas of education and economics. Inform world community about new amendments and changes in government policies to get more business and investment. Historical and cultural relations with countries, regional and international relief and rescue operations. Tweets are normally based on partnership and strategic relationship with countries, economic interaction between strategic partners, extending support to valued partners, collaborating for progress.

Strengthening cooperation on security challenges, informing about new government policies for business and investment which India has adopted, new flagship program and achievements of the government in periodic assessments of government work and achievements, regional and global perspective. humanitarian issue, regional and global issues, high degree of trust and mutual respect, deepening developmental cooperation, elevating relationships to heights on the bedrock of our traditional links, framework agreements, development activities, strengthening wide ranging activities and cooperation, relationship marked by age old ties of friendship and deep mutual respect, long standing friends, engagement with the diaspora, India's role as first responders in crisis, partnership for progress and prosperity, relationship characterized by shared beliefs in democracy, providing helpline numbers of local embassies to the Indian living at the time of crisis.

The positive side of using e diplomacy with contemporary practices is that it has given a new platform to new actors to take part in the international affairs. It has given a humanitarian face to the diplomacy through which you can take and solve soft issues and develop a trust and confidence among the citizens and state. In todays time, when global powers are engaged and trying hard to show their military and Nuclear power to the world. When pictures of hard faces of world leaders and other non state actors comes on TV screen and on social media gives us a scary indication of our future. When we check, our phone in the morning and see innocent children's dying in wars and we get very cruel pictures of wars and conflicts. In such time, its really soothing and relieving when we read a message of External Affairs Minister of a country who is very much concerned for the safety and security of not only people of her own country living miles away but also security and good health of people of a country which is constantly creating problems for our security. It is interesting to know that a cabinet minister of a country is active 24/7 to solve the problems of her people. E diplomacy has definitely changed the face of diplomacy in India, which is more people friendly and humanistic in nature and that is a revolutionary change in our perspective towards international affairs and diplomatic relations with world community.

REFERENCES

Arora, N. (2016, June 17). Translating Modi's Social Media Prowess Into Effective Governance is Easier Tweeted than Done. *The Wire*. Retrieved from https://thewire.in/43460/the-difficult-task-of-translating-modi-govts-social-media-prowess-into-effective-governance/

Bagchi, I. (2015, April 7). How Narendra Modi government rescued 3,500 Indians from war zone Yemen. *Times News Network, Economic Times*. Retrieved from http://www.economictimes.indiatimes.com

Basu, I. (2015, April 4). Yemen crisis: India rescued almost 2,000 foreign nationals, says Sushma Swaraj. *Huffpost India*. Retrieved from http://www.huffingtonpost.in/2015/04/20/yemen-crisis-india_n_7098856.html

Ben-Zvi, A., & Klieman, A. (2016). *Global Politics-Essays in Honour of David Vital*. London: Routledge.

Berkovitch, J., Kremenyuk, V., & Zartman, I. W. (2009). *The SAGE Handbook of Conflict Resolution*. SAGE Publications.

Chand, M. (2013). Thinking smart: A giant leap for India's foreign office. *India Writes*. Retrieved from http://mea.gov.in/in-focus-article.htm?21980/Thinking+Smart+A+giant+digital+leap+for+Indias+foreign+office

Chaudhary, D. R. (2016). India on top 10 ranking of global digital diplomacy: Diplomacy live. *Economic Times Bureau*. Retrieved from http://www.economictimes.indiatimes.com

Editorial. (2015, July 7). Just in time. *The Hindu*. Retrieved from http://www.thehindu.org

Gieboa, E. (2007, October 19). Diplomacy in the media age - Three models of uses and effects. *Diplomacy and Statecraft*, *12*(2). Retrieved from http://www.doi.org/10.1080/09592290108406201

Gupta, P. (interviewer), & Verma S. (interviewee). (2015). *Operation Rahat - The story of how India evacuated 7000 people from Yemen*. [Interview transcript]. Retrieved from https://silpnujs.wordpress.com/2015/05/12/interview-with-ambassador-sanjay-verma-on-operation-rahat-indias-rescue-operation-in-yemen/

Hocking, B., Melissen, J., Riordan, S., & Sharp, P. (2012, October 18). *Future for Diplomacy, Integrative Diplomacy in the 21st Century*. Netherlands Institute of International Relations 'Clingendael'. Retrieved from http://www.clingendael.org

HT Correspondent. (2016, July 14). Operation sankat mochas: Indians rescued from South Sudan to reach Delhi today. *Hindustan Times*. Retrieved from http://www.hindustantimes.com/india-news/op-sankat-mochan-over-500-indians-to-be-evacuated-from-south-sudan/story-RzrZ3gsFipBAWGe70pe4WP.html

Indian Public Diplomacy. (n.d.). Retrieved from http://www.en.m.wikipedia.org

Indo Asian News Service. (2014, October 13). *India's foreign policy a big draw on new and social media*. Retrieved from http://mea.gov.in/articles-in-indian-media.htm?dtl/24089/Indias+foreign+policy+a+big+draw+on+new+and+social+media

Issac, A., & Balan, S. S. (2017, March 30). As "Take Off" suggests, did a malayali businessman help in rescuing nurses from Iraq? *The NEWS Minute*. Retrieved from https://www.thenewsminute.com/article/take-suggests-did-malayali-businessman-help-rescuing-nurses-iraq-59511

Juneja, K. (2015). *Why operation rahat is a major achievement for India*. Observer Research Foundation. Retrieved from http://www.huffingtonpost.in/kabir-taneja/why-operation-rahat-is-a-_b_7023266.html

Kumar, K. J. (2012). *Mass communication in India*. Mumbai, India: JAICO Publishing House.

McQuail, D. (2005). McQuails mass communication theory, new media - New theory (5th ed.). Vistar Publication.

Murphy, M. (2013, July 3). How has social media affected diplomatic reporting? *DiPLO*. Retrieved from http://www.diplomacy.edu.in

Nandy, C. (2014, July 5). Evacuation of Indians from Iraq is a momentous diplomatic victory. India World. *Times of India*. Retrieved from https://blogs.timesofindia.indiatimes.com/nandygram/evacuation-of-indian-nurses-from-iraq-is-a-momentous-diplomatic-victory/

Rai, A. K. (2003, January). *Diplomacy and the news media: A comment on the Indian experience. Strategic analysis, volume 27*. Institute for Defence Studies and Analysis. Retrieved from http://www.idsa.in

Shukla, T. (2014, July 1). Govt. readies aircraft evacuation plan for Iraq, Govt. prepares plan to deploy aircraft to bring back Indians stranded in Iraq if the need arises. *Livemint*. Retrieved from http://www.livemint.com/Politics/nQ9bvIapoTAGVdtCraIuoI/Govt-readies-aircraft-evacuation-plan-for-Iraq.htm

Slaughter, A. M. (2009). America's Edge, Power in Networked Century. *Foreign Affairs*. Retrieved from http://www.foreignaffairs.com

Spencer, G. (2005). *The media and peace: From Vietnam to the "war of terror"*. Springer. doi:10.1057/9780230505506

Thakur, R. (2012, June 18). Effective diplomacy in the age of social media. Opinion. *The Japan Times*. Retrieved from http://www.japantimes.co.jp

Vijaykumar, N. (2016, October 17). How Sushma Swaraj means hope for Indians around the world. *The Week*. Retrieved from http://theweek.in

Xavier, C. (2016, December). India's expatriate evacuation operations - Bringing the diaspora home. *Carnegie India*. Retrieved from http://www.carnegieendowment.org

YKA Staff. (2016, March 11). *10 times Sushma Swaraj used Twitter like a boss and helped Indians from around the world*. Retrieved from http://www.youthkiawaaz.com

Chapter 7
Social Media Networking and the Future of Public Diplomacy in Black Africa:
Insights From Recent Research and Case Studies

Floribert Patrick C. Endong
University of Calabar, Nigeria

ABSTRACT

In spite of its global nature, digital diplomacy has mostly attracted the attention of Euro-centric scholars. Most studies on the issue have dominantly focused on the activities of western MFAs giving little or no attention to those of their African counterparts. This chapter attempts to fill this apparent gap in knowledge. Based on empirical understandings and secondary data, it critically examines how, and to what extent the digital technology paradigm has affected—or may affect—the conduct of public diplomacy particularly in Black African countries. The chapter is divided into four main sections. The first section provides a theoretical framework composed of the actors network theory and the digital divide theory. The second section provides a definition of e-diplomacy and traces its history. The third section examines African countries' progressive "appropriation" of this culture, and the fourth section highlights the prospects of e-diplomacy in Africa as well as major challenges faced by African countries in their deployment of digital diplomacy.

DOI: 10.4018/978-1-5225-3859-2.ch007

INTRODUCTION

Innovations in the realm of information and communication technologies – particularly the internet and the social media – have remarkably revolutionized international communication, the conduct of international relations and public diplomacy. From government organs through civil society organizations to private enterprises, almost all the social and political institutions in the world have recognized the imperative to adapt to the formidable mutations brought about by the ubiquity of the Internet, the World Wide Web and the social networks among others. One egregious evidence of this phenomenal shift is the increasing magnitude with which world countries have been resorting to digital diplomacy – otherwise called e-diplomacy, cyber-diplomacy, "numerical diplomacy" and twidiplomacy – as a paradigm to reconfigure and ameliorate their public diplomacy strategies in the world. Indeed, digital diplomacy is today envisaged as a universal tradition. It is equally envisaged as a realm where in, the digital divide between the North and the South seems considerably to be narrowing (Diplomacy School of Armenia, 2015; Manor 2016; Netherlands Institute of International Relations, 2015). According to scholars such as Flanagan (2015), the social media in particular have enabled or increased the ability of even common men to be both players and participants in the realm of public diplomacy. In effect, one does not need to be a government official or part of an international (intergovernmental) organization, an embassy or a transnational trade and cultural organization to be a digital diplomat. It will therefore not be surprising that even common men and small socio-political and economic institutions in Africa progressively have the potential to be participants in digital diplomacy.

According to popular imaginations, western countries constitute the hottest spot for the use of digital diplomacy by foreign ministries and diplomats (Center of International Governance and Innovation [CIGI], 2013; Williams, 2015). This means that they represent the part of the world considered as the leading force in the implementation of digital diplomacy as strategy to facilitate countries' foreign policies. This is perhaps due to a greater rate of penetration of the internet and social media in this hemisphere of the globe. In tandem with this, Flanagan (2015) contends that the above described situation (the west's dominant use or championing of digital diplomacy paradigm) may be the outcome of western countries' strong attachment to e-diplomacy and tremendous investments of resources in social media engagement around major diplomatic events in the world. Despite the pertinence of these speculations, more research is needed to understand all the nuances of this scenario (the West's leading position in the use off e-diplomacy) and other issues related to the practice and future of e-diplomacy in the world.

A striking issue – in the scholarship dedicated to postmodern forms of diplomacy – has been the fact that research on digital diplomacy has largely been Euro and American-centric. Such Euro and American-centrism is revealed by the fact that most scholars have given enormous attention to the proliferation of cyber-diplomacy in the West, giving somehow limited attention to Black African countries. Meanwhile, a number of evidences point to the fact that the phenomenon of e-diplomacy has quickly become a global tradition, involving even poor African nations. According to Manor (2016), digital diplomacy on Black African soil is clearly visible in the fact that, most Ministries of Foreign Affairs (MFAs) in such areas as East African countries have, with trepidation, migrated to social networking sites. They operate Facebook and Twitter accounts and implement multiple forms of cyber-diplomacy. A recent study by the Digital Diplomacy Review (2016) has somehow confirmed this observation by revealing that countries such as Egypt, South Africa and Ethiopia are ranked ahead of some western countries in the use of digital diplomacy.

Despite this study and similar ones, there still appears to be a big gap in knowledge, pertaining to the ways African governments come to terms with this post-modern phenomenon and other diplomatic exigencies of this digital era. Based on such premises, it is fair to enthuse that there is need for African or afro-centric scholars, to give a modicum of attention to the phenomenon of e-diplomacy in Black African countries. This chapter attempts to fill this gap. It specifically aims to explore secondary data (research works and cases studies) and use critical observations to examine how the digital technology has particularly affected – or may affect – the conduct of public diplomacy in Black African countries. It equally focuses on the prospects and challenges of e-diplomacy in Black African countries. Based on these objectives, the chapter is divided into five main sections. The first is devoted to defining a theoretical framework composed of the Actors Network Theory (ANT) and the digital divide theory. The second section endeavors to provide a definition of e-diplomacy and to trace its history. The third part focuses on African countries' appropriation of this culture. The fourth part highlights the prospects of e-diplomacy in Africa and the last section is devoted to major challenges faced by African countries in their deployment of digital diplomacy.

THEORETICAL FRAMEWORK

As earlier mentioned, this discourse is anchored on two theories namely the Actors Network Theory (ANT), and the digital divide theory. Given the fact that some of these theories are broad and complex, this section of the paper will underline specific tenets of the above mentioned theories that will be considered for the study.

The Actors Network Theory

The Actors Network Theory was developed in the 1980s by Bruno Latour, Michel Callon and John Law. It originates from the fields of science and technology and considers objects as components of a social system or network. The theory stresses the capacity of nonhuman entities to act or participate in complex systems or networks. It is equally associated with tenets of critical and conventional sociology. For a number of critics, the concept of Actor Network represents more a method/approach for conducting research than a theory (Nweke, 2012). In this respect, many authors define or describe it as the "material-semiotic" method. This means that it is an approach that maps relationships that are simultaneously material (that is between things) and semiotic (between concept). The method focuses on the connections between both human and nonhuman entities. It describes how such connections generate new entities that do not practice the characteristics of constituent entities. This can be likened to what happens when a chemist mixes two different chemicals.

ANT is therefore considered as a constructivist rather than an essentialist approach. It explains a successful theory by understanding the combinations and interactions of elements that make it successful, rather than saying it (the theory in question) is "true" and the others are "false. For instance, in studying the fusion of the two terms of "gun" and "man" into "gunman" an ANT researcher will be interested in the connections that bring the man and the gun together thereby creating a gunman. A gunman is, of course different from both a gun and a man in that, while a gunman can shoot and kill a human target, neither a man nor a gun can, *a priori*, do so. The plausible conclusion which could be drawn here is that neither man nor gun is responsible for outbreak of wars in the world. Rather it is the connection between the two entities which is at the root of the cruel incidences of wars. ANT seeks to establish the relationship between two central factors: the "actor" and the "actant". The former is the agency of nonhumans (for instance machines, text, information and communication technologies) while the later refers to any agent(s) which can individually or collectively associate or disassociate with other agents. Actants create network associations which in turn structure or shape their action and intention, and provide them with substance and subjectivity. Such network associations equally name and define the actants. This means that actants are foundationally indeterminate. They have no *a priori* substance and essence and derive their name and nature through the network in which they associate.

To relate this configuration to our study, one will say that ANT is a complex combination of conceptual, textual, social and technological actors and actants. While the actors represent the digital technology, the actants represent the government, the MFAs, the diplomats and the policymakers among others. Put differently the theory considers both the hard and software (actors) and the people destined to use and maintain these technologies (actants) namely the diplomats, government, telecom operators among others. In addition to this, the ANT theory equally considers the social, political and economic environment in which both actants and actors are made to operate. This environment can be considered at the institutional, national, or international level. The international level is a macro level in which socio-political and economic factors shape the proliferation of the digital technology and its application in the realm of diplomacy by states, international organizations and other cardinal players in international diplomacy. As put by Nweke (2012), ANT is apt in explaining and illustrating the ways in which actors and actants come together to reflect international relations. It specifically focuses on how diplomats and diplomatic bodies apply the digital technology (notably the internet and social media platforms) to network, inform and negotiate; as well as to achieve common purpose and interest in international scenes.

The Digital Divide Theory

The digital divide theory pertains to disparities in access to, and/or the inability to use communication technologies (Dominick, 2011; Pick & Sakar 2016). These disparities may exist between regions of the same country or between nations. In line with this, the Organization for Economic Cooperation and Development (OECD), defines the term digital divide as the "gap between individuals, households, businesses and geographic areas at different socio-economic levels with regard both to their opportunities to access ICTs and to their use of the Internet for a wide variety of activities" (OECD, 2011). The digital divide is predicated on a number of chief factors, one of which is the widening gap in level of income. It is therefore theorized that an increase in the level of income generally leads to increased acceptability and usage of information and communication technologies (notably the internet and the social media). It is equally theorized that poverty represents a serious barrier to the use of information and communication technologies in Third World countries.

According to theorists, there exist three principal determinants of digital divide. These include: (i) information accessibility, (ii) information utilization and (iii) information receptiveness. Based on these determinants two types of digital divide have been identified namely first order and second order digital divides. First order digital divides are related to access to information and communication technologies and cost associated with going online. Such divides are revealed by multiple factors, one of which is the varying rate of internet penetration across countries and continents. Studies have for instance demonstrated that western countries have greater accessibility to information and communication technologies than their counterparts in Africa and South Asian countries. The uneven spread of the internet in the world has represented an index of digital divide between poor and rich nations.

The second order digital divides deal with issues like digital literacy and digital capabilities among users of information and communication technologies. They focus on possible gaps between various categories of people in the ways they use digital technologies and online tools. A good example is the differences between digital natives and digital immigrants in the use of new communication technologies. The digital natives are users who generally are of younger generations and who, being born into the digital age, find it easy to use digital technologies. They have capabilities to use the digital technologies with relative ease and rapidity. The digital immigrants on the other hand are users who belong to older generations and who, being born to an "offline world", are forced – by circumstances – to migrate to the online world. Compared to digital natives, the digital immigrants are less capable of fully harnessing the potential of digital technologies.

A number of studies have demonstrated there exist both first and second orders of digital divide between African MFAs and their counterparts from western nation. While the first order digital divides may be narrowing, those of the second order are intensified. With close reference to the application of digital diplomacy in Africa, Manor (2016) shares corollaries. He notes that staffers at western countries' embassies and MFAs may have had access to the internet and other digital technologies for more than two decades as opposed to their counterparts in African MFAs.

Younger diplomats in Europe or North America may have opened a Hotmail email account while they were in Middle School and may have even used PCs throughout most of their education. This is not necessarily the case with MFA staffers in smaller and poorer African nations. Given that length of familiarity with the online environment may substantially increase one's digital capabilities and literacy, digital diplomacy may still be characterized by second order digital divides. As a result, African MFAs may find it harder to fully harness the potential of social media and use it as an effective tool for information gathering and policy making. (Manor, 2016, para 4)

It must be underlined that various perspectives have been adopted to test the digital divide theory. In view of this, authors such as Pick and Sakar (2016) prefer to talk of "digital divide theories" (plural) rather than "digital divide theory" (singular). In effect, one may mention at least four theories related to the concept of digital divide. These include (i) the Adoption and Diffusion theory (ADT), (ii) Van Dijk's Model of Digital Technology Access, (iii) the Unified Theory of Acceptance and Use of Technology (UTAUT), and (iv) Spatially Aware Technology Utilization Model (SATUM). In spite of this multiple facets of the theory, the present discourse will consider digital divides between the west and Africa.

DEFINING AND TRACING THE HISTORY OF DIGITAL DIPLOMACY

It may be tasking to provide a universally accepted definition of digital diplomacy. This is partly due to the fact that although the phenomenon has progressively become the talk of town in the corridors of international diplomacy, most Ministries of Foreign Affairs (MFAs), diplomatic missions, foreign policy practitioners and international relations critics have not bothered to clearly define the term. Difficulties to define the concept also stem from the fact that countries have adopted varied models in their implementation of digital diplomacy. So too have countries adopted varied terminologies to even refer to the phenomenon. While the U.S. State Department coined the term "21st Century Statesmanship", the U.K. Foreign Office preferred the substantive "Digital Diplomacy" and Russia's Ministry of Foreign Affairs used the term "Innovative Diplomacy" in reference to e-diplomacy. In addition to this, the theorization of the concept has been subject to controversy. As suggested by the Netherlands Institute of International Relations (2015), the term "digital diplomacy" is as problematic as the concept of "digital age" from which it is derived. Defining or theorizing it therefore has multiple ramifications. As the Institute notes,

The easiest course would be to focus on social media, but even here the picture is confused. For many, the role of digital media seems to be equated with the broader public diplomacy function, with diplomats embracing Twitter and Facebook, and their embassies engaging with local audiences in the digital domain. For others, digital media is loosely associated with general developments in world politics and foreign policy. Then there are disagreements as to the intensity of change in diplomatic practice wrought by technological change, not to mention clashes of opinion on their compatibility with diplomatic culture. (Netherlands Institute of International Relations, 2015, p. 19)

Nevertheless, there exists a number of perspectives on the concept. One of these perspectives simplistically construes digital diplomacy as a novel and postmodern tool in the conduct of public diplomacy while other perspectives describe the phenomenon as an interactive method of conducting public diplomacy. Such a method is aided by two way communication platforms such as social networks and the internet. Irrespective of perspectives, digital diplomacy can be viewed as the increasing use of Information and Communication Technologies (ICTs) and social media platforms by countries in view of achieving the ultimate targets of their foreign policies and implement their respective public diplomacy. In other words, it is the use of new information and communication technologies to deliver soft power and public diplomacy messages. Britain's Foreign Commonwealth Office puts it simple when it defines the concept of digital diplomacy as "solving foreign policy problems using the internet".

Digital diplomacy therefore entails the ability of countries (their Ministries of Foreign Affairs or Diplomatic Missions) to engage with a large pool of heterogeneous audiences of both state and non-state stakeholders and to utilize such feedback platforms to understand and fine tune public policy. Digital diplomats thus use social media networking to inform audiences (who are nationals of their countries) about various services as travel advice updates especially in contexts of crisis. They equally use such technologies to extend the influence of their respective countries, provide explanation about their course of action, keep records straight, answer queries and reinforce the targets or objectives of major diplomatic events and conferences among others. This specific perspective suggests that digital diplomacy is not limited to just being active on a social media platform through providing information. But it implies designing working machineries to pull online audiences. It therefore entails using the ICTs as tools to carry out a variety of diplomatic activities including negotiation, representation and communication. As put by the Diplomatic School of Armenia (2015), digital diplomacy, is typically conceptualized as a form of public diplomacy whose usefulness for states is understood "in speaking and listening terms". In effect, digital technologies - such as social media platforms Twitter, Facebook, and Weibo – allow government institutions or officials to enter into a kind of dialogic communication with foreign publics in a (usually) non-costly manner.

Digital diplomacy can therefore be viewed as a kind of revolution in the realm of international diplomacy. It is traceable to the end of the 20th century, and attributable to technological innovations in the domain of communication. In effect, before the 20th century, diplomacy was mainly conceived as a secretive intergovernmental communication. This tradition was in line with the Greek concept of "diploma" – the term from which diplomacy is derived. A "diploma" used to be a piece of folded paper containing a message destined to a specific and often well reduced number of people. The term thus symbolizes a form of diplomacy which entails a lot of secrecy. This form of diplomacy was practiced in the world from the Renaissance period to the First World War period. By this tradition, the concept (of diplomacy) was essentially interpreted as a cautious and circumspect endeavor, with meetings conducted mostly in secret. It was a process whereby a government sought to favorably affect its foreign counterpart(s) thereby indirectly and potentially affecting foreign populations. Direct communication between the government of one country and the population of another country was generally avoided as it was regarded by the international community as a bane to the principle of state sovereignty. However, with the advent and popularity of the radio and other sophisticated media of mass communication, it became possible and even strategic for world governments to directly communicate with and affect foreign populations. These formidable mutations led to the emergence of what is commonly called public diplomacy – the process whereby countries seek to attain their foreign policy goals by communicating with foreign publics or the acts by which a country seeks to create a positive climate among foreign populations in view of creating conditions favorable for the acceptance of its foreign policies. In the 1930s for instance, Nazis Germany and proponents of the Bolshevik Revolution in Russia used radio to talk to neighboring nations. Similarly, during the Cold War, both capitalist and communist nations saw the international media (international broadcasting) as tools par excellence for communicating directly with opponent populations and an infallible arsenal for international propaganda. This led to a paradigm shift in the realm of public diplomacy. In concrete terms, most nations began to see greater necessity to use latest communication technologies to achieve their foreign policy goals; hence the development by foreign policy practitioners of such neologisms as media diplomacy, "people diplomacy" and cultural diplomacy - among others – to refer to a new form of diplomacy.

The advent of digital diplomacy around the year 2001 has, of course, been a legacy of the technological innovations in the domain of ICTs and more precisely, the fruit of the proliferation of the internet and social media in the world. As put by Hilary Clinton, "just as the internet has changed virtually every aspect of how people worldwide live, learn, consume and communicate, connection technologies are changing the strategic context for diplomacy in the 21st century" (Cited in Kluz & Firlej, 2015). In the same line of argument, Amnon (cited in Tiedeman 2005) identifies over three ways in which advances in the domain of communication technologies have affected diplomacy in general and permitted the emergence of digital diplomacy. These ways include: (i) the displacement of traditional methods of conducting public diplomacy; (ii) the increase in the diplomatic influence of non-traditional sectors; and (iii), the acceleration of diplomacy's pace. It can be observed that technological innovations in the domain of communication have enabled the co-existence of the old/traditional face-to-face diplomacy and the new/electronic diplomacy. The old and new forms of diplomacy complement, rather than compete with one another. An egregious illustration of this verity is the fact that issues like negotiations are still conducted face-to-face in meetings, conventions and symposia around the world.

Since its advent, the digital diplomacy paradigm has largely been championed by the U.S.; with its State Department having an e-diplomacy office as early as 2003. Most of the major early initiatives which have enabled the popularization of digital diplomacy have been conceived in the U.S. A good example is Hilary Clinton's "21st Century Statecraft" project designed in 2009 to complement traditional tools of foreign policy. This project enabled the U.S. State Department to revolutionize its use of e-diplomacy through the management of 288 Facebook pages with 12.9 million fans; 196 Twitter accounts with 1.9 million followers; and 125 YouTube channels that have racked up 16.3 million views (Permyakova, 2014). Another positive evolution led by America in the realm of digital diplomacy has been the creation of the U.S. virtual embassy to Teheran in Iran. This project followed the closure of the American embassy to the Iranian capital. The virtual embassy played the same function as the traditional U.S. embassy. Perhaps the only difference was that it involved diplomacy at a virtual realm.

Other major western nations have initiated similar digital media-driven projects, for the sake of achieving their foreign policy aims. An egregious example is Russian Ministry of Foreign Affairs which in 2011 and 2012 respectively launched its official Twitter and YouTube accounts. Today e-diplomacy has impressively gone global. It has even become an imperative for virtually all the Ministries of Foreign Affairs and diplomats to operate efficiently. U.K. Ambassador to the Holy Seat (Nigel Baker) shares corollary as he notes that "the main question to be asked by any foreign service should not be: do we need to be digital? It should be: can we afford not to be in the digital space?" (GovUK, 2014).

The advent of the digital diplomacy paradigm only represents a revolution or evolution in the conduct of public diplomacy. Indeed, the phenomenon marks a change not in the message, but in the medium used for public diplomacy. This can be illustrated by the fact that instead of only using radio to talk to foreign audiences/publics, a diplomatic mission could now communicate with these publics through

Twitter, Youtube, or Facebook. Digital diplomacy equally ushered in interactive possibilities which, today, enable public diplomacy to remarkably mutate from a monologue to a dialogue. In view of all these indexes, it is generally believed that the keyword in "e-diplomacy" is not "electronic" or "digital" but "diplomacy". This is so as e-diplomacy remains diplomacy and not electronics. The concept (e-diplomacy) simply emphasizes the electronic as a tool deployed to achieve a state's national interest in the realm of international relations. No doubt a number of U.S. politicians (notably John Kerry), find the term "digital" – in the concept of "digital diplomacy" – as a mark of redundancy. According to such schools of thought, what is generally called "digital diplomacy" should simply be called "diplomacy" (Permyakova, 2014).

DIGITAL DIPLOMACY IN AFRICA

Digital diplomacy has quickly become a global phenomenon and Africa has not been left untouched by it. Though the rate of internet and social media penetration in the Black Continent is not as high as in the west, African MFAs have, over the years, become as adepts at using the social media as their western counterparts. Indeed, recent years have witnessed the phenomenal migration of many African MFAs to social networking sites. The MFAs and diplomatic missions of countries such as Ethiopia, Botswana, Somalia, Namibia and Uganda manage websites and Facebook accounts while their counterparts from countries such as the Democratic Republic of Congo, Mali, Rwanda and the like are more and more active on Twitter. According to some recent studies, countries such as South Africa, Egypt, Ethiopia, Rwanda and Kenya lead the way in digital diplomacy on African soil. According to a 2016 survey conducted by the Digital Diplomacy Review (2016), these five countries are respectively 51st, 63rd, 76th, 80th and 82nd in the world in terms of digital diplomacy. South Africa in particular is even more digitally diplomatic than some western nations such as Ireland. In the 2016 survey carried out by Digital Diplomacy Review, South Africa is ranked ahead of Ireland and some other western countries. Digital Diplomacy Review's rating was based on an integrated methodological design focusing on presence, customization, "up-to-dateness", strategy, influence, engagement, analytics, security, content, audience, transparency and innovation among other variables.

In a similar study aimed at examining the extent to which e-diplomacy is adopted by African countries, Manor (2016) demonstrates that MFAs from countries such as Kenya are as active on social media as their Western counterparts. He particularly notes that Kenya even has greater engagement on the social networks than the U.S. Based on this, he concludes that some African MFAs exhibit a more savvy use of digital diplomacy than their western peers in terms of diversity of content and engagement. This, to some extent, tends to suggest that, though African nations are not leading the way in digital diplomacy in the world, a number of countries within the Black Continent constitute a good case study of progressive migration to the use of social networking as tools to achieve international aims. The above-mentioned observations equally tend to rationalize the theory which stipulates that the digital divide between the west and Africa is considerably reducing.

Despite these encouraging indexes, it must be underlined that a good number of African countries have still not seen the rationale of digital diplomacy and so, are still seriously lagging behind. This can mainly be evidenced by the fact that they (African countries) constitute the bulk of countries featuring at the bottom of Digital Diplomacy Review's (2016) rankings. Digital diplomacy thus has both prospects and challenges in Africa which require specific strategies by African governments.

Prospects of Digital Diplomacy in Africa

The prospects of digital diplomacy in Africa can be seen in a plurality of domains including nation branding, Diaspora diplomacy, networked diplomacy, and Information and knowledge management by diplomatic missions among others. It goes without saying that the appropriate use of the social media by African MFAs may enable African countries to have greater media visibility in the international sphere and spread their soft power in the world. Such a use of digital diplomacy may help them manage their image, thereby correcting the stereotypical views the world – particularly the west – has often had of the continent. These negative views include the idea that Africa is a land of poverty, corruption and bad governance, dreadful epidemics and multiple sufferings among others. Conscious of the above-mentioned potential of digital diplomacy, the Kenyan government used Obama's visit to the country in July 2015 to launch a series of online nation branding campaigns. In effect, Obama's visit was given a relatively heavy media coverage by the international press, given the fact that it was part of the Global Entrepreneurial Summit. This attracted the attention of both national and international publics, offering the Kenyan government an excellent opportunity to deliver nation branding messages to this foreign publics via the social media. The country thus deployed various social media accounts and other digital diplomacy tactics to launder its image, branding itself as a rising economy and a land of prosperity. By this process, the Kenyan government indirectly challenged stereotypical views/myths which present the country as a "hotbed of terror" following insurgent and terrorist activities by the Al-Shabaab movement. Kenya, in this occasion, used Obama hashtag alongside a designated hashtag (#chooseKenya) and intensified its activities on four Twitter channels created for the circumstance. The four Twitter channels included the channel of the Kenyan Ministry of Foreign Affairs, the official channel of the President of the Republic, his personal channel and that of the Kenyan Minister of Foreign Affairs. The Kenyan government's digital diplomacy tactics were equally apt in countering image tarnishing initiatives by the western press notably CNN's Kenyan On Twitter (#KOT) which, though presented by this American media house as a platform to gauge Kenyan impressions about Obama's visit to Kenya, was profiled by most members of the Kenyan Intelligentsia as a sustained campaign aimed at presenting the country in a bad light. As put by Kenyan Interior Cabinet Secretary Joseph Nkaissery, CNN's #KOT was based on lies. "It demonstrates heightened irresponsibility by the media network and smacks of arrogance" (Zoker, 2015).

The social media can equally be used for Diaspora diplomacy. This involves the creation by African countries of social media channels via Twitter or Facebook to maintain ties with their global Diasporas and potentially attract tourists. Such social media channels may be vibrant hubs where information about embassies' activities and services are delivered to Diasporas as well as expatriates. They can equally be platforms through which experts are given consular assistance as well as directives on business and investment opportunities in African countries. Such use of the social media has been observed among few African countries, two of which are Rwanda and Ethiopia. In a comparative study of digital diplomacy activities of some African countries' embassies to a sample of western and Middle-East countries, Manor (2016) found that Ethiopian embassies to U.K., U.S., Canada, Israel, Lebanon and Saudi Arabia have high levels of online activities on both Twitter and Facebook. He equally found that in the U.S., the Ethiopian embassy has more than 30,000 followers on Facebook, while the country's embassy to the U.K. boasts of more than 10,000 followers on Facebook and 7,000 on Twitter.

Additionally, the use social media may equally enable African Ministries of Foreign Affairs to network with their counterparts from other continents thereby re-enforcing their ties with these foreign diplomatic institutions and ensuring greater negotiation/dialogue on crucial issues. It goes without saying that by being very active on social media, African MFAs may attract the attention of their western or Asian peers and voice their opinions on sensitive issues of global concern and eventually shape international debate on a variety of topics. The social media can therefore enable African MFAs to initiate initial bi or multilateral dialogues with their counterparts ahead of major summits or other meetings. Such initial dialogue may enable them influence decisions in these summits. Manor (2016) highlights social media networking's potential to enable African Ministries of Foreign Affairs to network with their counterparts thus:

The ability of smaller nations to leverage their position through online activity may be imagined as a form of social media mobility. Recent evaluations have shown that African MFAs have been able to use SNS [social networks sites] to elicit such mobility. For instance, when analyzing the social network of foreign ministers on Twitter, [...] I found that Kenya's foreign minister (Ambassador Amina Mohamed) serves as an important hub of information, as she connects ministers that do not follow one another directly. Thus, Ambassador Mohamed is now an information junction in this network, attracting attention from her peers around the globe. (p.34)

The new diplomatic paradigm of networked diplomacy is becoming a practical strategy among MFAs in the world. In other words, most ambassadors and policymakers use social networks such as twitter and Facebook to interact with peers, citizens and officials. It becomes imperative for the staffers of African MFAs to key into this paradigm. In the preface of *Twitter for Diplomacy*, former Italian Minister of Foreign Affairs Giulio Terzi stresses such imperative as he notes that: "Twitter has two big positive effects on foreign policy: It fosters a beneficial exchange of ideas between policymakers and civil society and enhances diplomats' ability to gather information and to anticipate, analyze, manage, and react to events" (@ andreas212nyc, 2013, p.2). Indeed, Twitters has enabled the re-invention of the art of public diplomacy. The 140 characters digital technology has revolutionized the way politicians and policymakers communicate with each other.

Another important prospect of digital diplomacy in Africa lies in the fact that it is relatively cost effective to practice diplomacy through social media platforms. In effect, for embassies with very limited resources (notably the ones opened by African countries), the internet and social media represent an excellent way to get messages out to a wider audience; as well as an excellent methodology to initiate a dialogue with various pockets of this audience. It does this much faster than the traditional media platforms. However, it must be underscored that the thesis supporting the cost effectiveness of digital diplomacy is plausible just to an extent. As has been enthused by number of foreign policy theorists, the cost-effectiveness of twidiplomacy depends principally on the type of digital diplomacy one country wishes to practice. Classical models of digital diplomacy which mainly consist of information dissemination through monologue sprinkled with well-crafted infographics, bullet points and videos may be said to be cost effective. However, when comprising giant projects (such as the White House's "@TheIranDeal social media campaign"), digital diplomacy may rather be very demanding in terms of finances and conceptualization. The type of social media campaigns undertaken by big countries like the U.S., Britain and Israel among others generally involve enormous human and economic resources which many African government may not afford.

Challenges of Digital Diplomacy in Africa

Digital diplomacy has a number of challenges which require the adoption of special strategies. Some of these challenges include digital divide, the lack of public trust in African politicians and policymakers, the top-bottom process of foreign policymaking and questionable regulations and censorship of social media and internet by African governments among others. The digital divide remains a serious impediment to the proliferation and effectiveness of digital diplomacy in Black African countries. The rate of internet penetration in Africa remains the lowest in the world. It is estimated at 26.5% as against 70.5% and 87.7% respectively in Europe and North America. African countries having the lowest rate of internet penetration include Ethiopia (1.9%), Ivory Coast (4.2%), Eritrea (5.9%) and Rwanda (9.0%) (Alliance for Affordability of Internet, 2016). What even makes the situation worse is the fact that African governments are yet to invest in the infrastructure needed to reduce the digital divide. They are yet to adopt suitable policies to ameliorate the situation. As enthused by Dahir (2017), national broadband plans either sit unendorsed (in countries like Mali), or are outdated, like in The Gambia. Out of the 58 African countries, only Mauritius features in the top 10 of the index tracking "affordability drivers". Internet connection is not affordable for most Africans.

Though many studies have proven that the rate of internet penetration in a country does not always determine the level of online activities by such a country's MFAs, it remains clear that the digital divide seriously affects the ability of African countries' MFAs to effectively converse and engage with their own citizens. Though they may reach out to large foreign peoples or diasporas (audiences in western countries with high rate of internet penetration) they have a considerably limited reach in Africa. Meanwhile, dialogue with national audiences (through online platforms) is a cardinal aspect of diplomacy in the 21st century.

Most, if not all African governments have access to the internet. They equally have means to support the use of social media channels and other digital instruments for diplomatic activities. However, there still exists what is usually called "second order digital divide" between MFAs in African countries and their counterparts in western countries. Diplomats in the western world have a greater familiarity with the online environment than their counterparts in African countries. This second order digital divide seriously handicaps African MFAs' effective deployment of digital technologies in the realm of diplomacy. They most often find it difficult to fully harness the potential of the social media and to utilize them as strategic instrument in information gathering and policy making.

Another challenge to the effective implementation of digital diplomacy in Africa is the lack of public trust in government officials and policymakers. Though the trend tends to be a global phenomenon – as 60% of the population in most countries do not trust government –it has been found to be more accentuated in Africa (Alliance for Affordability of Internet, 2016; OECD, 2016). Decades of bad governance, un-free and unfair elections, corruption, undemocratic rule and embezzlement of public funds by government officials have affected people's trust in policymakers and government officials in many Black African countries. So too have the foreign policies adopted by African countries often been subject to acerb criticism by home and host country nationals.

It is actually common in many African countries to find large pockets of audiences who – as a matter of compulsion – do not believe in their country or government and who are likely to view pronouncements authored by government officials as "half-truths", mere propaganda or distortions aimed to conceal unpleasant truths or/and launder the image of the government. Such popular sentiments and myths are observable particularly in situation of crisis. These popular myths often affect audiences' reception or perceptions of diplomacy messages transmitted in online channels by African MFAs. With this, most African audiences will likely doubt or resort to the triangulation of the content of online messages constructed by the foreign ministries and diplomats from their respective countries. This, they sometimes do, by comparing MFAs' version of the truth with the perspectives of citizen journalists, perspectives which might as well not be accurate and credible. As enthused by WPPGov (2016), falling levels of trust in government represents a serious impediment to the effectiveness of government communication, in the following ways: (i) It limits cut-through of government messages, (ii) Inhibits two-way dialogue, (iii) Contributes to detachment and disengagement from government and (iv) Inhibits the success of policies that depend on behavioral responses from the public. In the same line of argument, the OECD (2016) notes that the lack of trust in government compromises the willingness of citizens to favorably respond to public policies and foreign policies. This may affect the contribution of such citizens to contribute to the spreading of their countries' soft power in foreign climes.

A similar phenomenon is the host of negative stereotypes most foreign peoples (particularly western audiences) have associated Africa with. African governmental organs – including foreign ministries and diplomatic missions – are often viewed as veritable mouthpieces and advocates of corrupt governments or of political parties which are illegitimately in power. Their communications on sensitive political issues and diplomacy most often seek to protect the interests of particular quarters (the party in power) to the detriment of the general interest (the common good in their countries). These stereotypical images have the potential to affect foreign audiences' reception of diplomacy messages by African MFAs especially in contexts of crisis, thereby rendering some of Africans MFAs' online communications unfruitful.

The absolute top-bottom process of public diplomacy largely adopted by Black African countries coupled with the phenomenon of diplomatic secrecy constitutes another factor that may reduce or hamper the effectiveness of digital diplomacy by many African countries. In effect, most foreign offices and diplomatic missions from the continent function according to centralism paradigms that enable government to fully control the countries' respective diplomatic narratives (CIGI, 2013; Kate, 2016). Such paradigms do not tolerate unauthorized communications by ambassadors and/or junior diplomats/staffers. In tandem with this, some African foreign affairs Ministers and diplomats function on the bases of slow authorization processes which seriously hamper timely communication of their governments' views, particularly in situation of serious crisis. It was for instance observed that, Sierra Leonean Government officials, MFAs and diplomats were very slow in giving credible updates about the 2015 Ebola crisis which cleared the lives of many in their country. Government officials were actually slow to issue warnings to the local population sparking all sorts of virulent rumors and speculations on both the social networks and the traditional media (Kate, 2016).

A similar situation was observed at the end of the year 2016 in Malawi with the "mysterious" disappearance of President Peter Mutharika. The disappearance was actually concealed from the public by government officials and the country's diplomats. In effect, Mutharika left his country to attend the United Nation General Assembly scheduled to take place in mid-September and returned home only on the 6th of October, after rumors of his death had spread and seriously corroded people's trust in his government. His communications team endeavored not to divulgate his itinerary, sparking up waves of rumors particularly the famous hashtag #bringbackMutharika (Chutel, 2016). The above-mentioned indexes constitute a serious impediment to the strategic application of digital diplomacy, particularly in crisis management contexts. This is so as communication gaps always give way to rumors and misinformation.

African MFAs or diplomats are therefore compelled to inform the public on time to limit or curb incidences of misinformation or disinformation by concurrent/adversarial sources (citizen journalists). Besides that, we live in an era when citizens more and more demand speedy delivery of government services that meet both the technological standards set by society and human touch.

Last – but not least – in the list of challenges to be discussed here is African governments' drastic and muscled approaches to regulating or censoring internet and social networks in their respective countries. By such muscled approaches, African governments are quick to shut down the internet at will and mount serious pressure on telecom operators to cut off access or give government officials access to user's private information. Egregious illustrations of these approaches have been observed in Cameroon in 2011 and 2016-2017 when the government shut down Twitter and the internet to strategically bar the way to online anti-government activism by citizen journalists. By shutting down the internet from 2016 to 2017 (during the Anglophone Crisis in Cameroon) the Biya government hoped to strategically hamper digitally driven activism and political agitation by some Anglophone Cameroonians and their sympathizers. It goes without saying that the practice of occasionally shutting down the internet does not only give credence to negative stereotypes associated with African governments but hampers constant internet connectivity in African countries. This fanciful act of hampering internet connectivity is a serious challenge to digital diplomacy as it occasionally limits the reach of digitally enabled communications – thus, online diplomatic messages – by both government and non-government actors.

CONCLUSION

Technological innovations in the domains of information and communication have affected virtually the aspects of human life including international relations. Such innovations have been at the root of new traditions in the realm of diplomacy, one of which is digital diplomacy. Digital diplomacy is today becoming a universal phenomenon. Politicians and policymakers needs to be "pop stars", digital literate and marketed on social network sites to hope to catch the attention of various public. As argued by many critics, "demands of political correctness probably result in a skewed picture of who in diplomacy is using social networking sites, how, and with what aims and objectives" (Netherland Institute of International Relations, 2015). In view of all these contemporary trends, African governments (MFAs, diplomats and policymakers) cannot afford not to be part of this veritable bandwagon. A number of indexes point to the fact that despite the digital divide between Africa and the west, digital diplomacy is progressively embraced by African countries, particularly African MFAs and diplomatic missions. This chapter has critically reviewed a number of research works that confirm this observation and which reveal multiple prospects of digital diplomacy in Africa. Some of these prospects are observable in the domains of nation branding, Diaspora diplomacy, consular diplomacy and networked diplomacy among others.

Despite these positive developments, it must be recognized that Africa continues to remain at the bottom of global digital diplomacy rankings. There still persist multiple challenges to the effective application of the paradigm in the continent. Some of these challenges include the digital divide, the absolute top-to-bottom process of public diplomacy adopted by most countries of the continent, the abusive application of diplomatic secrecy, the relatively staunch and questionable approaches adopted by African governments to regulate and censor internet on the continent among others. These challenges, of course, call for the adoption of specific and well-conceived strategies by the government and civil society.

The issue of digital divide can be reduced or surmounted through intensive investment in information and communication technologies. African governments should therefore adopt policies aimed at enabling affordability of, and equal access to internet in their respective countries. Such policies should, among other things, ensure the upgrading of network operators' services and institute programs such as free wifi spots in public places, as observed in some South African cities. In addition to these, African governments should invest in the training and the recycling of their foreign offices personnel. This will enable them to reduce second order digital divide among African diplomats or foreign offices' staffers. Digital diplomacy should be a key component in the training of diplomats in African universities and specialized institutes; and research in this field should be encouraged and supported by African governments.

The absolute top-to-bottom process of public diplomacy should likewise be jettisoned in favor of an open policy approach. Such a shift has the potential to increase African MFAs and diplomats' capabilities to timely respond to specific crises and inform both foreign peoples and home audiences about their governments' views and positions over burning issues. As earlier explained, the absolute top-to-bottom process of public diplomacy coupled with the concept of diplomatic secret often hampers prompt communications by government officials and diplomats, given way to rumors and misinformation campaigns by citizen journalists. The open policy paradigm on the other hand facilitates a synergy of efforts involving both non-governmental and governmental stakeholders. It recognizes that good ideas emanate from foreign offices' staffers, irrespective of whether they are junior or senior.

REFERENCES

Alliance for Affordable Internet. (2016). World off-track to achieve UN internet access as broadband prices remain high. New York: Alliance for Affordable Internet (A4AI).

@andreas212nyc. (2013). *Twitter for Diplomats. Diplo Foundation*. Retrieved from https://issuu.com/diplo/docs/twitter_for_diplomats

Center for International Governance Innovation. (2013). *Constructive power initiative: Internet governance, cyber security and digital diplomacy*. Toronto: CIGI.

Chutel, L. (2016, October 19). The mystery of Africa's disappearing Presidents. *Quartz Africa*, 18-23.

Dahir, A. L. (2017, February). Government dithering prevents millions of Africans from accessing the internet. *Quartz Africa*, 21-27.

Digital Diplomacy Review. (2016). *Ranking and rating*. Retrieved February 18, 2017, from http://digital.diplomacy.live/ranking-and-rating/

Diplomacy School of Armenia. (2015). *Digital diplomacy: Prospects and challenges*. Yerevan: DSA.

Dominik, R. J. (2011). *The dynamics of mass communication*. New York: Grawhill.

Flanagan, M. (2015). Foreword. In Digital Diplomacy & the # G8 (pp. 2-3). London: Portland.

Fletcher, T. (2015). Naked diplomacy. In Digital diplomacy & the # G8 (pp. 9-11). London: Portland.

Fung, B. (2012). Digital diplomacy: Why is it tough for embassies to get social media right. *The Atlantic*. Retrieved January 24, from http://www.theatlantic.com/international/archive/2012/10/digital-diplomacy-why-its-so-tough-for-embassies-to-get-social-media-right/263744/

GovUk. (2014). Transcript of Ambassador Nigel Baker's interview with Fr. Antonio Spadaro. *Cyberteologia* Retrieved February 24, 2017, from https://www.gov.uk/government/world-location-news/digital-diplomacy-social-media-and-the-holy-see

Kate, T. (2016). *The West Africa Ebola crisis*. New York: Ebola Deeply.

Kluz, A., & Firlej, M. (2015). *The impact of technology on foreign affairs*. FPA: Foreign Policy Association. Retrieved January 12, 2016 from http://foreignpolicyblogs.com/2015/12/22/the-impact-of-technology-on-foreign-affairs-five-challenges/

Leach, J. (2015). Diplomacy – facing a future without borders. In Digital diplomacy & the # G8 (pp. 15-17). London: Portland.

Manor, I. (2015). Between two digital divides. *Exploring digital diplomacy*. Retrieved January 24, 2017, from https://digdipblog.com/2016/01/27/between-two-digital-divides/

Manor, I. (2015). In digital diplomacy, a narrowing digital divide. *Exploring digital diplomacy*. Retrieved January 24 from https://digdipblog.com/2015/01/19/divide/

Manor, I. (2016). *Digital diplomacy in Africa: A research agenda*. USC Center on Public Diplomacy.

Melissen, J. (2005). The New diplomacy: Between theory and practice. In M. Jan (Ed.), *The New public diplomacy. Soft power in international relations* (pp. 3–27). Hampshire: Palgrave Macmillan. doi:10.1057/9780230554931_1

Metzger, E. T. (2012). Is it the medium or the message? Social media, American public relations & Iran. *Global Media Journal*, *15*, 1–16.

Netherlands, Institute of International Relations. (2015). *Diplomacy in the digital age. Clingedael Report*. The Hague: Clingendael Institute.

Organization for Economic Co-operation and Development. (2011). Understanding the digital divide. In *OECD Digital Economy Papers 49*. Paris: OECD Publishing.

Organization for Economic Co-operation and Development. (2016). *People trust in government*. Retrieved January 20, 2017, from http://www.oecd.org/gov/trust-in-government.htm

Permyakova, L. (2014, January 2). The Future of digital diplomacy. *Russia Direct*, 23-30.

Rito, L. (2013). *Diplomacy and its practices. Digital diplomacy*. ISPD: Protocol and Diplomacy. Retrieved 24 January 2017, from http://ispdnetwork.org/2014/08/diplomacy-and-its-practice-v-digital-diplomacy/

Shenhav, S. R., Sheafer, T., & Gabay, I. (2010). Incoherent narrator: Israeli public diplomacy during the disengagement and the elections in the Palestinian Authority. *Israel Studies*, *15*(3), 143–162. doi:10.2979/isr.2010.15.3.143

Sileshie, S. K. (2014). Challenges and opportunities of Facebook as a media platform in Ethiopia. *JMCS: Journal of Media Communication Studies*, *6*(7), 99–110.

Tiedeman, A. (2005). Islamic republic of Iran broadcasting: Public diplomacy or propaganda? *Al Nakhalali: The Fletcher School Online Journal for Issues Related to South West Asia and Islamic Civilization*, *5*(1), 1–7.

Williams, L. (2015). Disruptive diplomacy. In Digital diplomacy & the # G8 (pp. 12-14). London: Portland.

WPPGov. (2016). Executive Summary. The Government and public sector practice. *The Leaders' Reporter*, p. 2.

Zoker, Y. (2015, July 23). Here is how Kenyans on Twitter are responding to CNN's coverage of Obama's first presidential visit to Kenya. *OkayAfrica*, 16-22.

KEY TERMS AND DEFINITIONS

Digital Diplomacy: It is the systematic use of ICTs and social networking sites by a country in order to achieve its foreign policy goals.

Digital Divide: This term refers to unequally in access to, and capabilities to use information and communication technologics. Such incqualitics arc caused by economic and social factors. Most often, the term is used in reference to the uneven spread of the internet across countries of the world, illustrated by low internet penetration and low level of affordability of the internet in developing countries, compared to their western counterparts.

Digital Literacy: This refers to the skill necessary for individual to use the internet and the social networks to effectively search, retrieve, analyze, contextualize, visualize, and synthesize information.

Diplomatic Secrecy: Otherwise called secret diplomacy, this term is used in reference to the act of concealing particular—and often sensitive information—from the general public. Over three types of secret diplomacy may be identified namely strategic secrecy, operational secrecy and official secrecy. *Strategic secrecy* pertains to the concealment of major agreements and commitments. *Operational secrecy* refers to the concealment of diplomatic negotiations, relations between diplomats, and information of interest to diplomats while *Official secrecy* refers to "known unknowns," things that are known but are treated as if they are unknown.

Nation Branding: It refers to the application of branding principles and techniques to a country's external communication for desired perception and understanding. The concept equally refers to how branding is applied to individual communication endeavors that produce and accrue benefits to the aggregate entity of a nation's image.

Public Diplomacy: A term often used to refer to communications that are aimed at foreign publics and designed to inform, influence and open up a dialogue with the latter (such publics). It is also known as the act and practice of promoting the national interest and the national security of a country through understanding, informing, and influencing foreign publics and broadening dialogue between the citizens and institutions of that country and their counterparts from other countries.

Soft Power: A country's ability to achieve desired aims in international affairs through attraction rather than coercion. It is equally the systematic use of information by a state to convince its counterparts to agree to a number of principles and institutions that yield desired behavior.

Chapter 8
The Age of the Internet:
A Tech Savvy World and New Diplomacy

Aakriti Sethi
Jawaharlal Nehru University, India

ABSTRACT

The bittersweet characteristics of internet and social media have caught the imagination of the era we live in. No orb of this society is untouched by the marvels of information and communication technologies (ICT). The evolution of internet from ARPANET to social media sites like Facebook, Twitter, Instagram, or apps like Watsapp has changed the modern world from its core, impacting every nook of every society. These tools and services have made individuals way more involved in political, social, cultural, and economic happenings around the globe, making them feel authorized to send their message/opinion beyond their computer/phone screen. Amidst this backdrop, state and traditional diplomacy has seen remarkable technological changes. The birth of digital diplomacy has opened a plethora of opportunities for the people as well as the state. Postmodern understanding of a state's power beyond the realm of its military capabilities (hard power) and through the lens of soft power has led to many countries trying to win "hearts and minds" across the globe. But, the interaction of state and newer technologies in the midst of labyrinth unconventional threats has changed the traditional rules of the game.

DOI: 10.4018/978-1-5225-3859-2.ch008

The speed of communications is wondrous to behold. It is also true that speed can multiply the distribution of information that we know to be untrue. -Edward R Murrow, 28 October 1964

INTRODUCTION

Evolution of Internet

Internet has expanded into a dynamic and nebulous phenomenon. Many have started believing that its current features, potential and broadened approach has led it to exceed its once simple definition. People from technical background might stress that internet is what it was back in the early days i.e. a worldwide communication network of computers. But, what the educated public has come to think of 'the internet' has evolved to encompass not just the hardware and software of the network itself but the mind-boggling diverse variety of human activities conducted over it. (Haigh, Russell & Dutton, 2015) Daily means of technology like television, refrigerators, railways, airlines etc have not only connected themselves to internet but have also reinvented themselves because of an internet-driven market. The dot com revolution and the technological boom have created 'tech elite' which produces finer technology to the masses (like various types of social media). This refined access of technology has expeditiously reformed the political, cultural, economic and societal fabric of the world. The current expansion has hit its zenith with the development of 'mobile internet' and 'smart phones' which forecasts to connect hundreds of billions of people in the coming decades.

Since the beginning of time, humans have developed networks for exclusive communications. Earlier technologies such as lines of fire beacons, smoke signals, the passing of written messages and later technologies like optical telegraph, semaphore tower network, electric telegraph, telephone, and radio were most highly developed in support of military ends. (Everard, 2013) Not surprisingly, Internet was too initiated with military purposes as its larger goal. Post Second World War, the world saw itself being divided in two blocs led by US and USSR. The ideological friction between the two led to reshaping of the modern world. The 1950s were times of high tension as both the sides prepared to indulge in Nuclear War which could've led to unthinkable human casualty. During John F Kennedy presidency, it was realized that for the US president to make a nuclear decision in a possible nuclear exchange scenario, he needed a nuclear proof method of communication with his nuclear strike forces. The need to maintain and secure lines of communication was discussed ten years before, during Harry S Truman presidency. But nobody in the administration had any clue as to how to safeguard these lines of communications. Paul Baran, (a researcher working at RAND Corporation, US), came up with a solution in his memorandum 'On Distributed Communication Networks' in 1962 for the US Air Force. He describes his communication network with no pre-decided route between sender and receiver. He further explained his hot potato (deflection) routing doctrine- "to achieve real-time operation it is desirable to respond to change in network status as quickly as possible, so we shall seek to derive the network status information directly from each message block". Every message would contain a "to", "from" and a handover number tag which would indicate the length of time on the network or path length. (Baran, 1964)

His suggestions were not only radical but also way ahead of its time. For the first time, Baran's proposal brought together two earlier unrelated spheres i.e. computers and communications. This network was focused on user to user rather than centre to centre communication. As a sign of how this would eventually empower Internet users en masse, he noted that the administrative censorship that had occurred in previous military communications systems would not be possible on the new system. What he had produced was a new mechanism for relaying vast quantities of data across a cheap network while benefiting from nuclear-proof resilience. (Ryan, 2010) When the US Air Force took this idea to telecommunications conglomerate AT&T, they objected vehemently. On the other hand in the UK, researcher named Donald Davies proved that packet switching (breaking of a message into number of parts) is possible at National Physics Laboratory in 1965. In a 1967 symposium, Advanced Research Projects Agency or ARPA brought together university and commercial (US defense contractors) experts to discuss proposals for a protocol for exchanging messages between computers. From this meeting came the concept for the ARPA Network or ARPANET packet-switch using the information message processor (IMP). (Everard, 2013) Though this discovery was widely appreciated, funding became an issue for ARPA. During 1965-1967, ARPA enjoyed its prestige within defense establishment, but, witnessed its decline due to Vietnam War absorbing its resources. Nevertheless, the theory was quickly becoming a reality, and in 1969, the year of the first manned lunar landing, ARPANET was born. It began with a node at the University of California at Los Angeles (UCLA) and soon afterwards connected with the Stanford Research Institute (SRI), University of California at Santa Barbara (UCSB) and the University of Utah. (Ryan, 2010)

ARPANET was a sort of *lingua franca* for computers that would not only link defense establishment's computers but also computers of research faculties and universities. By late 1974, ARPANET had grown beyond the umbrella of defense contractors and defense funded institutions. There was a clear demand for ARPANET to grow beyond the purview of military circles. In an effort to stem this pressure, on 1 June 1975 the US Defense Communications Agency took over the operational management of ARPANET. A month later, Bolt, Beranek and Newman (BBN-American high-tech company) opened Telenet, a commercial version of ARPANET. (Ryan, 2010) Though ARPANET was revolutionary, it wasn't useful until unless you weren't from a military or scientific sector. Connecting with ARPANET from one's network was not possible, no matter where the network was. The scientists saw this vacuum which didn't let the larger public to have such a networking system. They wanted an overarching grid which could let anyone to interact irrespective of what network they had. By mid 1980s, with massive funding an 'inter- network' was formed or as we know it, internet. This connected all big universities and institutes in the country and with some overseas ones too.

Though Internet was bigger and comparatively much more accessible than ARPANET, it was still complicating to use. British computer scientist Tim Berners Lee figured that people wanted to access these networks for other larger purposes rather than simply connecting to another computer. With the help of French scientist Robert Cailliau at European Organization for Nuclear Research or CERN designed a system that used the Internet to store, receive, and send documents, and he called his invention the "World Wide Web. (Poe, 2013) Realizing the growing demand of PCs manufactured by Microsoft and Macintosh, the students at National Center for Supercomputing Applications (NCSA) at the University of Illinois created an imaginative 'Web Browser' under the name of 'Mosaic'. By the 1990s, surfing the net became an activity like reading newspaper or watching television. The usability of internet has only grown with the introduction of smartphones. Earlier smartphones by IBM, Blackberry and Nokia only helped in fueling technological advancements and finally reached its peak with Apple and Samsung entering in this field. The iOs and Android operating systems were eventually introduced by these two.

Building on the revolution of internet, social media mushroomed, ultimately shaping the society in a detrimental way. A new infrastructure for online sociality and creativity has emerged, penetrating every fiber of culture today. Social media, roughly defined as "a group of Internet-based applications that build on the ideological and technological foundations of Web 2.0, and that allow the creation and exchange of user-generated content", form a new online layer through which people organize their lives. (Dijick, 2013) Large and influential platforms such as Facebook, Twitter, YouTube, and LinkedIn exploded in terms of users and monetizing potential, alongside countless smaller profit and nonprofit sites. (Dijick, 2013) This resulted in the development of an eco system with interconnection of various platforms. The transformation from networked communication to "platformed" sociality, and from a participatory culture to a culture of connectivity, took place in a relatively short time span of ten years. (Dijick, 2013) Social media websites have found larger base in masses across the world, seeping in various parts of one's life. Smartphones have only strengthened their popularity and usage, enabling social media to become the centre of an individual's social, cultural and professional activities.

Internet: A Double-Edged Sword

The 1990s saw, Blogger (1999),Wikipedia (2001), Myspace (2003), Facebook (2004), Flickr (2004), YouTube (2005), Twitter (2006), and a wide array of platforms to offer web tools that mixed old and new online communication forms. These websites offer micro blogging, video sharing, video conferencing, chatting etc. and have become mainstream platforms to do so. The apex of a brand's success is reached when its tag becomes a verb, e.g. tweeting (Twitter), YouTubing (YouTube) etc. But the earliest such phenomenon was that of Google or 'googling' which has become synonymous with online searching. In today's time the concept of 'digital citizenship' i.e. citizens who use internet regularly, effectively and daily, has garnered mainstream discussion. In much the same way that education has promoted democracy and economic growth, the Internet has been viewed to benefit society as a whole, and facilitate the membership and participation of individuals within society. (Mossberger, Tolbert & McNeal, 2008) It has been seen as a technology that can positively impact individuals' life. Being a global repository of information, internet has revolutionized information sharing and availability of data. The instant access factor and anytime-anywhere characteristic of it has been a boon for researchers, students, scholars etc. The empowering ability to connect people from various parts of the world and lessening miles of distance between them has especially been taken ahead by social media platforms. Real time conversations have metamorphosed the communication technology. On an economic level, online banking has made transactions easier for common citizens. The swiftness and time saving act of digital transactions has reformed the overall international banking system. Online shopping of various products has become a new and dynamic platform to bring buyers and sellers together. E-commerce websites like Amazon, E-Bay and Flipkart have become successful models for online commerce and have established 'market' in the virtual world. Furthermore, entertainment sector has become multifaceted with the help of internet. Gaming, movies, music industry etc. have tapped the vast reach and profitability of internet.

Table 1. Most popular social networks worldwide

Social Network Sites Worldwide	Number of Active Users (in Millions) (till January 2017)
Facebook	1871
WhatsApp	1000
Facebook Messenger	1000
QQ	877
WeChat	846
QZone	632
Instagram	600
Tumblr	550
Twitter	317
Baidu Tieba	300
Snapchat	300
Skype	300
Sina Weibo	297
Viber	249
Line	217
Pinterest	150
YY	122
LinkedIn	106
BBM	100
Telegram	100
VKontakte	90
Kakaotalk	49

(Source: adapted from Statista: The Statistics Portal, 2018)

But as the newer generation has adjusted to this technological revolution, we are coming in terms with Internet's dark side and various challenges it poses for the individuals and state. Easy information sharing at social media platforms enables any individual to view content. This issue has been a primary catalyst to the growing 'privacy concerns of the people'. In the age of 'Edward Snowden Scandal', people have come to terms that their lives are not as private as it once was. Social media has also become the hub of manipulation and defamation. Fake profiles, hacked profiles and cheating incidences online have become a routine activity on these platforms. Though many social media websites have taken steps to strengthen their privacy policy, multiple such cases manage to occur on a daily basis.

Table 2. Internet usage: Regional overview

World Region	Population	Population % of the World	Internet Users (as of 31 March 2017) (in Millions)	Penetration Rate (% of Population)
Asia	4,148,177,672	55.2%	1874	45.2%
Europe	822,710,362	10.9%	637	77.4%
Latin American/Caribbean	647,604,645	8.6%	386	59.6%
Africa	1,246,504,865	16.6%	346	27.7%
North America	363,224,006	4.8%	320	88.1%
Middle East	250,327,574	3.3%	142	56.7%
Oceania/Australia	40,479,846	0.5%	28	68.1%

*Please note that the regions are in descending order based on the internet users.
(Source: adapted from Internet World Stats, 2017)

All these issues are more associated to people at an individual level. From a macro perspective, this technological boom has reshaped the world landscape. Newer technologies and their role in political movements, terrorist activities, cyber fraud, cyber espionage, political movements etc have posed new set of issues for the state. Since ages, state has undergone multiple tests in face of modified and newer technologies. Thirty years ago, cable television sparked transformations; twenty years ago, the communications satellite did the same. In the last ten years the Internet and the convergence of new technologies have invited wholesale restructuring. (Monroe, 2002) The Arab Spring (2011) was first political upheaval which highlighted the importance of new technologies. In covering what some deemed the Facebook or Twitter revolutions, the media focused heavily on young protesters mobilizing in the streets in political opposition, smartphones in hand. (Brown, Guskin & Mitchell, 2012, para. 1) This event made the world realize the plausible impact technology, internet and social media can have on the politico-socio framework of the society. The ever-growing virtual world has blurred the lines between states, leading to debates about whether nation states are still relevant- and if so, to what degree. But many have also countered that 'the death of the state' phenomenon is highly exaggerated.

Nevertheless, growth of technology and internet in particular, has kick started a discussion on its larger impact on nation states. The overwhelming power internet has given to terrorist organizations like ISIS has not only multiplied their ability to execute violent operations across the world but has also given them an easy platform to hire new people. Their propaganda mechanisms are primarily implemented via internet, also social media websites have given them easy access to voice and spread their opinions. Cyber threats are another daunting challenge which the nation states look eye to eye. These attacks in the form of hacking, espionage etc can come from either other states or non-state actors. Recently, Russian cyber hacking during the 2016 US Presidential Elections has created a storm of controversies. In past, cyber-attacks by China and North Korea have also been a serious cause of worry. These new developments have pushed the technological and information revolution debates into new realms where states have to maneuver their future discourse. According to Giampiero Giacomello, the evolution and ultimate shape of a mature digital information network will be decided by a three-way political struggle between states, firms and individuals. But furthermore, the three-player structure can only occur under the condition of democracy. States are not all the same. Public opinion in democratic states has far more 'access points' to government, than its counterparts in autocratic regimes. (Giacomello, 2003) Both China and Cuba have taken a proactive approach, using the Internet to disseminate propaganda and making plans for national intranets that will allow access to only officially approved material. In China particularly, the state relies on filtering technology and self-censorship to keep out threatening content. Web sites are frequently blocked or summarily shut down, and chat rooms are policed by "Big Mamas," who quickly delete "offensive" material. (Yester, 2009, para. 2)

ADJUSTING IN A TECH SAVVY WORLD: DIPLOMACY TO DIGITAL DIPLOMACY

Headley Bull's definition of diplomacy as "the conduct of relations between states and other entities with standing in world politics by official agents and by peaceful means," (Bull, 1997) has been widely accepted. According to him, it is one of the five major institutions of international society which helps in the maintenance of international order. The latter is the 'fortiori in world politics', (Bull, 1997). In many ways diplomacy is still the same. Diplomats and global leaders continue touring around the globe, just as their predecessors did to take their country's policies ahead. Tele-conferencing and Information, Communication and Technology (ICT) have radically changed the execution of these businesses, yet the basic component of negotiations to come to a mutual conclusion remains imperative. Not exactly in a core way, but ICT has impacted how the state and foreign departments of various countries go ahead with their work. With introduction of internet and the expansion of Diplomacy into Digital Diplomacy or e-diplomacy has led to communication technologies as an important tool for acquiring diplomatic objectives. The information revolution has compressed the time and distance which once separated countries in all parts of the globe. More important, it has changed the character and dimension of the problems governments must confront. Increasingly, these problems cannot be confined within the borders of a single country, nor blamed on the malfeasance of a single country, nor adequately dealt with by a single government acting alone. (Walter, 1991) Whether in such area as defense and security, human rights, trade and investment, industrial and immigration policies, the protection of the environment, or the advancement of science and technology, governments today must increasingly come to grips with issues that arouse the concerns, impinge on the interests, and even threaten the goals and values not just of their own country but of individuals and constituencies across national lines. (Walter, 1991) These changes have led to 'international-isation of demands' for action from the governments by not only once own public but also from international audiences.

Digital diplomacy has managed to bring widespread change in the fundamental understanding of traditional diplomacy. Two themes, in particular, stand out. First, at the policy level, social media affects the ways that diplomats and other leaders do their jobs. Second, at the institutional level, diverse organizations from foreign ministries to NGOs and international organizations are being reshaped and re-imagined due to the revolution in digital technologies. (Holmes, 2015) But digital platforms are not entirely positive in its impact or outreach. Lately, social media platforms have been used for 'word violence' where actors are involved in insults, molding of truth and intimidation which can harm relations. The overwhelming example of word violence has been associated with the newly elected President of US Donald Trump who has used Twitter as a platform to voice his opinions on countries like China, Russia, Mexico, Pakistan etc. One of his tweet resulted to the cancelation of Mexican President Enrique Pena Nieto's visit to Washington DC. (Campoy, 2017, para. 1)

People-to-people interaction has been reformed drastically via the new technologies under the ambit of cultural diplomacy. The way a country is presented to the world is very important in the success or failure of one's larger foreign policy. Internet and social media act as windows for the world to understand the other nation. The rapid access of information about any incident happening in one corner of the world can impact the overall image of country. For example, isolated violent incidents on few tourists in India quickly escalated as an important issue because of social and foreign media. This led to government intervention and the reintroduction of the

'Incredible India' campaign to attract foreign tourists. But not always this 'instant info' characteristic of new age media helps countries. Many times media themselves play along the prejudices and stereotypes amidst the backdrop of global interdependence, without being fully aware of other societies. The new media is more international and instantaneous in nature, but their ability to play up differences can sometime lead to policy ineffectiveness.

Gaining a better understanding of foreign publics, projecting an image of the self to other states, enhancing legitimacy through more intensive communication and information dissemination and so forth imply important relationships between key variables in international politics, such as the form of diplomacy undertaken and variation in received state images. (Holmes, 2015) But because newer technologies are ubiquitously omnipresent in today's society or day to day life, constructing a tangible understanding of digital diplomacy becomes difficult. To disentangle information or the impact of digital diplomacy is not as easy as it once used to be. Though diplomats operate in a currently vulnerable world where terrorist attacks and cyber hackings are a routine affair, their role is albeit relevant. The area of diplomacy has got new actors (NGOs, civic society) because of globalization and ICT, but it has also enlarged the scope of interaction with the rest of the world. The traditional forums have found themselves to benefit with a dynamic navigation of contemporary forms of media, leading countries to formidably actualize their foreign policy goals.

The erratic unpredictability of international politics has always caught actors by surprise. Though historically events have never occurred in a vacuum, but this is truer now than ever. Diplomats try to have a polished foresight about the world and anticipate events or political behaviors but many a times one cannot foresee. 'Real-Time Diplomacy' because of the digital revolution has increased the possibility of back-and-forth of information which has changed the rules of diplomacy. During much of the twentieth century, speed steadily encroached on diplomatic process as radio, television, and then the Internet were increasingly relied upon by the public and policymakers as principal sources of information. The diplomatic pouch become largely obsolete as foreign ministries turn first to open sources such as the BBC, CNN, and, more recently, Twitter and other social media to find out what is going on in distant parts of the world. (Seib, 2012) Therefore, the task to embrace and adjust to the swift availability and exchange of information at various technological platforms lies on respective countries'.

Soft Power Rivalry: Information Age, Media and Digital Diplomacy

Diplomacy as a practice has grown and changed not only with time but also with new discoveries made by people. Not until when printing press was discovered, any kind of official communication with other foreign public was almost obscure. During the 20th century and the development of fascism and Nazism as a means to strengthen national identity, directly gave a stronger impetus to democratic nations for initiating the 'international mission' to win 'hearts and minds'. By the time Joseph Nye Jr introduced the concept of Soft Power in the post-modern world, it has become increasingly a well accepted phenomenon by countries in a world environment of interdependence, transnational connectivity and global information age. According to Nye, this 'second face of power' (first face being Hard Power or the military power) rests on the ability to shape the preferences of people, i.e. co-opting rather than coercing them. (Nye, 2004) Culture, political values and foreign policy are important resources for a nation's soft power. Furthermore, under the ambit of soft power, public diplomacy can be seen as a very important instrument for wielding international power and attraction, recognized officially since the Cold War times (and in actuality since the World Wars) as a potent tool of influence in world politics for the governments amidst a plethora of hard power choices. Nye argues that countries that are likely to be more attractive in postmodern international relations are those that help to frame issues, whose culture and ideas are closer to prevailing international norms, and whose credibility abroad is reinforced by their values and policies. (Nye, 2004)

In the midst of this background, a new understanding of power has been associated with public diplomacy, digital diplomacy or e-diplomacy, cultural diplomacy and all other recently discovered diplomacies. The post 9/11 era has seen a renewed debate about various dimensions of public diplomacy and the digital-ness of diplomacy. With intercultural clashes around the world, nontraditional security threats, rising powers in various geopolitical regions and economic crisis, countries have started competing ferociously to win the hearts and minds of the world, and secure a strong soft power base. To have an assertive role in the global order, various governments of the world are realizing ways to bolster their soft power and public diplomacy initiatives in this digital era. America being the home for biggest digital platforms in the world like Facebook, Twitter etc, has set the stage for digital diplomacy. Many embassies now use these digital platforms to interact with the local people. Following this suit, China's Weibo or WeChat is changing the way foreign embassies are communicating in China. In 'Social Media and E-Diplomacy: Scanning Embassies on Weibo', author Ying Jiang states that "top three social media platforms most frequently used in China by foreign embassies are Sina Weibo, Tencent Weibo and WeChat". Compared with conventional offline public diplomacy, reaching out to target group via social media is much more cost effective and efficient. Embassies of countries like US, UK, Canada and South Korea are conversationally active on Weibo and engage with their followers. Especially South Korea, as it is able to tap in its vast Soft Power base in China, thanks to the devout KPop or Korean Pop music following amongst young Chinese. (Jiang, 2017) With bigger powers realizing the potential and importance of media in today's time, China in 2009 declared to spend 45 billion yuan (HK $51 billion) on the overseas expansion of its main media organizations in an attempt to improve its country's image abroad. This move has been seen as an ambitious drive by China to build an internationally acclaimed media station, something similar to the Qatar based Al-Jazeera model. ("Beijing in 45b Yuan Global Media Drive", 2009) According to William Brooks, a US State Department veteran and an adjunct professor of Japanese studies at SAIS, John Hopkins University, Japan has been losing on to China in the information war, especially in America. He states that China through its sophisticated CCTV World Channel has emerged as the clear technological leader in the de facto information providing rivalry with Japan. "It has set up a Washington Bureau and state of the art programming that is as sophisticated as CNN's, even to the extent of adding top-notch American anchors and reporters to present hard-hitting balanced news and features to a world audience…Japan has no comparable US based programming." (Kingston, 2015, para. 13)

During the 1930s, Soviet Union had one of the best propaganda run systems in the world. Currently, Vladmir Putin's following in the world, or specifically amongst the nationalists and populists, can easily remind anyone of the Russia in the 1920s and 1930s, when it had embarked on the role of being anti-establishment during the Bolshevik Revolution. But this fervor of admiration towards Putin has a lot to do with its well weave of e- diplomacy, media and digital presentation of Russia and its leaders abroad. In 2005, Putin founded RT, Russian Government run global news network with a mere budget of 30 million dollars. By 2010, this budget rose to 300 million dollars a year, very close to BBC International Service's budget (376 million dollars) which is the biggest news gathering broadcast in the world. The RT network has already gone a long way toward "breaking the Anglo Saxon monopoly on global information streams", as Putin ordered it to do during a visit to RT's brand new studios in Moscow in 2013. (Shuster, 2015, para. 5)

Soft power and digital diplomacy has become an integral point of focus for countries across the globe. Soft Power 30, a ranking of global soft power index by Portland, lists yearly 30 top countries with the best soft power influence in the world based on seven categories namely- digital, culture, enterprise, engagement, education, government and polling. Currently, America ranks number one on the soft power ranking, and also earned number one spot in the digital category. The ranking stated-"Home to many of the biggest tech brands in the world, the US is the global leader in digital technology and innovation….the Obama Administration and State Department developed the theory and practice of online-driven campaigning and 'digital diplomacy'….the way the US has developed and leveraged digital diplomacy, gives the nation a significant soft power boost". (Index Result, 2016) Other countries with formidable digital ratings according to the soft power rankings were Canada, United Kingdom, Germany, France, Singapore, Australia Sweden, Norway, Netherlands, Russia and Japan.

Table 3. Youtube subscribers of prominent media broadcasters (till June 2017)

Channel	Subscribers
ABC News	2,651,093
RT	2,143,888
CNN	2,116,374
BBC	1,384,524
Al Jazeera English	1,436,887
CCTV English	49,784

Comprehending Future

Internet and social media will only continue to be more central to international happenings. Today, more than 50 percent of the world's population has access to some combination of cell phones (five billion users) and the Internet (two billion). These people communicate within and across borders, forming virtual communities that empower citizens at the (sometimes) expense of governments. (Schmidt & Cohen, 2010, para. 2)Connection technologies will eventually carve out opportunities for growth and huge challenges for nation states. Diplomacy has always evolved with new technologies, whether because of telegraph, postal messages or radio. Earlier messages between states used to take days for it to reach and eventually act upon. States had to rely on this two and fro method of messages which were not only time consuming but also cumbersome. Just as newer technologies have eased individual life in various spheres; it has also absorbed itself in the political discourse of the world. When US President Bill Clinton sent his first electronic message to the Swedish Prime Minister Carl Bildt in 1994, the diplomatic community was gradually embracing itself for a wave of change.

Dear Carl:

I appreciate your support for my decision to end trade embargo on Vietnam....... thank you for all that Sweden has done......I share your enthusiasm for the potential of emerging communications technologies. This demonstration of electronic communications is an important step toward building a global information superhighway.

Sincerely

Bill

(*Source:* US Government Publishing Office, 1994)

The tech savvy-ness of governments helps them to connect well with not only their own masses but also internationally. Prime Minister Narendra Modi's overwhelming acceptance for newer technologies and its importance in his popularity within the Indian society is a classic example of positively scooping the benefits of digital age. Never before has an Indian Prime Minister opened multiple digital avenues for the public to connect easily to the government. The Ministry of External Affairs of India under his leadership has been making positive headlines for its swift responses to public problems on social media websites like twitter. With a more determined approach in helping Indian Diaspora across the globe, External Affairs Minister Sushma Swaraj has been utilizing these new age tools of communication. In another example of exploiting the pros of digital platforms, former US President Barack Obama was able to lock his win in the 2008 US Presidential election due to fierce online marketing strategy resulting to mass individual donations for his election campaign. Internet and new technologies are revamping the world in every sphere it's interacting with. The socio-politico-economic areas have become increasingly intertwined and interdependent with new media platforms.

Amidst the cluster of its usefulness, newer technologies bring with them unprecedented challenges as well. When the beheading of many Westerners was video recorded and uploaded by ISIS on internet, just like any other music video for the world to see, states and individuals were unimaginably appalled. The technology that brought people together was a prism for witnessing unthinkable violence with any kind of hesitance. Such incidents remind the world about the dark usage of ICT for achieving corrupt goals. The threat of violent non-state actors has opened a new chapter on terrorism and modern media platforms. The duality of ISIS as not only a fighting force but also a media conglomerate poses unique threats to the world order which begs diplomatic and technological innovation on the parts of leaders to deal with this threat.

Cyberattacks pose exclusive challenges for the state. Not only the confidential information and security of critical infrastructure can be compromised, but the plausibility of nuclear framework being threatened is apocalyptic in thinking. Cyber threats from whether individuals, non state actors or states themselves can either damage key national security data or lead to cyber espionage. In short span of time, the world has journeyed from digital diplomacy to cyber warfare, which throws light on the speed at which international order is evolving. All these issues are unique in nature which hasn't been faced by nations before. Therefore, apart from innovation, they would require conscious will and coming together of states, corporations, civic society, NGOs and international organizations for a long-term solution.

Internet and the dot com boom make 21st century light years ahead from past centuries. Its beneficial factors transcend manmade boundaries and introduce us to an evolved lifestyle our forefathers never thought off. Political actors, diplomatic agents and state have tried to adapt and make its way through these technological changes. Face-to-face diplomacy has not evaporated from the diplomatic circuits, but the utility of ICT in this field has been overwhelmingly realized. With complex challenges and threats beyond the traditional boundaries of states emanating, the field of diplomacy and statecraft has to evolve further so that it counters them.

REFERENCES

Abbate, J. (2000). *Inventing the Internet*. Cambridge, MA: MIT Press.

Briggs, A., & Burke, P. (2009). A Social History of the Media: From Gutenberg to the Internet. Cambridge, UK: Polity Press.

Brunton, F. (2013). *Spam: A Shadow History of the Internet*. Cambridge, MA: MIT Press.

Castells, M. (2001). *The Internet Galaxy: Reflections on the Internet, Business, and Society*. New York: Oxford University Press. doi:10.1007/978-3-322-89613-1

Deruda, A. (2014). *The Digital Diplomacy Handbook: How to Use Social Media to Engage with Global Audiences*. Create Space Independent Publishing Platform.

Fuchs, C. (2011). *Internet and Society: Social Theory in the Information Age*. New York: Routledge.

Graham, M., & Dutton, W. H. (2014). *Society and the Internet; How Networks of Information and Communication are Changing Our Lives*. New York: Oxford University Press. doi:10.1093/acprof:oso/9780199661992.001.0001

Internet Usage Statistics. (2017). *Internet World Stats: Usage and Population Statistics*. Retrieved from http://www.internetworldstats.com/stats.htm

Sandre, A. (2015). *Digital Diplomacy: Conversations on Innovation in Foreign Policy*. London: Rowman and Littlefield.

Shorter, C. R. (2014). *Digital Diplomacy in an Era of Rising Social Powers: How New Media Impacted the Practice of Public Diplomacy by Empowering Citizens and Terrorist Organizations*. London: Webster University.

Statista: The Statistics Portal. (2018). *Most famous social network sites worldwide as of January 2017, ranked by number of active users (in millions)*. Retrieved from https://www.statista.com/statistics/272014/global-social-networks-ranked-by-number-of-users/

United States Government Publishing Office. (1994). *1994 Public Papers 273 - Electronic Mail Message to Prime Minister Carl Bildt of Sweden*. Retrieved from https://www.gpo.gov/fdsys/granule/PPP-1994-book1/PPP-1994-book1-doc-pg273/content-detail.html

Related References

To continue our tradition of advancing academic research, we have compiled a list of recommended IGI Global readings. These references will provide additional information and guidance to further enrich your knowledge and assist you with your own research and future publications.

Adeyemo, O. (2013). The nationwide health information network: A biometric approach to prevent medical identity theft. In *User-driven healthcare: Concepts, methodologies, tools, and applications* (pp. 1636–1649). Hershey, PA: IGI Global. doi:10.4018/978-1-4666-2770-3.ch081

Adler, M., & Henman, P. (2009). Justice beyond the courts: The implications of computerisation for procedural justice in social security. In A. Martínez & P. Abat (Eds.), *E-justice: Using information communication technologies in the court system* (pp. 65–86). Hershey, PA: IGI Global. doi:10.4018/978-1-59904-998-4.ch005

Aflalo, E., & Gabay, E. (2013). An information system for coping with student dropout. In L. Tomei (Ed.), *Learning tools and teaching approaches through ICT advancements* (pp. 176–187). Hershey, PA: IGI Global. doi:10.4018/978-1-4666-2017-9.ch016

Ahmed, M. A., Janssen, M., & van den Hoven, J. (2012). Value sensitive transfer (VST) of systems among countries: Towards a framework. *International Journal of Electronic Government Research*, *8*(1), 26–42. doi:10.4018/jegr.2012010102

Aikins, S. K. (2008). Issues and trends in internet-based citizen participation. In G. Garson & M. Khosrow-Pour (Eds.), *Handbook of research on public information technology* (pp. 31–40). Hershey, PA: IGI Global. doi:10.4018/978-1-59904-857-4.ch004

Aikins, S. K. (2009). A comparative study of municipal adoption of internet-based citizen participation. In C. Reddick (Ed.), *Handbook of research on strategies for local e-government adoption and implementation: Comparative studies* (pp. 206–230). Hershey, PA: IGI Global. doi:10.4018/978-1-60566-282-4.ch011

Aikins, S. K. (2012). Improving e-government project management: Best practices and critical success factors. In *Digital democracy: Concepts, methodologies, tools, and applications* (pp. 1314–1332). Hershey, PA: IGI Global. doi:10.4018/978-1-4666-1740-7.ch065

Akabawi, M. S. (2011). Ghabbour group ERP deployment: Learning from past technology failures. In E. Business Research and Case Center (Ed.), Cases on business and management in the MENA region: New trends and opportunities (pp. 177-203). Hershey, PA: IGI Global. doi:10.4018/978-1-60960-583-4.ch012

Akabawi, M. S. (2013). Ghabbour group ERP deployment: Learning from past technology failures. In *Industrial engineering: Concepts, methodologies, tools, and applications* (pp. 933–958). Hershey, PA: IGI Global. doi:10.4018/978-1-4666-1945-6.ch051

Akbulut, A. Y., & Motwani, J. (2008). Integration and information sharing in e-government. In G. Putnik & M. Cruz-Cunha (Eds.), *Encyclopedia of networked and virtual organizations* (pp. 729–734). Hershey, PA: IGI Global. doi:10.4018/978-1-59904-885-7.ch096

Akers, E. J. (2008). Technology diffusion in public administration. In G. Garson & M. Khosrow-Pour (Eds.), *Handbook of research on public information technology* (pp. 339–348). Hershey, PA: IGI Global. doi:10.4018/978-1-59904-857-4.ch033

Al-Shafi, S. (2008). Free wireless internet park services: An investigation of technology adoption in Qatar from a citizens' perspective. *Journal of Cases on Information Technology*, *10*(3), 21–34. doi:10.4018/jcit.2008070103

Al-Shafi, S., & Weerakkody, V. (2009). Implementing free wi-fi in public parks: An empirical study in Qatar. *International Journal of Electronic Government Research*, *5*(3), 21–35. doi:10.4018/jegr.2009070102

Aladwani, A. M. (2002). Organizational actions, computer attitudes and end-user satisfaction in public organizations: An empirical study. In C. Snodgrass & E. Szewczak (Eds.), *Human factors in information systems* (pp. 153–168). Hershey, PA: IGI Global. doi:10.4018/978-1-931777-10-0.ch012

Aladwani, A. M. (2002). Organizational actions, computer attitudes, and end-user satisfaction in public organizations: An empirical study. *Journal of Organizational and End User Computing*, *14*(1), 42–49. doi:10.4018/joeuc.2002010104

Allen, B., Juillet, L., Paquet, G., & Roy, J. (2005). E-government and private-public partnerships: Relational challenges and strategic directions. In M. Khosrow-Pour (Ed.), *Practicing e-government: A global perspective* (pp. 364–382). Hershey, PA: IGI Global. doi:10.4018/978-1-59140-637-2.ch016

Alshawaf, A., & Knalil, O. E. (2008). IS success factors and IS organizational impact: Does ownership type matter in Kuwait? *International Journal of Enterprise Information Systems*, *4*(2), 13–33. doi:10.4018/jeis.2008040102

Ambali, A. R. (2009). Digital divide and its implication on Malaysian e-government: Policy initiatives. In H. Rahman (Ed.), *Social and political implications of data mining: Knowledge management in e-government* (pp. 267–287). Hershey, PA: IGI Global. doi:10.4018/978-1-60566-230-5.ch016

Amoretti, F. (2007). Digital international governance. In A. Anttiroiko & M. Malkia (Eds.), *Encyclopedia of digital government* (pp. 365–370). Hershey, PA: IGI Global. doi:10.4018/978-1-59140-789-8.ch056

Amoretti, F. (2008). Digital international governance. In A. Anttiroiko (Ed.), *Electronic government: Concepts, methodologies, tools, and applications* (pp. 688–696). Hershey, PA: IGI Global. doi:10.4018/978-1-59904-947-2.ch058

Amoretti, F. (2008). E-government at supranational level in the European Union. In A. Anttiroiko (Ed.), *Electronic government: Concepts, methodologies, tools, and applications* (pp. 1047–1055). Hershey, PA: IGI Global. doi:10.4018/978-1-59904-947-2.ch079

Amoretti, F. (2008). E-government regimes. In A. Anttiroiko (Ed.), *Electronic government: Concepts, methodologies, tools, and applications* (pp. 3846–3856). Hershey, PA: IGI Global. doi:10.4018/978-1-59904-947-2.ch280

Amoretti, F. (2009). Electronic constitution: A Braudelian perspective. In F. Amoretti (Ed.), *Electronic constitution: Social, cultural, and political implications* (pp. 1–19). Hershey, PA: IGI Global. doi:10.4018/978-1-60566-254-1.ch001

Amoretti, F., & Musella, F. (2009). Institutional isomorphism and new technologies. In M. Khosrow-Pour (Ed.), *Encyclopedia of information science and technology* (2nd ed.; pp. 2066–2071). Hershey, PA: IGI Global. doi:10.4018/978-1-60566-026-4.ch325

Andersen, K. V., & Henriksen, H. Z. (2007). E-government research: Capabilities, interaction, orientation, and values. In D. Norris (Ed.), *Current issues and trends in e-government research* (pp. 269–288). Hershey, PA: IGI Global. doi:10.4018/978-1-59904-283-1.ch013

Anderson, K. V., & Henriksen, H. Z. (2005). The first leg of e-government research: Domains and application areas 1998-2003. *International Journal of Electronic Government Research, 1*(4), 26–44. doi:10.4018/jegr.2005100102

Anttiroiko, A. (2009). Democratic e-governance. In M. Khosrow-Pour (Ed.), *Encyclopedia of information science and technology* (2nd ed.; pp. 990–995). Hershey, PA: IGI Global. doi:10.4018/978-1-60566-026-4.ch158

Association, I. R. (2010). *Networking and telecommunications: Concepts, methodologies, tools and applications* (Vols. 1–3). Hershey, PA: IGI Global. doi:10.4018/978-1-60566-986-1

Association, I. R. (2010). *Web-based education: Concepts, methodologies, tools and applications* (Vols. 1–3). Hershey, PA: IGI Global. doi:10.4018/978-1-61520-963-7

Baker, P. M., Bell, A., & Moon, N. W. (2009). Accessibility issues in municipal wireless networks. In C. Reddick (Ed.), *Handbook of research on strategies for local e-government adoption and implementation: Comparative studies* (pp. 569–588). Hershey, PA: IGI Global. doi:10.4018/978-1-60566-282-4.ch030

Becker, S. A., Keimer, R., & Muth, T. (2010). A case on university and community collaboration: The sci-tech entrepreneurial training services (ETS) program. In S. Becker & R. Niebuhr (Eds.), *Cases on technology innovation: Entrepreneurial successes and pitfalls* (pp. 68–90). Hershey, PA: IGI Global. doi:10.4018/978-1-61520-609-4.ch003

Becker, S. A., Keimer, R., & Muth, T. (2012). A case on university and community collaboration: The sci-tech entrepreneurial training services (ETS) program. In Regional development: Concepts, methodologies, tools, and applications (pp. 947-969). Hershey, PA: IGI Global. doi:10.4018/978-1-4666-0882-5.ch507

Bernardi, R. (2012). Information technology and resistance to public sector reforms: A case study in Kenya. In T. Papadopoulos & P. Kanellis (Eds.), *Public sector reform using information technologies: Transforming policy into practice* (pp. 59–78). Hershey, PA: IGI Global. doi:10.4018/978-1-60960-839-2.ch004

Bernardi, R. (2013). Information technology and resistance to public sector reforms: A case study in Kenya. In *User-driven healthcare: Concepts, methodologies, tools, and applications* (pp. 14–33). Hershey, PA: IGI Global. doi:10.4018/978-1-4666-2770-3.ch002

Bolívar, M. P., Pérez, M. D., & Hernández, A. M. (2012). Municipal e-government services in emerging economies: The Latin-American and Caribbean experiences. In Y. Chen & P. Chu (Eds.), *Electronic governance and cross-boundary collaboration: Innovations and advancing tools* (pp. 198–226). Hershey, PA: IGI Global. doi:10.4018/978-1-60960-753-1.ch011

Borycki, E. M., & Kushniruk, A. W. (2010). Use of clinical simulations to evaluate the impact of health information systems and ubiquitous computing devices upon health professional work. In S. Mohammed & J. Fiaidhi (Eds.), *Ubiquitous health and medical informatics: The ubiquity 2.0 trend and beyond* (pp. 552–573). Hershey, PA: IGI Global. doi:10.4018/978-1-61520-777-0.ch026

Borycki, E. M., & Kushniruk, A. W. (2011). Use of clinical simulations to evaluate the impact of health information systems and ubiquitous computing devices upon health professional work. In *Clinical technologies: Concepts, methodologies, tools and applications* (pp. 532–553). Hershey, PA: IGI Global. doi:10.4018/978-1-60960-561-2.ch220

Buchan, J. (2011). Developing a dynamic and responsive online learning environment: A case study of a large Australian university. In B. Czerkawski (Ed.), *Free and open source software for e-learning: Issues, successes and challenges* (pp. 92–109). Hershey, PA: IGI Global. doi:10.4018/978-1-61520-917-0.ch006

Buenger, A. W. (2008). Digital convergence and cybersecurity policy. In G. Garson & M. Khosrow-Pour (Eds.), *Handbook of research on public information technology* (pp. 395–405). Hershey, PA: IGI Global. doi:10.4018/978-1-59904-857-4.ch038

Burn, J. M., & Loch, K. D. (2002). The societal impact of world wide web - Key challenges for the 21st century. In A. Salehnia (Ed.), *Ethical issues of information systems* (pp. 88–106). Hershey, PA: IGI Global. doi:10.4018/978-1-931777-15-5.ch007

Burn, J. M., & Loch, K. D. (2003). The societal impact of the world wide web-Key challenges for the 21st century. In M. Khosrow-Pour (Ed.), *Advanced topics in information resources management* (Vol. 2, pp. 32–51). Hershey, PA: IGI Global. doi:10.4018/978-1-59140-062-2.ch002

Bwalya, K. J., Du Plessis, T., & Rensleigh, C. (2012). The "quicksilver initiatives" as a framework for e-government strategy design in developing economies. In K. Bwalya & S. Zulu (Eds.), *Handbook of research on e-government in emerging economies: Adoption, e-participation, and legal frameworks* (pp. 605–623). Hershey, PA: IGI Global. doi:10.4018/978-1-4666-0324-0.ch031

Cabotaje, C. E., & Alampay, E. A. (2013). Social media and citizen engagement: Two cases from the Philippines. In S. Saeed & C. Reddick (Eds.), *Human-centered system design for electronic governance* (pp. 225–238). Hershey, PA: IGI Global. doi:10.4018/978-1-4666-3640-8.ch013

Camillo, A., Di Pietro, L., Di Virgilio, F., & Franco, M. (2013). Work-groups conflict at PetroTech-Italy, S.R.L.: The influence of culture on conflict dynamics. In B. Christiansen, E. Turkina, & N. Williams (Eds.), *Cultural and technological influences on global business* (pp. 272–289). Hershey, PA: IGI Global. doi:10.4018/978-1-4666-3966-9.ch015

Capra, E., Francalanci, C., & Marinoni, C. (2008). Soft success factors for m-government. In A. Anttiroiko (Ed.), *Electronic government: Concepts, methodologies, tools, and applications* (pp. 1213–1233). Hershey, PA: IGI Global. doi:10.4018/978-1-59904-947-2.ch089

Cartelli, A. (2009). The implementation of practices with ICT as a new teaching-learning paradigm. In A. Cartelli & M. Palma (Eds.), *Encyclopedia of information communication technology* (pp. 413–417). Hershey, PA: IGI Global. doi:10.4018/978-1-59904-845-1.ch055

Charalabidis, Y., Lampathaki, F., & Askounis, D. (2010). Investigating the landscape in national interoperability frameworks. *International Journal of E-Services and Mobile Applications*, *2*(4), 28–41. doi:10.4018/jesma.2010100103

Charalabidis, Y., Lampathaki, F., & Askounis, D. (2012). Investigating the landscape in national interoperability frameworks. In A. Scupola (Ed.), *Innovative mobile platform developments for electronic services design and delivery* (pp. 218–231). Hershey, PA: IGI Global. doi:10.4018/978-1-4666-1568-7.ch013

Chen, I. (2005). Distance education associations. In C. Howard, J. Boettcher, L. Justice, K. Schenk, P. Rogers, & G. Berg (Eds.), *Encyclopedia of distance learning* (pp. 599–612). Hershey, PA: IGI Global. doi:10.4018/978-1-59140-555-9.ch087

Chen, I. (2008). Distance education associations. In L. Tomei (Ed.), *Online and distance learning: Concepts, methodologies, tools, and applications* (pp. 562–579). Hershey, PA: IGI Global. doi:10.4018/978-1-59904-935-9.ch048

Chen, Y. (2008). Managing IT outsourcing for digital government. In A. Anttiroiko (Ed.), *Electronic government: Concepts, methodologies, tools, and applications* (pp. 3107–3114). Hershey, PA: IGI Global. doi:10.4018/978-1-59904-947-2.ch229

Chen, Y., & Dimitrova, D. V. (2006). Electronic government and online engagement: Citizen interaction with government via web portals. *International Journal of Electronic Government Research, 2*(1), 54–76. doi:10.4018/jegr.2006010104

Chen, Y., & Knepper, R. (2005). Digital government development strategies: Lessons for policy makers from a comparative perspective. In W. Huang, K. Siau, & K. Wei (Eds.), *Electronic government strategies and implementation* (pp. 394–420). Hershey, PA: IGI Global. doi:10.4018/978-1-59140-348-7.ch017

Chen, Y., & Knepper, R. (2008). Digital government development strategies: Lessons for policy makers from a comparative perspective. In H. Rahman (Ed.), *Developing successful ICT strategies: Competitive advantages in a global knowledge-driven society* (pp. 334–356). Hershey, PA: IGI Global. doi:10.4018/978-1-59904-654-9.ch017

Cherian, E. J., & Ryan, T. W. (2014). Incongruent needs: Why differences in the iron-triangle of priorities make health information technology adoption and use difficult. In C. El Morr (Ed.), *Research perspectives on the role of informatics in health policy and management* (pp. 209–221). Hershey, PA: IGI Global. doi:10.4018/978-1-4666-4321-5.ch012

Cho, H. J., & Hwang, S. (2010). Government 2.0 in Korea: Focusing on e-participation services. In C. Reddick (Ed.), *Politics, democracy and e-government: Participation and service delivery* (pp. 94–114). Hershey, PA: IGI Global. doi:10.4018/978-1-61520-933-0.ch006

Chorus, C., & Timmermans, H. (2010). Ubiquitous travel environments and travel control strategies: Prospects and challenges. In M. Wachowicz (Ed.), *Movement-aware applications for sustainable mobility: Technologies and approaches* (pp. 30–51). Hershey, PA: IGI Global. doi:10.4018/978-1-61520-769-5.ch003

Chuanshen, R. (2007). E-government construction and China's administrative litigation act. In A. Anttiroiko & M. Malkia (Eds.), *Encyclopedia of digital government* (pp. 507–510). Hershey, PA: IGI Global. doi:10.4018/978-1-59140-789-8.ch077

Ciaghi, A., & Villafiorita, A. (2012). Law modeling and BPR for public administration improvement. In K. Bwalya & S. Zulu (Eds.), *Handbook of research on e-government in emerging economies: Adoption, e-participation, and legal frameworks* (pp. 391–410). Hershey, PA: IGI Global. doi:10.4018/978-1-4666-0324-0.ch019

Ciaramitaro, B. L., & Skrocki, M. (2012). mHealth: Mobile healthcare. In B. Ciaramitaro (Ed.), Mobile technology consumption: Opportunities and challenges (pp. 99-109). Hershey, PA: IGI Global. doi:10.4018/978-1-61350-150-4.ch007

Comite, U. (2012). Innovative processes and managerial effectiveness of e-procurement in healthcare. In A. Manoharan & M. Holzer (Eds.), *Active citizen participation in e-government: A global perspective* (pp. 206–229). Hershey, PA: IGI Global. doi:10.4018/978-1-4666-0116-1.ch011

Cordella, A. (2013). E-government success: How to account for ICT, administrative rationalization, and institutional change. In J. Gil-Garcia (Ed.), *E-government success factors and measures: Theories, concepts, and methodologies* (pp. 40–51). Hershey, PA: IGI Global. doi:10.4018/978-1-4666-4058-0.ch003

Cropf, R. A. (2009). ICT and e-democracy. In M. Khosrow-Pour (Ed.), *Encyclopedia of information science and technology* (2nd ed.; pp. 1789–1793). Hershey, PA: IGI Global. doi:10.4018/978-1-60566-026-4.ch281

Cropf, R. A. (2009). The virtual public sphere. In M. Pagani (Ed.), *Encyclopedia of multimedia technology and networking* (2nd ed.; pp. 1525–1530). Hershey, PA: IGI Global. doi:10.4018/978-1-60566-014-1.ch206

D'Abundo, M. L. (2013). Electronic health record implementation in the United States healthcare industry: Making the process of change manageable. In V. Wang (Ed.), *Handbook of research on technologies for improving the 21st century workforce: Tools for lifelong learning* (pp. 272–286). Hershey, PA: IGI Global. doi:10.4018/978-1-4666-2181-7.ch018

Damurski, L. (2012). E-participation in urban planning: Online tools for citizen engagement in Poland and in Germany. *International Journal of E-Planning Research, 1*(3), 40–67. doi:10.4018/ijepr.2012070103

de Almeida, M. O. (2007). E-government strategy in Brazil: Increasing transparency and efficiency through e-government procurement. In M. Gascó-Hernandez (Ed.), *Latin America online: Cases, successes and pitfalls* (pp. 34–82). Hershey, PA: IGI Global. doi:10.4018/978-1-59140-974-8.ch002

de Juana Espinosa, S. (2008). Empirical study of the municipalitites' motivations for adopting online presence. In A. Anttiroiko (Ed.), *Electronic government: Concepts, methodologies, tools, and applications* (pp. 3593–3608). Hershey, PA: IGI Global. doi:10.4018/978-1-59904-947-2.ch262 de Souza Dias, D. (2002). Motivation for using information technology. In C. Snodgrass & E. Szewczak (Eds.), *Human factors in information systems* (pp. 55–60). Hershey, PA: IGI Global. doi:10.4018/978-1-931777-10-0.ch005

Demediuk, P. (2006). Government procurement ICT's impact on the sustainability of SMEs and regional communities. In S. Marshall, W. Taylor, & X. Yu (Eds.), *Encyclopedia of developing regional communities with information and communication technology* (pp. 321–324). Hershey, PA: IGI Global. doi:10.4018/978-1-59140-575-7.ch056

Devonshire, E., Forsyth, H., Reid, S., & Simpson, J. M. (2013). The challenges and opportunities of online postgraduate coursework programs in a traditional university context. In B. Tynan, J. Willems, & R. James (Eds.), *Outlooks and opportunities in blended and distance learning* (pp. 353–368). Hershey, PA: IGI Global. doi:10.4018/978-1-4666-4205-8.ch026

Di Cerbo, F., Scotto, M., Sillitti, A., Succi, G., & Vernazza, T. (2007). Toward a GNU/Linux distribution for corporate environments. In S. Sowe, I. Stamelos, & I. Samoladas (Eds.), *Emerging free and open source software practices* (pp. 215–236). Hershey, PA: IGI Global. doi:10.4018/978-1-59904-210-7.ch010

Diesner, J., & Carley, K. M. (2005). Revealing social structure from texts: Meta-matrix text analysis as a novel method for network text analysis. In V. Narayanan & D. Armstrong (Eds.), *Causal mapping for research in information technology* (pp. 81–108). Hershey, PA: IGI Global. doi:10.4018/978-1-59140-396-8.ch004

Dologite, D. G., Mockler, R. J., Bai, Q., & Viszhanyo, P. F. (2006). IS change agents in practice in a US-Chinese joint venture. In M. Hunter & F. Tan (Eds.), *Advanced topics in global information management* (Vol. 5, pp. 331–352). Hershey, PA: IGI Global. doi:10.4018/978-1-59140-923-6.ch015

Drnevich, P., Brush, T. H., & Luckock, G. T. (2011). Process and structural implications for IT-enabled outsourcing. *International Journal of Strategic Information Technology and Applications*, *2*(4), 30–43. doi:10.4018/jsita.2011100103

Dwivedi, A. N. (2009). *Handbook of research on information technology management and clinical data administration in healthcare* (Vols. 1–2). Hershey, PA: IGI Global. doi:10.4018/978-1-60566-356-2

Elbeltagi, I., McBride, N., & Hardaker, G. (2006). Evaluating the factors affecting DSS usage by senior managers in local authorities in Egypt. In M. Hunter & F. Tan (Eds.), *Advanced topics in global information management* (Vol. 5, pp. 283–307). Hershey, PA: IGI Global. doi:10.4018/978-1-59140-923-6.ch013

Eom, S., & Fountain, J. E. (2013). Enhancing information services through public-private partnerships: Information technology knowledge transfer underlying structures to develop shared services in the U.S. and Korea. In J. Gil-Garcia (Ed.), *E-government success around the world: Cases, empirical studies, and practical recommendations* (pp. 15–40). Hershey, PA: IGI Global. doi:10.4018/978-1-4666-4173-0.ch002

Esteves, T., Leuenberger, D., & Van Leuven, N. (2012). Reaching citizen 2.0: How government uses social media to send public messages during times of calm and times of crisis. In K. Kloby & M. D'Agostino (Eds.), *Citizen 2.0: Public and governmental interaction through web 2.0 technologies* (pp. 250–268). Hershey, PA: IGI Global. doi:10.4018/978-1-4666-0318-9.ch013

Estevez, E., Fillottrani, P., Janowski, T., & Ojo, A. (2012). Government information sharing: A framework for policy formulation. In Y. Chen & P. Chu (Eds.), *Electronic governance and cross-boundary collaboration: Innovations and advancing tools* (pp. 23–55). Hershey, PA: IGI Global. doi:10.4018/978-1-60960-753-1.ch002

Ezz, I. E. (2008). E-governement emerging trends: Organizational challenges. In A. Anttiroiko (Ed.), *Electronic government: Concepts, methodologies, tools, and applications* (pp. 3721–3737). Hershey, PA: IGI Global. doi:10.4018/978-1-59904-947-2.ch269

Fabri, M. (2009). The Italian style of e-justice in a comparative perspective. In A. Martínez & P. Abat (Eds.), *E-justice: Using information communication technologies in the court system* (pp. 1–19). Hershey, PA: IGI Global. doi:10.4018/978-1-59904-998-4.ch001

Fagbe, T., & Adekola, O. D. (2010). Workplace safety and personnel well-being: The impact of information technology. *International Journal of Green Computing, 1*(1), 28–33. doi:10.4018/jgc.2010010103

Fagbe, T., & Adekola, O. D. (2011). Workplace safety and personnel well-being: The impact of information technology. In *Global business: Concepts, methodologies, tools and applications* (pp. 1438–1444). Hershey, PA: IGI Global. doi:10.4018/978-1-60960-587-2.ch509

Farmer, L. (2008). Affective collaborative instruction with librarians. In S. Kelsey & K. St.Amant (Eds.), *Handbook of research on computer mediated communication* (pp. 15–24). Hershey, PA: IGI Global. doi:10.4018/978-1-59904-863-5.ch002

Favier, L., & Mekhantar, J. (2007). Use of OSS by local e-administration: The French situation. In K. St.Amant & B. Still (Eds.), *Handbook of research on open source software: Technological, economic, and social perspectives* (pp. 428–444). Hershey, PA: IGI Global. doi:10.4018/978-1-59140-999-1.ch033

Fernando, S. (2009). Issues of e-learning in third world countries. In M. Khosrow-Pour (Ed.), *Encyclopedia of information science and technology* (2nd ed.; pp. 2273–2277). Hershey, PA: IGI Global. doi:10.4018/978-1-60566-026-4.ch360

Filho, J. R., & dos Santos, J. R. Jr. (2009). Local e-government in Brazil: Poor interaction and local politics as usual. In C. Reddick (Ed.), *Handbook of research on strategies for local e-government adoption and implementation: Comparative studies* (pp. 863–878). Hershey, PA: IGI Global. doi:10.4018/978-1-60566-282-4.ch045

Fletcher, P. D. (2004). Portals and policy: Implications of electronic access to U.S. federal government information services. In A. Pavlichev & G. Garson (Eds.), *Digital government: Principles and best practices* (pp. 52–62). Hershey, PA: IGI Global. doi:10.4018/978-1-59140-122-3.ch004

Fletcher, P. D. (2008). Portals and policy: Implications of electronic access to U.S. federal government information services. In A. Anttiroiko (Ed.), *Electronic government: Concepts, methodologies, tools, and applications* (pp. 3970–3979). Hershey, PA: IGI Global. doi:10.4018/978-1-59904-947-2.ch289

Forlano, L. (2004). The emergence of digital government: International perspectives. In A. Pavlichev & G. Garson (Eds.), *Digital government: Principles and best practices* (pp. 34–51). Hershey, PA: IGI Global. doi:10.4018/978-1-59140-122-3.ch003

Franzel, J. M., & Coursey, D. H. (2004). Government web portals: Management issues and the approaches of five states. In A. Pavlichev & G. Garson (Eds.), *Digital government: Principles and best practices* (pp. 63–77). Hershey, PA: IGI Global. doi:10.4018/978-1-59140-122-3.ch005

Gaivéo, J. M. (2013). Security of ICTs supporting healthcare activities. In M. Cruz-Cunha, I. Miranda, & P. Gonçalves (Eds.), *Handbook of research on ICTs for human-centered healthcare and social care services* (pp. 208–228). Hershey, PA: IGI Global. doi:10.4018/978-1-4666-3986-7.ch011

Garson, G. D. (1999). *Information technology and computer applications in public administration: Issues and trends*. Hershey, PA: IGI Global. doi:10.4018/978-1-87828-952-0

Garson, G. D. (2003). Toward an information technology research agenda for public administration. In G. Garson (Ed.), *Public information technology: Policy and management issues* (pp. 331–357). Hershey, PA: IGI Global. doi:10.4018/978-1-59140-060-8.ch014

Garson, G. D. (2004). The promise of digital government. In A. Pavlichev & G. Garson (Eds.), *Digital government: Principles and best practices* (pp. 2–15). Hershey, PA: IGI Global. doi:10.4018/978-1-59140-122-3.ch001

Garson, G. D. (2007). An information technology research agenda for public administration. In G. Garson (Ed.), *Modern public information technology systems: Issues and challenges* (pp. 365–392). Hershey, PA: IGI Global. doi:10.4018/978-1-59904-051-6.ch018

Gasco, M. (2007). Civil servants' resistance towards e-government development. In A. Anttiroiko & M. Malkia (Eds.), *Encyclopedia of digital government* (pp. 190–195). Hershey, PA: IGI Global. doi:10.4018/978-1-59140-789-8.ch028

Gasco, M. (2008). Civil servants' resistance towards e-government development. In A. Anttiroiko (Ed.), *Electronic government: Concepts, methodologies, tools, and applications* (pp. 2580–2588). Hershey, PA: IGI Global. doi:10.4018/978-1-59904-947-2.ch190

Ghere, R. K. (2010). Accountability and information technology enactment: Implications for social empowerment. In E. Ferro, Y. Dwivedi, J. Gil-Garcia, & M. Williams (Eds.), *Handbook of research on overcoming digital divides: Constructing an equitable and competitive information society* (pp. 515–532). Hershey, PA: IGI Global. doi:10.4018/978-1-60566-699-0.ch028

Gibson, I. W. (2012). Simulation modeling of healthcare delivery. In A. Kolker & P. Story (Eds.), *Management engineering for effective healthcare delivery: Principles and applications* (pp. 69–89). Hershey, PA: IGI Global. doi:10.4018/978-1-60960-872-9.ch003

Gil-Garcia, J. R. (2007). Exploring e-government benefits and success factors. In A. Anttiroiko & M. Malkia (Eds.), *Encyclopedia of digital government* (pp. 803–811). Hershey, PA: IGI Global. doi:10.4018/978-1-59140-789-8.ch122

Gil-Garcia, J. R., & González Miranda, F. (2010). E-government and opportunities for participation: The case of the Mexican state web portals. In C. Reddick (Ed.), *Politics, democracy and e-government: Participation and service delivery* (pp. 56–74). Hershey, PA: IGI Global. doi:10.4018/978-1-61520-933-0.ch004

Goldfinch, S. (2012). Public trust in government, trust in e-government, and use of e-government. In Z. Yan (Ed.), *Encyclopedia of cyber behavior* (pp. 987–995). Hershey, PA: IGI Global. doi:10.4018/978-1-4666-0315-8.ch081

Goodyear, M. (2012). Organizational change contributions to e-government project transitions. In S. Aikins (Ed.), *Managing e-government projects: Concepts, issues, and best practices* (pp. 1–21). Hershey, PA: IGI Global. doi:10.4018/978-1-4666-0086-7.ch001

Gordon, S., & Mulligan, P. (2003). Strategic models for the delivery of personal financial services: The role of infocracy. In S. Gordon (Ed.), *Computing information technology: The human side* (pp. 220–232). Hershey, PA: IGI Global. doi:10.4018/978-1-93177-752-0.ch014

Gordon, T. F. (2007). Legal knowledge systems. In A. Anttiroiko & M. Malkia (Eds.), *Encyclopedia of digital government* (pp. 1161–1166). Hershey, PA: IGI Global. doi:10.4018/978-1-59140-789-8.ch175

Graham, J. E., & Semich, G. W. (2008). Integrating technology to transform pedagogy: Revisiting the progress of the three phase TUI model for faculty development. In L. Tomei (Ed.), *Adapting information and communication technologies for effective education* (pp. 1–12). Hershey, PA: IGI Global. doi:10.4018/978-1-59904-922-9.ch001

Grandinetti, L., & Pisacane, O. (2012). Web services for healthcare management. In D. Prakash Vidyarthi (Ed.), *Technologies and protocols for the future of internet design: Reinventing the web* (pp. 60–94). Hershey, PA: IGI Global. doi:10.4018/978-1-4666-0203-8.ch004

Groenewegen, P., & Wagenaar, F. P. (2008). VO as an alternative to hierarchy in the Dutch police sector. In G. Putnik & M. Cruz-Cunha (Eds.), *Encyclopedia of networked and virtual organizations* (pp. 1851–1857). Hershey, PA: IGI Global. doi:10.4018/978-1-59904-885-7.ch245

Gronlund, A. (2001). Building an infrastructure to manage electronic services. In S. Dasgupta (Ed.), *Managing internet and intranet technologies in organizations: Challenges and opportunities* (pp. 71–103). Hershey, PA: IGI Global. doi:10.4018/978-1-878289-95-7.ch006

Gronlund, A. (2002). Introduction to electronic government: Design, applications and management. In Å. Grönlund (Ed.), *Electronic government: Design, applications and management* (pp. 1–21). Hershey, PA: IGI Global. doi:10.4018/978-1-930708-19-8.ch001

Gupta, A., Woosley, R., Crk, I., & Sarnikar, S. (2009). An information technology architecture for drug effectiveness reporting and post-marketing surveillance. In J. Tan (Ed.), *Medical informatics: Concepts, methodologies, tools, and applications* (pp. 631–646). Hershey, PA: IGI Global. doi:10.4018/978-1-60566-050-9.ch047

Hallin, A., & Lundevall, K. (2007). mCity: User focused development of mobile services within the city of Stockholm. In I. Kushchu (Ed.), Mobile government: An emerging direction in e-government (pp. 12-29). Hershey, PA: IGI Global. doi:10.4018/978-1-59140-884-0.ch002

Hallin, A., & Lundevall, K. (2009). mCity: User focused development of mobile services within the city of Stockholm. In S. Clarke (Ed.), Evolutionary concepts in end user productivity and performance: Applications for organizational progress (pp. 268-280). Hershey, PA: IGI Global. doi:10.4018/978-1-60566-136-0.ch017

Hallin, A., & Lundevall, K. (2009). mCity: User focused development of mobile services within the city of Stockholm. In D. Taniar (Ed.), Mobile computing: Concepts, methodologies, tools, and applications (pp. 3455-3467). Hershey, PA: IGI Global. doi:10.4018/978-1-60566-054-7.ch253

Hanson, A. (2005). Overcoming barriers in the planning of a virtual library. In M. Khosrow-Pour (Ed.), *Encyclopedia of information science and technology* (pp. 2255–2259). Hershey, PA: IGI Global. doi:10.4018/978-1-59140-553-5.ch397

Haque, A. (2008). Information technology and surveillance: Implications for public administration in a new word order. In T. Loendorf & G. Garson (Eds.), *Patriotic information systems* (pp. 177–185). Hershey, PA: IGI Global. doi:10.4018/978-1-59904-594-8.ch008

Hauck, R. V., Thatcher, S. M., & Weisband, S. P. (2012). Temporal aspects of information technology use: Increasing shift work effectiveness. In J. Wang (Ed.), *Advancing the service sector with evolving technologies: Techniques and principles* (pp. 87–104). Hershey, PA: IGI Global. doi:10.4018/978-1-4666-0044-7.ch006

Hawk, S., & Witt, T. (2006). Telecommunications courses in information systems programs. *International Journal of Information and Communication Technology Education*, *2*(1), 79–92. doi:10.4018/jicte.2006010107

Helms, M. M., Moore, R., & Ahmadi, M. (2009). Information technology (IT) and the healthcare industry: A SWOT analysis. In J. Tan (Ed.), *Medical informatics: Concepts, methodologies, tools, and applications* (pp. 134–152). Hershey, PA: IGI Global. doi:10.4018/978-1-60566-050-9.ch012

Hendrickson, S. M., & Young, M. E. (2014). Electronic records management at a federally funded research and development center. In J. Krueger (Ed.), *Cases on electronic records and resource management implementation in diverse environments* (pp. 334–350). Hershey, PA: IGI Global. doi:10.4018/978-1-4666-4466-3.ch020

Henman, P. (2010). Social policy and information communication technologies. In J. Martin & L. Hawkins (Eds.), *Information communication technologies for human services education and delivery: Concepts and cases* (pp. 215–229). Hershey, PA: IGI Global. doi:10.4018/978-1-60566-735-5.ch014

Hismanoglu, M. (2011). Important issues in online education: E-pedagogy and marketing. In U. Demiray & S. Sever (Eds.), *Marketing online education programs: Frameworks for promotion and communication* (pp. 184–209). Hershey, PA: IGI Global. doi:10.4018/978-1-60960-074-7.ch012

Ho, K. K. (2008). The e-government development, IT strategies, and portals of the Hong Kong SAR government. In A. Anttiroiko (Ed.), *Electronic government: Concepts, methodologies, tools, and applications* (pp. 715–733). Hershey, PA: IGI Global. doi:10.4018/978-1-59904-947-2.ch060

Holden, S. H. (2003). The evolution of information technology management at the federal level: Implications for public administration. In G. Garson (Ed.), *Public information technology: Policy and management issues* (pp. 53–73). Hershey, PA: IGI Global. doi:10.4018/978-1-59140-060-8.ch003

Holden, S. H. (2007). The evolution of federal information technology management literature: Does IT finally matter? In G. Garson (Ed.), *Modern public information technology systems: Issues and challenges* (pp. 17–34). Hershey, PA: IGI Global. doi:10.4018/978-1-59904-051-6.ch002

Holland, J. W. (2009). Automation of American criminal justice. In M. Khosrow-Pour (Ed.), *Encyclopedia of information science and technology* (2nd ed.; pp. 300–302). Hershey, PA: IGI Global. doi:10.4018/978-1-60566-026-4.ch051

Holloway, K. (2013). Fair use, copyright, and academic integrity in an online academic environment. In *Digital rights management: Concepts, methodologies, tools, and applications* (pp. 917–928). Hershey, PA: IGI Global. doi:10.4018/978-1-4666-2136-7.ch044

Horiuchi, C. (2005). E-government databases. In L. Rivero, J. Doorn, & V. Ferraggine (Eds.), *Encyclopedia of database technologies and applications* (pp. 206–210). Hershey, PA: IGI Global. doi:10.4018/978-1-59140-560-3.ch035

Horiuchi, C. (2006). Creating IS quality in government settings. In E. Duggan & J. Reichgelt (Eds.), *Measuring information systems delivery quality* (pp. 311–327). Hershey, PA: IGI Global. doi:10.4018/978-1-59140-857-4.ch014

Hsiao, N., Chu, P., & Lee, C. (2012). Impact of e-governance on businesses: Model development and case study. In *Digital democracy: Concepts, methodologies, tools, and applications* (pp. 1407–1425). Hershey, PA: IGI Global. doi:10.4018/978-1-4666-1740-7.ch070

Huang, T., & Lee, C. (2010). Evaluating the impact of e-government on citizens: Cost-benefit analysis. In C. Reddick (Ed.), *Citizens and e-government: Evaluating policy and management* (pp. 37–52). Hershey, PA: IGI Global. doi:10.4018/978-1-61520-931-6.ch003

Hunter, M. G., Diochon, M., Pugsley, D., & Wright, B. (2002). Unique challenges for small business adoption of information technology: The case of the Nova Scotia ten. In S. Burgess (Ed.), *Managing information technology in small business: Challenges and solutions* (pp. 98–117). Hershey, PA: IGI Global. doi:10.4018/978-1-930708-35-8.ch006

Hurskainen, J. (2003). Integration of business systems and applications in merger and alliance: Case metso automation. In T. Reponen (Ed.), *Information technology enabled global customer service* (pp. 207–225). Hershey, PA: IGI Global. doi:10.4018/978-1-59140-048-6.ch012

Iazzolino, G., & Pietrantonio, R. (2011). The soveria.it project: A best practice of e-government in southern Italy. In D. Piaggesi, K. Sund, & W. Castelnovo (Eds.), *Global strategy and practice of e-governance: Examples from around the world* (pp. 34–56). Hershey, PA: IGI Global. doi:10.4018/978-1-60960-489-9.ch003

Imran, A., & Gregor, S. (2012). A process model for successful e-government adoption in the least developed countries: A case of Bangladesh. In F. Tan (Ed.), *International comparisons of information communication technologies: Advancing applications* (pp. 321–350). Hershey, PA: IGI Global. doi:10.4018/978-1-61350-480-2.ch014

Inoue, Y., & Bell, S. T. (2005). Electronic/digital government innovation, and publishing trends with IT. In M. Khosrow-Pour (Ed.), *Encyclopedia of information science and technology* (pp. 1018–1023). Hershey, PA: IGI Global. doi:10.4018/978-1-59140-553-5.ch180

Islam, M. M., & Ehsan, M. (2013). Understanding e-governance: A theoretical approach. In M. Islam & M. Ehsan (Eds.), *From government to e-governance: Public administration in the digital age* (pp. 38–49). Hershey, PA: IGI Global. doi:10.4018/978-1-4666-1909-8.ch003

Jaeger, B. (2009). E-government and e-democracy in the making. In M. Khosrow-Pour (Ed.), *Encyclopedia of information science and technology* (2nd ed.; pp. 1318–1322). Hershey, PA: IGI Global. doi:10.4018/978-1-60566-026-4.ch208

Jain, R. B. (2007). Revamping the administrative structure and processes in India for online diplomacy. In A. Anttiroiko & M. Malkia (Eds.), *Encyclopedia of digital government* (pp. 1418–1423). Hershey, PA: IGI Global. doi:10.4018/978-1-59140-789-8.ch217

Jain, R. B. (2008). Revamping the administrative structure and processes in India for online diplomacy. In A. Anttiroiko (Ed.), *Electronic government: Concepts, methodologies, tools, and applications* (pp. 3142–3149). Hershey, PA: IGI Global. doi:10.4018/978-1-59904-947-2.ch233

Jauhiainen, J. S., & Inkinen, T. (2009). E-governance and the information society in periphery. In C. Reddick (Ed.), *Handbook of research on strategies for local e-government adoption and implementation: Comparative studies* (pp. 497–514). Hershey, PA: IGI Global. doi:10.4018/978-1-60566-282-4.ch026

Jensen, M. J. (2009). Electronic democracy and citizen influence in government. In C. Reddick (Ed.), *Handbook of research on strategies for local e-government adoption and implementation: Comparative studies* (pp. 288–305). Hershey, PA: IGI Global. doi:10.4018/978-1-60566-282-4.ch015

Jiao, Y., Hurson, A. R., Potok, T. E., & Beckerman, B. G. (2009). Integrating mobile-based systems with healthcare databases. In J. Erickson (Ed.), *Database technologies: Concepts, methodologies, tools, and applications* (pp. 484–504). Hershey, PA: IGI Global. doi:10.4018/978-1-60566-058-5.ch031

Joia, L. A. (2002). A systematic model to integrate information technology into metabusinesses: A case study in the engineering realms. In F. Tan (Ed.), *Advanced topics in global information management* (Vol. 1, pp. 250–267). Hershey, PA: IGI Global. doi:10.4018/978-1-930708-43-3.ch016

Jones, T. H., & Song, I. (2000). Binary equivalents of ternary relationships in entity-relationship modeling: A logical decomposition approach. *Journal of Database Management, 11*(2), 12–19. doi:10.4018/jdm.2000040102

Juana-Espinosa, S. D. (2007). Empirical study of the municipalitites' motivations for adopting online presence. In L. Al-Hakim (Ed.), *Global e-government: Theory, applications and benchmarking* (pp. 261–279). Hershey, PA: IGI Global. doi:10.4018/978-1-59904-027-1.ch015

Jun, K., & Weare, C. (2012). Bridging from e-government practice to e-government research: Past trends and future directions. In K. Bwalya & S. Zulu (Eds.), *Handbook of research on e-government in emerging economies: Adoption, e-participation, and legal frameworks* (pp. 263–289). Hershey, PA: IGI Global. doi:10.4018/978-1-4666-0324-0.ch013

Junqueira, A., Diniz, E. H., & Fernandez, M. (2010). Electronic government implementation projects with multiple agencies: Analysis of the electronic invoice project under PMBOK framework. In J. Cordoba-Pachon & A. Ochoa-Arias (Eds.), *Systems thinking and e-participation: ICT in the governance of society* (pp. 135–153). Hershey, PA: IGI Global. doi:10.4018/978-1-60566-860-4.ch009

Juntunen, A. (2009). Joint service development with the local authorities. In C. Reddick (Ed.), *Handbook of research on strategies for local e-government adoption and implementation: Comparative studies* (pp. 902–920). Hershey, PA: IGI Global. doi:10.4018/978-1-60566-282-4.ch047

Kamel, S. (2001). *Using DSS for crisis management.* Hershey, PA: IGI Global. doi:10.4018/978-1-87828-961-2.ch020

Kamel, S. (2006). DSS for strategic decision making. In M. Khosrow-Pour (Ed.), *Cases on information technology and organizational politics & culture* (pp. 230–246). Hershey, PA: IGI Global. doi:10.4018/978-1-59904-411-8.ch015

Kamel, S. (2009). The software industry in Egypt as a potential contributor to economic growth. In M. Khosrow-Pour (Ed.), *Encyclopedia of information science and technology* (2nd ed.; pp. 3531–3537). Hershey, PA: IGI Global. doi:10.4018/978-1-60566-026-4.ch562

Kamel, S., & Hussein, M. (2008). Xceed: Pioneering the contact center industry in Egypt. *Journal of Cases on Information Technology, 10*(1), 67–91. doi:10.4018/jcit.2008010105

Kamel, S., & Wahba, K. (2003). The use of a hybrid model in web-based education: "The Global campus project. In A. Aggarwal (Ed.), *Web-based education: Learning from experience* (pp. 331–346). Hershey, PA: IGI Global. doi:10.4018/978-1-59140-102-5.ch020

Kardaras, D. K., & Papathanassiou, E. A. (2008). An exploratory study of the e-government services in Greece. In G. Garson & M. Khosrow-Pour (Eds.), *Handbook of research on public information technology* (pp. 162–174). Hershey, PA: IGI Global. doi:10.4018/978-1-59904-857-4.ch016

Kassahun, A. E., Molla, A., & Sarkar, P. (2012). Government process reengineering: What we know and what we need to know. In *Digital democracy: Concepts, methodologies, tools, and applications* (pp. 1730–1752). Hershey, PA: IGI Global. doi:10.4018/978-1-4666-1740-7.ch086

Khan, B. (2005). Technological issues. In B. Khan (Ed.), *Managing e-learning strategies: Design, delivery, implementation and evaluation* (pp. 154–180). Hershey, PA: IGI Global. doi:10.4018/978-1-59140-634-1.ch004

Khasawneh, A., Bsoul, M., Obeidat, I., & Al Azzam, I. (2012). Technology fears: A study of e-commerce loyalty perception by Jordanian customers. In J. Wang (Ed.), *Advancing the service sector with evolving technologies: Techniques and principles* (pp. 158–165). Hershey, PA: IGI Global. doi:10.4018/978-1-4666-0044-7.ch010

Khatibi, V., & Montazer, G. A. (2012). E-research methodology. In A. Juan, T. Daradoumis, M. Roca, S. Grasman, & J. Faulin (Eds.), *Collaborative and distributed e-research: Innovations in technologies, strategies and applications* (pp. 62–81). Hershey, PA: IGI Global. doi:10.4018/978-1-4666-0125-3.ch003

Kidd, T. (2011). The dragon in the school's backyard: A review of literature on the uses of technology in urban schools. In L. Tomei (Ed.), *Online courses and ICT in education: Emerging practices and applications* (pp. 242–257). Hershey, PA: IGI Global. doi:10.4018/978-1-60960-150-8.ch019

Kidd, T. T. (2010). My experience tells the story: Exploring technology adoption from a qualitative perspective - A pilot study. In H. Song & T. Kidd (Eds.), *Handbook of research on human performance and instructional technology* (pp. 247–262). Hershey, PA: IGI Global. doi:10.4018/978-1-60566-782-9.ch015

Kieley, B., Lane, G., Paquet, G., & Roy, J. (2002). e-Government in Canada: Services online or public service renewal? In Å. Grönlund (Ed.), Electronic government: Design, applications and management (pp. 340-355). Hershey, PA: IGI Global. doi:10.4018/978-1-930708-19-8.ch016

Kim, P. (2012). "Stay out of the way! My kid is video blogging through a phone!": A lesson learned from math tutoring social media for children in underserved communities. In *Wireless technologies: Concepts, methodologies, tools and applications* (pp. 1415–1428). Hershey, PA: IGI Global. doi:10.4018/978-1-61350-101-6.ch517

Kirlidog, M. (2010). Financial aspects of national ICT strategies. In S. Kamel (Ed.), *E-strategies for technological diffusion and adoption: National ICT approaches for socioeconomic development* (pp. 277–292). Hershey, PA: IGI Global. doi:10.4018/978-1-60566-388-3.ch016

Kisielnicki, J. (2006). Transfer of information and knowledge in the project management. In E. Coakes & S. Clarke (Eds.), *Encyclopedia of communities of practice in information and knowledge management* (pp. 544–551). Hershey, PA: IGI Global. doi:10.4018/978-1-59140-556-6.ch091

Kittner, M., & Van Slyke, C. (2006). Reorganizing information technology services in an academic environment. In M. Khosrow-Pour (Ed.), *Cases on the human side of information technology* (pp. 49–66). Hershey, PA: IGI Global. doi:10.4018/978-1-59904-405-7.ch004

Knoell, H. D. (2008). Semi virtual workplaces in German financial service enterprises. In P. Zemliansky & K. St.Amant (Eds.), *Handbook of research on virtual workplaces and the new nature of business practices* (pp. 570–581). Hershey, PA: IGI Global. doi:10.4018/978-1-59904-893-2.ch041

Koh, S. L., & Maguire, S. (2009). Competing in the age of information technology in a developing economy: Experiences of an Indian bank. In S. Koh & S. Maguire (Eds.), *Information and communication technologies management in turbulent business environments* (pp. 326–350). Hershey, PA: IGI Global. doi:10.4018/978-1-60566-424-8.ch018

Kollmann, T., & Häsel, M. (2009). Competence of information technology professionals in internet-based ventures. In I. Lee (Ed.), *Electronic business: Concepts, methodologies, tools, and applications* (pp. 1905–1919). Hershey, PA: IGI Global. doi:10.4018/978-1-60566-056-1.ch118

Kollmann, T., & Häsel, M. (2009). Competence of information technology professionals in internet-based ventures. In A. Cater-Steel (Ed.), *Information technology governance and service management: Frameworks and adaptations* (pp. 239–253). Hershey, PA: IGI Global. doi:10.4018/978-1-60566-008-0.ch013

Kollmann, T., & Häsel, M. (2010). Competence of information technology professionals in internet-based ventures. In *Electronic services: Concepts, methodologies, tools and applications* (pp. 1551–1565). Hershey, PA: IGI Global. doi:10.4018/978-1-61520-967-5.ch094

Kraemer, K., & King, J. L. (2006). Information technology and administrative reform: Will e-government be different? *International Journal of Electronic Government Research, 2*(1), 1–20. doi:10.4018/jegr.2006010101

Kraemer, K., & King, J. L. (2008). Information technology and administrative reform: Will e-government be different? In D. Norris (Ed.), *E-government research: Policy and management* (pp. 1–20). Hershey, PA: IGI Global. doi:10.4018/978-1-59904-913-7.ch001

Lampathaki, F., Tsiakaliaris, C., Stasis, A., & Charalabidis, Y. (2011). National interoperability frameworks: The way forward. In Y. Charalabidis (Ed.), *Interoperability in digital public services and administration: Bridging e-government and e-business* (pp. 1–24). Hershey, PA: IGI Global. doi:10.4018/978-1-61520-887-6.ch001

Lan, Z., & Scott, C. R. (1996). The relative importance of computer-mediated information versus conventional non-computer-mediated information in public managerial decision making. *Information Resources Management Journal*, *9*(1), 27–0. doi:10.4018/irmj.1996010103

Law, W. (2004). *Public sector data management in a developing economy*. Hershey, PA: IGI Global. doi:10.4018/978-1-59140-259-6.ch034

Law, W. K. (2005). Information resources development challenges in a cross-cultural environment. In M. Khosrow-Pour (Ed.), *Encyclopedia of information science and technology* (pp. 1476–1481). Hershey, PA: IGI Global. doi:10.4018/978-1-59140-553-5.ch259

Law, W. K. (2009). Cross-cultural challenges for information resources management. In M. Khosrow-Pour (Ed.), *Encyclopedia of information science and technology* (2nd ed.; pp. 840–846). Hershey, PA: IGI Global. doi:10.4018/978-1-60566-026-4.ch136

Law, W. K. (2011). Cross-cultural challenges for information resources management. In *Global business: Concepts, methodologies, tools and applications* (pp. 1924–1932). Hershey, PA: IGI Global. doi:10.4018/978-1-60960-587-2.ch704

Malkia, M., & Savolainen, R. (2004). eTransformation in government, politics and society: Conceptual framework and introduction. In M. Malkia, A. Anttiroiko, & R. Savolainen (Eds.), eTransformation in governance: New directions in government and politics (pp. 1-21). Hershey, PA: IGI Global. doi:10.4018/978-1-59140-130-8.ch001

Mandujano, S. (2011). Network manageability security. In D. Kar & M. Syed (Eds.), *Network security, administration and management: Advancing technology and practice* (pp. 158–181). Hershey, PA: IGI Global. doi:10.4018/978-1-60960-777-7.ch009

Marich, M. J., Schooley, B. L., & Horan, T. A. (2012). A normative enterprise architecture for guiding end-to-end emergency response decision support. In M. Jennex (Ed.), *Managing crises and disasters with emerging technologies: Advancements* (pp. 71–87). Hershey, PA: IGI Global. doi:10.4018/978-1-4666-0167-3.ch006

Markov, R., & Okujava, S. (2008). Costs, benefits, and risks of e-government portals. In G. Putnik & M. Cruz-Cunha (Eds.), *Encyclopedia of networked and virtual organizations* (pp. 354–363). Hershey, PA: IGI Global. doi:10.4018/978-1-59904-885-7.ch047

Martin, N., & Rice, J. (2013). Evaluating and designing electronic government for the future: Observations and insights from Australia. In V. Weerakkody (Ed.), *E-government services design, adoption, and evaluation* (pp. 238–258). Hershey, PA: IGI Global. doi:10.4018/978-1-4666-2458-0.ch014

i. Martinez, A. C. (2008). Accessing administration's information via internet in Spain. In F. Tan (Ed.), *Global information technologies: Concepts, methodologies, tools, and applications* (pp. 2558–2573). Hershey, PA: IGI Global. doi:10.4018/978-1-59904-939-7.ch186

Mbarika, V. W., Meso, P. N., & Musa, P. F. (2006). A disconnect in stakeholders' perceptions from emerging realities of teledensity growth in Africa's least developed countries. In M. Hunter & F. Tan (Eds.), *Advanced topics in global information management* (Vol. 5, pp. 263–282). Hershey, PA: IGI Global. doi:10.4018/978-1-59140-923-6.ch012

Mbarika, V. W., Meso, P. N., & Musa, P. F. (2008). A disconnect in stakeholders' perceptions from emerging realities of teledensity growth in Africa's least developed countries. In F. Tan (Ed.), *Global information technologies: Concepts, methodologies, tools, and applications* (pp. 2948–2962). Hershey, PA: IGI Global. doi:10.4018/978-1-59904-939-7.ch209

Means, T., Olson, E., & Spooner, J. (2013). Discovering ways that don't work on the road to success: Strengths and weaknesses revealed by an active learning studio classroom project. In A. Benson, J. Moore, & S. Williams van Rooij (Eds.), *Cases on educational technology planning, design, and implementation: A project management perspective* (pp. 94–113). Hershey, PA: IGI Global. doi:10.4018/978-1-4666-4237-9.ch006

Melitski, J., Holzer, M., Kim, S., Kim, C., & Rho, S. (2008). Digital government worldwide: An e-government assessment of municipal web sites. In G. Garson & M. Khosrow-Pour (Eds.), *Handbook of research on public information technology* (pp. 790–804). Hershey, PA: IGI Global. doi:10.4018/978-1-59904-857-4.ch069

Memmola, M., Palumbo, G., & Rossini, M. (2009). Web & RFID technology: New frontiers in costing and process management for rehabilitation medicine. In L. Al-Hakim & M. Memmola (Eds.), *Business web strategy: Design, alignment, and application* (pp. 145–169). Hershey, PA: IGI Global. doi:10.4018/978-1-60566-024-0.ch008

Meng, Z., Fahong, Z., & Lei, L. (2008). Information technology and environment. In Y. Kurihara, S. Takaya, H. Harui, & H. Kamae (Eds.), *Information technology and economic development* (pp. 201–212). Hershey, PA: IGI Global. doi:10.4018/978-1-59904-579-5.ch014

Mentzingen de Moraes, A. J., Ferneda, E., Costa, I., & Spinola, M. D. (2011). Practical approach for implementation of governance process in IT: Information technology areas. In N. Shi & G. Silvius (Eds.), *Enterprise IT governance, business value and performance measurement* (pp. 19–40). Hershey, PA: IGI Global. doi:10.4018/978-1-60566-346-3.ch002

Merwin, G. A. Jr, McDonald, J. S., & Odera, L. C. (2008). Economic development: Government's cutting edge in IT. In M. Raisinghani (Ed.), *Handbook of research on global information technology management in the digital economy* (pp. 1–37). Hershey, PA: IGI Global. doi:10.4018/978-1-59904-875-8.ch001

Meso, P., & Duncan, N. (2002). Can national information infrastructures enhance social development in the least developed countries? An empirical investigation. In M. Dadashzadeh (Ed.), *Information technology management in developing countries* (pp. 23–51). Hershey, PA: IGI Global. doi:10.4018/978-1-931777-03-2.ch002

Meso, P. N., & Duncan, N. B. (2002). Can national information infrastructures enhance social development in the least developed countries? In F. Tan (Ed.), *Advanced topics in global information management* (Vol. 1, pp. 207–226). Hershey, PA: IGI Global. doi:10.4018/978-1-930708-43-3.ch014

Middleton, M. (2008). Evaluation of e-government web sites. In G. Garson & M. Khosrow-Pour (Eds.), *Handbook of research on public information technology* (pp. 699–710). Hershey, PA: IGI Global. doi:10.4018/978-1-59904-857-4.ch063

Mingers, J. (2010). Pluralism, realism, and truth: The keys to knowledge in information systems research. In D. Paradice (Ed.), *Emerging systems approaches in information technologies: Concepts, theories, and applications* (pp. 86–98). Hershey, PA: IGI Global. doi:10.4018/978-1-60566-976-2.ch006

Mital, K. M. (2012). ICT, unique identity and inclusive growth: An Indian perspective. In A. Manoharan & M. Holzer (Eds.), *E-governance and civic engagement: Factors and determinants of e-democracy* (pp. 584–612). Hershey, PA: IGI Global. doi:10.4018/978-1-61350-083-5.ch029

Mizell, A. P. (2008). Helping close the digital divide for financially disadvantaged seniors. In F. Tan (Ed.), *Global information technologies: Concepts, methodologies, tools, and applications* (pp. 2396–2402). Hershey, PA: IGI Global. doi:10.4018/978-1-59904-939-7.ch173

Molinari, F., Wills, C., Koumpis, A., & Moumtzi, V. (2011). A citizen-centric platform to support networking in the area of e-democracy. In H. Rahman (Ed.), *Cases on adoption, diffusion and evaluation of global e-governance systems: Impact at the grass roots* (pp. 282–302). Hershey, PA: IGI Global. doi:10.4018/978-1-61692-814-8.ch014

Molinari, F., Wills, C., Koumpis, A., & Moumtzi, V. (2013). A citizen-centric platform to support networking in the area of e-democracy. In H. Rahman (Ed.), *Cases on progressions and challenges in ICT utilization for citizen-centric governance* (pp. 265–297). Hershey, PA: IGI Global. doi:10.4018/978-1-4666-2071-1.ch013

Monteverde, F. (2010). The process of e-government public policy inclusion in the governmental agenda: A framework for assessment and case study. In J. Cordoba-Pachon & A. Ochoa-Arias (Eds.), *Systems thinking and e-participation: ICT in the governance of society* (pp. 233–245). Hershey, PA: IGI Global. doi:10.4018/978-1-60566-860-4.ch015

Moodley, S. (2008). Deconstructing the South African government's ICT for development discourse. In A. Anttiroiko (Ed.), *Electronic government: Concepts, methodologies, tools, and applications* (pp. 622–631). Hershey, PA: IGI Global. doi:10.4018/978-1-59904-947-2.ch053

Moodley, S. (2008). Deconstructing the South African government's ICT for development discourse. In C. Van Slyke (Ed.), *Information communication technologies: Concepts, methodologies, tools, and applications* (pp. 816–825). Hershey, PA: IGI Global. doi:10.4018/978-1-59904-949-6.ch052

Mora, M., Cervantes-Perez, F., Gelman-Muravchik, O., Forgionne, G. A., & Mejia-Olvera, M. (2003). DMSS implementation research: A conceptual analysis of the contributions and limitations of the factor-based and stage-based streams. In G. Forgionne, J. Gupta, & M. Mora (Eds.), *Decision-making support systems: Achievements and challenges for the new decade* (pp. 331–356). Hershey, PA: IGI Global. doi:10.4018/978-1-59140-045-5.ch020

Mörtberg, C., & Elovaara, P. (2010). Attaching people and technology: Between e and government. In S. Booth, S. Goodman, & G. Kirkup (Eds.), *Gender issues in learning and working with information technology: Social constructs and cultural contexts* (pp. 83–98). Hershey, PA: IGI Global. doi:10.4018/978-1-61520-813-5.ch005

Murphy, J., Harper, E., Devine, E. C., Burke, L. J., & Hook, M. L. (2011). Case study: Lessons learned when embedding evidence-based knowledge in a nurse care planning and documentation system. In A. Cashin & R. Cook (Eds.), *Evidence-based practice in nursing informatics: Concepts and applications* (pp. 174–190). Hershey, PA: IGI Global. doi:10.4018/978-1-60960-034-1.ch014

Mutula, S. M. (2013). E-government's role in poverty alleviation: Case study of South Africa. In H. Rahman (Ed.), *Cases on progressions and challenges in ICT utilization for citizen-centric governance* (pp. 44–68). Hershey, PA: IGI Global. doi:10.4018/978-1-4666-2071-1.ch003

Nath, R., & Angeles, R. (2005). Relationships between supply characteristics and buyer-supplier coupling in e-procurement: An empirical analysis. *International Journal of E-Business Research, 1*(2), 40–55. doi:10.4018/jebr.2005040103

Nissen, M. E. (2006). Application cases in government. In M. Nissen (Ed.), *Harnessing knowledge dynamics: Principled organizational knowing & learning* (pp. 152–181). Hershey, PA: IGI Global. doi:10.4018/978-1-59140-773-7.ch008

Norris, D. F. (2003). Leading-edge information technologies and American local governments. In G. Garson (Ed.), *Public information technology: Policy and management issues* (pp. 139–169). Hershey, PA: IGI Global. doi:10.4018/978-1-59140-060-8.ch007

Norris, D. F. (2008). Information technology among U.S. local governments. In G. Garson & M. Khosrow-Pour (Eds.), *Handbook of research on public information technology* (pp. 132–144). Hershey, PA: IGI Global. doi:10.4018/978-1-59904-857-4.ch013

Northrop, A. (1999). The challenge of teaching information technology in public administration graduate programs. In G. Garson (Ed.), *Information technology and computer applications in public administration: Issues and trends* (pp. 1–22). Hershey, PA: IGI Global. doi:10.4018/978-1-87828-952-0.ch001

Northrop, A. (2003). Information technology and public administration: The view from the profession. In G. Garson (Ed.), *Public information technology: Policy and management issues* (pp. 1–19). Hershey, PA: IGI Global. doi:10.4018/978-1-59140-060-8.ch001

Northrop, A. (2007). Lip service? How PA journals and textbooks view information technology. In G. Garson (Ed.), *Modern public information technology systems: Issues and challenges* (pp. 1–16). Hershey, PA: IGI Global. doi:10.4018/978-1-59904-051-6.ch001

Null, E. (2013). Legal and political barriers to municipal networks in the United States. In A. Abdelaal (Ed.), *Social and economic effects of community wireless networks and infrastructures* (pp. 27–56). Hershey, PA: IGI Global. doi:10.4018/978-1-4666-2997-4.ch003

Okunoye, A., Frolick, M., & Crable, E. (2006). ERP implementation in higher education: An account of pre-implementation and implementation phases. *Journal of Cases on Information Technology*, *8*(2), 110–132. doi:10.4018/jcit.2006040106

Olasina, G. (2012). A review of egovernment services in Nigeria. In A. Tella & A. Issa (Eds.), *Library and information science in developing countries: Contemporary issues* (pp. 205–221). Hershey, PA: IGI Global. doi:10.4018/978-1-61350-335-5.ch015

Orgeron, C. P. (2008). A model for reengineering IT job classes in state government. In G. Garson & M. Khosrow-Pour (Eds.), *Handbook of research on public information technology* (pp. 735–746). Hershey, PA: IGI Global. doi:10.4018/978-1-59904-857-4.ch066

Owsinski, J. W., & Pielak, A. M. (2011). Local authority websites in rural areas: Measuring quality and functionality, and assessing the role. In Z. Andreopoulou, B. Manos, N. Polman, & D. Viaggi (Eds.), *Agricultural and environmental informatics, governance and management: Emerging research applications* (pp. 39–60). Hershey, PA: IGI Global. doi:10.4018/978-1-60960-621-3.ch003

Owsiński, J. W., Pielak, A. M., Sęp, K., & Stańczak, J. (2014). Local web-based networks in rural municipalities: Extension, density, and meaning. In Z. Andreopoulou, V. Samathrakis, S. Louca, & M. Vlachopoulou (Eds.), *E-innovation for sustainable development of rural resources during global economic crisis* (pp. 126–151). Hershey, PA: IGI Global. doi:10.4018/978-1-4666-4550-9.ch011

Pagani, M., & Pasinetti, C. (2008). Technical and functional quality in the development of t-government services. In A. Anttiroiko (Ed.), *Electronic government: Concepts, methodologies, tools, and applications* (pp. 2943–2965). Hershey, PA: IGI Global. doi:10.4018/978-1-59904-947-2.ch220

Pani, A. K., & Agrahari, A. (2005). On e-markets in emerging economy: An Indian experience. In M. Khosrow-Pour (Ed.), *Advanced topics in electronic commerce* (Vol. 1, pp. 287–299). Hershey, PA: IGI Global. doi:10.4018/978-1-59140-819-2.ch015

Papadopoulos, T., Angelopoulos, S., & Kitsios, F. (2011). A strategic approach to e-health interoperability using e-government frameworks. In A. Lazakidou, K. Siassiakos, & K. Ioannou (Eds.), *Wireless technologies for ambient assisted living and healthcare: Systems and applications* (pp. 213–229). Hershey, PA: IGI Global. doi:10.4018/978-1-61520-805-0.ch012

Papadopoulos, T., Angelopoulos, S., & Kitsios, F. (2013). A strategic approach to e-health interoperability using e-government frameworks. In *User-driven healthcare: Concepts, methodologies, tools, and applications* (pp. 791–807). Hershey, PA: IGI Global. doi:10.4018/978-1-4666-2770-3.ch039

Papaleo, G., Chiarella, D., Aiello, M., & Caviglione, L. (2012). Analysis, development and deployment of statistical anomaly detection techniques for real e-mail traffic. In T. Chou (Ed.), *Information assurance and security technologies for risk assessment and threat management: Advances* (pp. 47–71). Hershey, PA: IGI Global. doi:10.4018/978-1-61350-507-6.ch003

Papp, R. (2003). Information technology & FDA compliance in the pharmaceutical industry. In M. Khosrow-Pour (Ed.), *Annals of cases on information technology* (Vol. 5, pp. 262–273). Hershey, PA: IGI Global. doi:10.4018/978-1-59140-061-5.ch017

Parsons, T. W. (2007). Developing a knowledge management portal. In A. Tatnall (Ed.), *Encyclopedia of portal technologies and applications* (pp. 223–227). Hershey, PA: IGI Global. doi:10.4018/978-1-59140-989-2.ch039

Passaris, C. E. (2007). Immigration and digital government. In A. Anttiroiko & M. Malkia (Eds.), *Encyclopedia of digital government* (pp. 988–994). Hershey, PA: IGI Global. doi:10.4018/978-1-59140-789-8.ch148

Pavlichev, A. (2004). The e-government challenge for public administration. In A. Pavlichev & G. Garson (Eds.), *Digital government: Principles and best practices* (pp. 276–290). Hershey, PA: IGI Global. doi:10.4018/978-1-59140-122-3.ch018

Penrod, J. I., & Harbor, A. F. (2000). Designing and implementing a learning organization-oriented information technology planning and management process. In L. Petrides (Ed.), *Case studies on information technology in higher education: Implications for policy and practice* (pp. 7–19). Hershey, PA: IGI Global. doi:10.4018/978-1-878289-74-2.ch001

Planas-Silva, M. D., & Joseph, R. C. (2011). Perspectives on the adoption of electronic resources for use in clinical trials. In M. Guah (Ed.), *Healthcare delivery reform and new technologies: Organizational initiatives* (pp. 19–28). Hershey, PA: IGI Global. doi:10.4018/978-1-60960-183-6.ch002

Pomazalová, N., & Rejman, S. (2013). The rationale behind implementation of new electronic tools for electronic public procurement. In N. Pomazalová (Ed.), *Public sector transformation processes and internet public procurement: Decision support systems* (pp. 85–117). Hershey, PA: IGI Global. doi:10.4018/978-1-4666-2665-2.ch006

Postorino, M. N. (2012). City competitiveness and airport: Information science perspective. In M. Bulu (Ed.), *City competitiveness and improving urban subsystems: Technologies and applications* (pp. 61–83). Hershey, PA: IGI Global. doi:10.4018/978-1-61350-174-0.ch004

Poupa, C. (2002). Electronic government in Switzerland: Priorities for 2001-2005 - Electronic voting and federal portal. In Å. Grönlund (Ed.), *Electronic government: Design, applications and management* (pp. 356–369). Hershey, PA: IGI Global. doi:10.4018/978-1-930708-19-8.ch017

Powell, S. R. (2010). Interdisciplinarity in telecommunications and networking. In *Networking and telecommunications: Concepts, methodologies, tools and applications* (pp. 33–40). Hershey, PA: IGI Global. doi:10.4018/978-1-60566-986-1.ch004

Priya, P. S., & Mathiyalagan, N. (2011). A study of the implementation status of two e-governance projects in land revenue administration in India. In M. Shareef, V. Kumar, U. Kumar, & Y. Dwivedi (Eds.), *Stakeholder adoption of e-government services: Driving and resisting factors* (pp. 214–230). Hershey, PA: IGI Global. doi:10.4018/978-1-60960-601-5.ch011

Prysby, C., & Prysby, N. (2000). Electronic mail, employee privacy and the workplace. In L. Janczewski (Ed.), *Internet and intranet security management: Risks and solutions* (pp. 251–270). Hershey, PA: IGI Global. doi:10.4018/978-1-878289-71-1.ch009

Prysby, C. L., & Prysby, N. D. (2003). Electronic mail in the public workplace: Issues of privacy and public disclosure. In G. Garson (Ed.), *Public information technology: Policy and management issues* (pp. 271–298). Hershey, PA: IGI Global. doi:10.4018/978-1-59140-060-8.ch012

Prysby, C. L., & Prysby, N. D. (2007). You have mail, but who is reading it? Issues of e-mail in the public workplace. In G. Garson (Ed.), *Modern public information technology systems: Issues and challenges* (pp. 312–336). Hershey, PA: IGI Global. doi:10.4018/978-1-59904-051-6.ch016

Radl, A., & Chen, Y. (2005). Computer security in electronic government: A state-local education information system. *International Journal of Electronic Government Research, 1*(1), 79–99. doi:10.4018/jegr.2005010105

Rahman, H. (2008). Information dynamics in developing countries. In C. Van Slyke (Ed.), *Information communication technologies: Concepts, methodologies, tools, and applications* (pp. 104–114). Hershey, PA: IGI Global. doi:10.4018/978-1-59904-949-6.ch008

Ramanathan, J. (2009). Adaptive IT architecture as a catalyst for network capability in government. In P. Saha (Ed.), *Advances in government enterprise architecture* (pp. 149–172). Hershey, PA: IGI Global. doi:10.4018/978-1-60566-068-4.ch007

Ramos, I., & Berry, D. M. (2006). Social construction of information technology supporting work. In M. Khosrow-Pour (Ed.), *Cases on information technology: Lessons learned* (Vol. 7, pp. 36–52). Hershey, PA: IGI Global. doi:10.4018/978-1-59140-673-0.ch003

Ray, D., Gulla, U., Gupta, M. P., & Dash, S. S. (2009). Interoperability and constituents of interoperable systems in public sector. In V. Weerakkody, M. Janssen, & Y. Dwivedi (Eds.), *Handbook of research on ICT-enabled transformational government: A global perspective* (pp. 175–195). Hershey, PA: IGI Global. doi:10.4018/978-1-60566-390-6.ch010

Reddick, C. G. (2007). E-government and creating a citizen-centric government: A study of federal government CIOs. In G. Garson (Ed.), *Modern public information technology systems: Issues and challenges* (pp. 143–165). Hershey, PA: IGI Global. doi:10.4018/978-1-59904-051-6.ch008

Reddick, C. G. (2010). Citizen-centric e-government. In C. Reddick (Ed.), *Homeland security preparedness and information systems: Strategies for managing public policy* (pp. 45–75). Hershey, PA: IGI Global. doi:10.4018/978-1-60566-834-5.ch002

Reddick, C. G. (2010). E-government and creating a citizen-centric government: A study of federal government CIOs. In C. Reddick (Ed.), *Homeland security preparedness and information systems: Strategies for managing public policy* (pp. 230–250). Hershey, PA: IGI Global. doi:10.4018/978-1-60566-834-5.ch012

Reddick, C. G. (2010). Perceived effectiveness of e-government and its usage in city governments: Survey evidence from information technology directors. In C. Reddick (Ed.), *Homeland security preparedness and information systems: Strategies for managing public policy* (pp. 213–229). Hershey, PA: IGI Global. doi:10.4018/978-1-60566-834-5.ch011

Reddick, C. G. (2012). Customer relationship management adoption in local governments in the United States. In S. Chhabra & M. Kumar (Eds.), *Strategic enterprise resource planning models for e-government: Applications and methodologies* (pp. 111–124). Hershey, PA: IGI Global. doi:10.4018/978-1-60960-863-7.ch008

Reeder, F. S., & Pandy, S. M. (2008). Identifying effective funding models for e-government. In A. Anttiroiko (Ed.), *Electronic government: Concepts, methodologies, tools, and applications* (pp. 1108–1138). Hershey, PA: IGI Global. doi:10.4018/978-1-59904-947-2.ch083

Riesco, D., Acosta, E., & Montejano, G. (2003). An extension to a UML activity graph from workflow. In L. Favre (Ed.), *UML and the unified process* (pp. 294–314). Hershey, PA: IGI Global. doi:10.4018/978-1-93177-744-5.ch015

Ritzhaupt, A. D., & Gill, T. G. (2008). A hybrid and novel approach to teaching computer programming in MIS curriculum. In S. Negash, M. Whitman, A. Woszczynski, K. Hoganson, & H. Mattord (Eds.), *Handbook of distance learning for real-time and asynchronous information technology education* (pp. 259–281). Hershey, PA: IGI Global. doi:10.4018/978-1-59904-964-9.ch014

Roche, E. M. (1993). International computing and the international regime. *Journal of Global Information Management, 1*(2), 33–44. doi:10.4018/jgim.1993040103

Rocheleau, B. (2007). Politics, accountability, and information management. In G. Garson (Ed.), *Modern public information technology systems: Issues and challenges* (pp. 35–71). Hershey, PA: IGI Global. doi:10.4018/978-1-59904-051-6.ch003

Rodrigues Filho, J. (2010). E-government in Brazil: Reinforcing dominant institutions or reducing citizenship? In C. Reddick (Ed.), *Politics, democracy and e-government: Participation and service delivery* (pp. 347–362). Hershey, PA: IGI Global. doi:10.4018/978-1-61520-933-0.ch021

Rodriguez, S. R., & Thorp, D. A. (2013). eLearning for industry: A case study of the project management process. In A. Benson, J. Moore, & S. Williams van Rooij (Eds.), Cases on educational technology planning, design, and implementation: A project management perspective (pp. 319-342). Hershey, PA: IGI Global. doi:10.4018/978-1-4666-4237-9.ch017

Roman, A. V. (2013). Delineating three dimensions of e-government success: Security, functionality, and transformation. In J. Gil-Garcia (Ed.), *E-government success factors and measures: Theories, concepts, and methodologies* (pp. 171–192). Hershey, PA: IGI Global. doi:10.4018/978-1-4666-4058-0.ch010

Ross, S. C., Tyran, C. K., & Auer, D. J. (2008). Up in smoke: Rebuilding after an IT disaster. In H. Nemati (Ed.), *Information security and ethics: Concepts, methodologies, tools, and applications* (pp. 3659–3675). Hershey, PA: IGI Global. doi:10.4018/978-1-59904-937-3.ch248

Ross, S. C., Tyran, C. K., Auer, D. J., Junell, J. M., & Williams, T. G. (2005). Up in smoke: Rebuilding after an IT disaster. *Journal of Cases on Information Technology*, *7*(2), 31–49. doi:10.4018/jcit.2005040103

Roy, J. (2008). Security, sovereignty, and continental interoperability: Canada's elusive balance. In T. Loendorf & G. Garson (Eds.), *Patriotic information systems* (pp. 153–176). Hershey, PA: IGI Global. doi:10.4018/978-1-59904-594-8.ch007

Rubeck, R. F., & Miller, G. A. (2009). vGOV: Remote video access to government services. In A. Scupola (Ed.), Cases on managing e-services (pp. 253-268). Hershey, PA: IGI Global. doi:10.4018/978-1-60566-064-6.ch017

Saekow, A., & Boonmee, C. (2011). The challenges of implementing e-government interoperability in Thailand: Case of official electronic correspondence letters exchange across government departments. In Y. Charalabidis (Ed.), *Interoperability in digital public services and administration: Bridging e-government and e-business* (pp. 40–61). Hershey, PA: IGI Global. doi:10.4018/978-1-61520-887-6.ch003

Saekow, A., & Boonmee, C. (2012). The challenges of implementing e-government interoperability in Thailand: Case of official electronic correspondence letters exchange across government departments. In *Digital democracy: Concepts, methodologies, tools, and applications* (pp. 1883–1905). Hershey, PA: IGI Global. doi:10.4018/978-1-4666-1740-7.ch094

Sagsan, M., & Medeni, T. (2012). Understanding "knowledge management (KM) paradigms" from social media perspective: An empirical study on discussion group for KM at professional networking site. In M. Cruz-Cunha, P. Gonçalves, N. Lopes, E. Miranda, & G. Putnik (Eds.), *Handbook of research on business social networking: Organizational, managerial, and technological dimensions* (pp. 738–755). Hershey, PA: IGI Global. doi:10.4018/978-1-61350-168-9.ch039

Sahi, G., & Madan, S. (2013). Information security threats in ERP enabled e-governance: Challenges and solutions. In *Enterprise resource planning: Concepts, methodologies, tools, and applications* (pp. 825–837). Hershey, PA: IGI Global. doi:10.4018/978-1-4666-4153-2.ch048

Sanford, C., & Bhattacherjee, A. (2008). IT implementation in a developing country municipality: A sociocognitive analysis. *International Journal of Technology and Human Interaction*, *4*(3), 68–93. doi:10.4018/jthi.2008070104

Schelin, S. H. (2003). E-government: An overview. In G. Garson (Ed.), *Public information technology: Policy and management issues* (pp. 120–138). Hershey, PA: IGI Global. doi:10.4018/978-1-59140-060-8.ch006

Schelin, S. H. (2004). Training for digital government. In A. Pavlichev & G. Garson (Eds.), *Digital government: Principles and best practices* (pp. 263–275). Hershey, PA: IGI Global. doi:10.4018/978-1-59140-122-3.ch017

Schelin, S. H. (2007). E-government: An overview. In G. Garson (Ed.), *Modern public information technology systems: Issues and challenges* (pp. 110–126). Hershey, PA: IGI Global. doi:10.4018/978-1-59904-051-6.ch006

Schelin, S. H., & Garson, G. (2004). Theoretical justification of critical success factors. In G. Garson & S. Schelin (Eds.), *IT solutions series: Humanizing information technology: Advice from experts* (pp. 4–15). Hershey, PA: IGI Global. doi:10.4018/978-1-59140-245-9.ch002

Scime, A. (2002). Information systems and computer science model curricula: A comparative look. In M. Dadashzadeh, A. Saber, & S. Saber (Eds.), *Information technology education in the new millennium* (pp. 146–158). Hershey, PA: IGI Global. doi:10.4018/978-1-931777-05-6.ch018

Scime, A. (2009). Computing curriculum analysis and development. In M. Khosrow-Pour (Ed.), *Encyclopedia of information science and technology* (2nd ed.; pp. 667–671). Hershey, PA: IGI Global. doi:10.4018/978-1-60566-026-4.ch108

Scime, A., & Wania, C. (2008). Computing curricula: A comparison of models. In C. Van Slyke (Ed.), *Information communication technologies: Concepts, methodologies, tools, and applications* (pp. 1270–1283). Hershey, PA: IGI Global. doi:10.4018/978-1-59904-949-6.ch088

Seidman, S. B. (2009). An international perspective on professional software engineering credentials. In H. Ellis, S. Demurjian, & J. Naveda (Eds.), *Software engineering: Effective teaching and learning approaches and practices* (pp. 351–361). Hershey, PA: IGI Global. doi:10.4018/978-1-60566-102-5.ch018

Seifert, J. W. (2007). E-government act of 2002 in the United States. In A. Anttiroiko & M. Malkia (Eds.), *Encyclopedia of digital government* (pp. 476–481). Hershey, PA: IGI Global. doi:10.4018/978-1-59140-789-8.ch072

Seifert, J. W., & Relyea, H. C. (2008). E-government act of 2002 in the United States. In A. Anttiroiko (Ed.), *Electronic government: Concepts, methodologies, tools, and applications* (pp. 154–161). Hershey, PA: IGI Global. doi:10.4018/978-1-59904-947-2.ch013

Seufert, S. (2002). E-learning business models: Framework and best practice examples. In M. Raisinghani (Ed.), *Cases on worldwide e-commerce: Theory in action* (pp. 70–94). Hershey, PA: IGI Global. doi:10.4018/978-1-930708-27-3.ch004

Shareef, M. A., & Archer, N. (2012). E-government service development. In M. Shareef, N. Archer, & S. Dutta (Eds.), *E-government service maturity and development: Cultural, organizational and technological perspectives* (pp. 1–14). Hershey, PA: IGI Global. doi:10.4018/978-1-60960-848-4.ch001

Shareef, M. A., & Archer, N. (2012). E-government initiatives: Review studies on different countries. In M. Shareef, N. Archer, & S. Dutta (Eds.), *E-government service maturity and development: Cultural, organizational and technological perspectives* (pp. 40–76). Hershey, PA: IGI Global. doi:10.4018/978-1-60960-848-4.ch003

Shareef, M. A., Kumar, U., & Kumar, V. (2011). E-government development: Performance evaluation parameters. In M. Shareef, V. Kumar, U. Kumar, & Y. Dwivedi (Eds.), *Stakeholder adoption of e-government services: Driving and resisting factors* (pp. 197–213). Hershey, PA: IGI Global. doi:10.4018/978-1-60960-601-5.ch010

Shareef, M. A., Kumar, U., Kumar, V., & Niktash, M. (2012). Electronic-government vision: Case studies for objectives, strategies, and initiatives. In M. Shareef, N. Archer, & S. Dutta (Eds.), *E-government service maturity and development: Cultural, organizational and technological perspectives* (pp. 15–39). Hershey, PA: IGI Global. doi:10.4018/978-1-60960-848-4.ch002

Shukla, P., Kumar, A., & Anu Kumar, P. B. (2013). Impact of national culture on business continuity management system implementation. *International Journal of Risk and Contingency Management*, *2*(3), 23–36. doi:10.4018/ijrcm.2013070102

Shulman, S. W. (2007). The federal docket management system and the prospect for digital democracy in U S rulemaking. In G. Garson (Ed.), *Modern public information technology systems: Issues and challenges* (pp. 166–184). Hershey, PA: IGI Global. doi:10.4018/978-1-59904-051-6.ch009

Simonovic, S. (2007). Problems of offline government in e-Serbia. In A. Anttiroiko & M. Malkia (Eds.), *Encyclopedia of digital government* (pp. 1342–1351). Hershey, PA: IGI Global. doi:10.4018/978-1-59140-789-8.ch205

Simonovic, S. (2008). Problems of offline government in e-Serbia. In A. Anttiroiko (Ed.), *Electronic government: Concepts, methodologies, tools, and applications* (pp. 2929–2942). Hershey, PA: IGI Global. doi:10.4018/978-1-59904-947-2.ch219

Singh, A. M. (2005). Information systems and technology in South Africa. In M. Khosrow-Pour (Ed.), *Encyclopedia of information science and technology* (pp. 1497–1502). Hershey, PA: IGI Global. doi:10.4018/978-1-59140-553-5.ch263

Singh, S., & Naidoo, G. (2005). Towards an e-government solution: A South African perspective. In W. Huang, K. Siau, & K. Wei (Eds.), *Electronic government strategies and implementation* (pp. 325–353). Hershey, PA: IGI Global. doi:10.4018/978-1-59140-348-7.ch014

Snoke, R., & Underwood, A. (2002). Generic attributes of IS graduates: An analysis of Australian views. In F. Tan (Ed.), *Advanced topics in global information management* (Vol. 1, pp. 370–384). Hershey, PA: IGI Global. doi:10.4018/978-1-930708-43-3.ch023

Sommer, L. (2006). Revealing unseen organizations in higher education: A study framework and application example. In A. Metcalfe (Ed.), *Knowledge management and higher education: A critical analysis* (pp. 115–146). Hershey, PA: IGI Global. doi:10.4018/978-1-59140-509-2.ch007

Song, H., Kidd, T., & Owens, E. (2011). Examining technological disparities and instructional practices in English language arts classroom: Implications for school leadership and teacher training. In L. Tomei (Ed.), *Online courses and ICT in education: Emerging practices and applications* (pp. 258–274). Hershey, PA: IGI Global. doi:10.4018/978-1-60960-150-8.ch020

Speaker, P. J., & Kleist, V. F. (2003). Using information technology to meet electronic commerce and MIS education demands. In A. Aggarwal (Ed.), *Web-based education: Learning from experience* (pp. 280–291). Hershey, PA: IGI Global. doi:10.4018/978-1-59140-102-5.ch017

Spitler, V. K. (2007). Learning to use IT in the workplace: Mechanisms and masters. In M. Mahmood (Ed.), *Contemporary issues in end user computing* (pp. 292–323). Hershey, PA: IGI Global. doi:10.4018/978-1-59140-926-7.ch013

Stellefson, M. (2011). Considerations for marketing distance education courses in health education: Five important questions to examine before development. In U. Demiray & S. Sever (Eds.), *Marketing online education programs: Frameworks for promotion and communication* (pp. 222–234). Hershey, PA: IGI Global. doi:10.4018/978-1-60960-074-7.ch014

Straub, D. W., & Loch, K. D. (2006). Creating and developing a program of global research. *Journal of Global Information Management, 14*(2), 1–28. doi:10.4018/jgim.2006040101

Straub, D. W., Loch, K. D., & Hill, C. E. (2002). Transfer of information technology to the Arab world: A test of cultural influence modeling. In M. Dadashzadeh (Ed.), *Information technology management in developing countries* (pp. 92–134). Hershey, PA: IGI Global. doi:10.4018/978-1-931777-03-2.ch005

Straub, D. W., Loch, K. D., & Hill, C. E. (2003). Transfer of information technology to the Arab world: A test of cultural influence modeling. In F. Tan (Ed.), *Advanced topics in global information management* (Vol. 2, pp. 141–172). Hershey, PA: IGI Global. doi:10.4018/978-1-59140-064-6.ch009

Suki, N. M., Ramayah, T., Ming, M. K., & Suki, N. M. (2013). Factors enhancing employed job seekers intentions to use social networking sites as a job search tool. In A. Mesquita (Ed.), *User perception and influencing factors of technology in everyday life* (pp. 265–281). Hershey, PA: IGI Global. doi:10.4018/978-1-4666-1954-8.ch018

Suomi, R. (2006). Introducing electronic patient records to hospitals: Innovation adoption paths. In T. Spil & R. Schuring (Eds.), *E-health systems diffusion and use: The innovation, the user and the use IT model* (pp. 128–146). Hershey, PA: IGI Global. doi:10.4018/978-1-59140-423-1.ch008

Swim, J., & Barker, L. (2012). Pathways into a gendered occupation: Brazilian women in IT. *International Journal of Social and Organizational Dynamics in IT, 2*(4), 34–51. doi:10.4018/ijsodit.2012100103

Tarafdar, M., & Vaidya, S. D. (2006). Adoption and implementation of IT in developing nations: Experiences from two public sector enterprises in India. In M. Khosrow-Pour (Ed.), *Cases on information technology planning, design and implementation* (pp. 208–233). Hershey, PA: IGI Global. doi:10.4018/978-1-59904-408-8.ch013

Tarafdar, M., & Vaidya, S. D. (2008). Adoption and implementation of IT in developing nations: Experiences from two public sector enterprises in India. In G. Garson & M. Khosrow-Pour (Eds.), *Handbook of research on public information technology* (pp. 905–924). Hershey, PA: IGI Global. doi:10.4018/978-1-59904-857-4.ch076

Thesing, Z. (2007). Zarina thesing, pumpkin patch. In M. Hunter (Ed.), *Contemporary chief information officers: Management experiences* (pp. 83–94). Hershey, PA: IGI Global. doi:10.4018/978-1-59904-078-3.ch007

Thomas, J. C. (2004). Public involvement in public administration in the information age: Speculations on the effects of technology. In M. Malkia, A. Anttiroiko, & R. Savolainen (Eds.), *eTransformation in governance: New directions in government and politics* (pp. 67–84). Hershey, PA: IGI Global. doi:10.4018/978-1-59140-130-8.ch004

Treiblmaier, H., & Chong, S. (2013). Trust and perceived risk of personal information as antecedents of online information disclosure: Results from three countries. In F. Tan (Ed.), *Global diffusion and adoption of technologies for knowledge and information sharing* (pp. 341–361). Hershey, PA: IGI Global. doi:10.4018/978-1-4666-2142-8.ch015

van Grembergen, W., & de Haes, S. (2008). IT governance in practice: Six case studies. In W. van Grembergen & S. De Haes (Eds.), *Implementing information technology governance: Models, practices and cases* (pp. 125–237). Hershey, PA: IGI Global. doi:10.4018/978-1-59904-924-3.ch004

van Os, G., Homburg, V., & Bekkers, V. (2013). Contingencies and convergence in European social security: ICT coordination in the back office of the welfare state. In M. Cruz-Cunha, I. Miranda, & P. Gonçalves (Eds.), *Handbook of research on ICTs and management systems for improving efficiency in healthcare and social care* (pp. 268–287). Hershey, PA: IGI Global. doi:10.4018/978-1-4666-3990-4.ch013

Velloso, A. B., Gassenferth, W., & Machado, M. A. (2012). Evaluating IBMEC-RJ's intranet usability using fuzzy logic. In M. Cruz-Cunha, P. Gonçalves, N. Lopes, E. Miranda, & G. Putnik (Eds.), *Handbook of research on business social networking: Organizational, managerial, and technological dimensions* (pp. 185–205). Hershey, PA: IGI Global. doi:10.4018/978-1-61350-168-9.ch010

Villablanca, A. C., Baxi, H., & Anderson, K. (2009). Novel data interface for evaluating cardiovascular outcomes in women. In A. Dwivedi (Ed.), *Handbook of research on information technology management and clinical data administration in healthcare* (pp. 34–53). Hershey, PA: IGI Global. doi:10.4018/978-1-60566-356-2.ch003

Villablanca, A. C., Baxi, H., & Anderson, K. (2011). Novel data interface for evaluating cardiovascular outcomes in women. In *Clinical technologies: Concepts, methodologies, tools and applications* (pp. 2094–2113). Hershey, PA: IGI Global. doi:10.4018/978-1-60960-561-2.ch806

Virkar, S. (2011). Information and communication technologies in administrative reform for development: Exploring the case of property tax systems in Karnataka, India. In J. Steyn, J. Van Belle, & E. Mansilla (Eds.), *ICTs for global development and sustainability: Practice and applications* (pp. 127–149). Hershey, PA: IGI Global. doi:10.4018/978-1-61520-997-2.ch006

Virkar, S. (2013). Designing and implementing e-government projects: Actors, influences, and fields of play. In S. Saeed & C. Reddick (Eds.), *Human-centered system design for electronic governance* (pp. 88–110). Hershey, PA: IGI Global. doi:10.4018/978-1-4666-3640-8.ch007

Wallace, A. (2009). E-justice: An Australian perspective. In A. Martínez & P. Abat (Eds.), *E-justice: Using information communication technologies in the court system* (pp. 204–228). Hershey, PA: IGI Global. doi:10.4018/978-1-59904-998-4.ch014

Wang, G. (2012). E-democratic administration and bureaucratic responsiveness: A primary study of bureaucrats' perceptions of the civil service e-mail box in Taiwan. In K. Kloby & M. D'Agostino (Eds.), *Citizen 2.0: Public and governmental interaction through web 2.0 technologies* (pp. 146–173). Hershey, PA: IGI Global. doi:10.4018/978-1-4666-0318-9.ch009

Wangpipatwong, S., Chutimaskul, W., & Papasratorn, B. (2011). Quality enhancing the continued use of e-government web sites: Evidence from e-citizens of Thailand. In V. Weerakkody (Ed.), *Applied technology integration in governmental organizations: New e-government research* (pp. 20–36). Hershey, PA: IGI Global. doi:10.4018/978-1-60960-162-1.ch002

Wedemeijer, L. (2006). Long-term evolution of a conceptual schema at a life insurance company. In M. Khosrow-Pour (Ed.), *Cases on database technologies and applications* (pp. 202–226). Hershey, PA: IGI Global. doi:10.4018/978-1-59904-399-9.ch012

Whybrow, E. (2008). Digital access, ICT fluency, and the economically disadvantages: Approaches to minimize the digital divide. In F. Tan (Ed.), *Global information technologies: Concepts, methodologies, tools, and applications* (pp. 1409–1422). Hershey, PA: IGI Global. doi:10.4018/978-1-59904-939-7.ch102

Whybrow, E. (2008). Digital access, ICT fluency, and the economically disadvantages: Approaches to minimize the digital divide. In C. Van Slyke (Ed.), *Information communication technologies: Concepts, methodologies, tools, and applications* (pp. 764–777). Hershey, PA: IGI Global. doi:10.4018/978-1-59904-949-6.ch049

Wickramasinghe, N., & Geisler, E. (2010). Key considerations for the adoption and implementation of knowledge management in healthcare operations. In M. Saito, N. Wickramasinghe, M. Fuji, & E. Geisler (Eds.), *Redesigning innovative healthcare operation and the role of knowledge management* (pp. 125–142). Hershey, PA: IGI Global. doi:10.4018/978-1-60566-284-8.ch009

Wickramasinghe, N., & Geisler, E. (2012). Key considerations for the adoption and implementation of knowledge management in healthcare operations. In *Organizational learning and knowledge: Concepts, methodologies, tools and applications* (pp. 1316–1328). Hershey, PA: IGI Global. doi:10.4018/978-1-60960-783-8.ch405

Wickramasinghe, N., & Goldberg, S. (2007). A framework for delivering m-health excellence. In L. Al-Hakim (Ed.), *Web mobile-based applications for healthcare management* (pp. 36–61). Hershey, PA: IGI Global. doi:10.4018/978-1-59140-658-7.ch002

Wickramasinghe, N., & Goldberg, S. (2008). Critical success factors for delivering m-health excellence. In N. Wickramasinghe & E. Geisler (Eds.), *Encyclopedia of healthcare information systems* (pp. 339–351). Hershey, PA: IGI Global. doi:10.4018/978-1-59904-889-5.ch045

Wyld, D. (2009). Radio frequency identification (RFID) technology. In J. Symonds, J. Ayoade, & D. Parry (Eds.), *Auto-identification and ubiquitous computing applications* (pp. 279–293). Hershey, PA: IGI Global. doi:10.4018/978-1-60566-298-5.ch017

Yaghmaei, F. (2010). Understanding computerised information systems usage in community health. In J. Rodrigues (Ed.), *Health information systems: Concepts, methodologies, tools, and applications* (pp. 1388–1399). Hershey, PA: IGI Global. doi:10.4018/978-1-60566-988-5.ch088

Yee, G., El-Khatib, K., Korba, L., Patrick, A. S., Song, R., & Xu, Y. (2005). Privacy and trust in e-government. In W. Huang, K. Siau, & K. Wei (Eds.), *Electronic government strategies and implementation* (pp. 145–190). Hershey, PA: IGI Global. doi:10.4018/978-1-59140-348-7.ch007

Yeh, S., & Chu, P. (2010). Evaluation of e-government services: A citizen-centric approach to citizen e-complaint services. In C. Reddick (Ed.), *Citizens and e-government: Evaluating policy and management* (pp. 400–417). Hershey, PA: IGI Global. doi:10.4018/978-1-61520-931-6.ch022

Young-Jin, S., & Seang-tae, K. (2008). E-government concepts, measures, and best practices. In A. Anttiroiko (Ed.), *Electronic government: Concepts, methodologies, tools, and applications* (pp. 32–57). Hershey, PA: IGI Global. doi:10.4018/978-1-59904-947-2.ch004

Yun, H. J., & Opheim, C. (2012). New technology communication in American state governments: The impact on citizen participation. In K. Bwalya & S. Zulu (Eds.), *Handbook of research on e-government in emerging economies: Adoption, e-participation, and legal frameworks* (pp. 573–590). Hershey, PA: IGI Global. doi:10.4018/978-1-4666-0324-0.ch029

Zhang, N., Guo, X., Chen, G., & Chau, P. Y. (2011). User evaluation of e-government systems: A Chinese cultural perspective. In F. Tan (Ed.), *International enterprises and global information technologies: Advancing management practices* (pp. 63–84). Hershey, PA: IGI Global. doi:10.4018/978-1-60960-605-3.ch004

Zuo, Y., & Hu, W. (2011). Trust-based information risk management in a supply chain network. In J. Wang (Ed.), *Supply chain optimization, management and integration: Emerging applications* (pp. 181–196). Hershey, PA: IGI Global. doi:10.4018/978-1-60960-135-5.ch013

Compilation of References

@andreas212nyc. (2013). *Twitter for Diplomats. Diplo Foundation*. Retrieved from https://issuu.com/diplo/docs/twitter_for_diplomats

Abbate, J. (2000). *Inventing the Internet*. Cambridge, MA: MIT Press.

Acharya, B. (2012). *Mass Communication & Journalism Study*. Kathmandu: Pradhan Book House.

Adhikari, D. (2016, September 13). Art of the Conscious. *Republica*. Retrieved December 19, 2016, from http://www.myrepublica.com/news/author/1221

Adhikari, D. (2017, January 17). On Media Writing – III. *Republica*. Retrieved January 20, 2017, from http://www.myrepublica.com/news/13197

Alliance for Affordable Internet. (2016). World off-track to achieve UN internet access as broadband prices remain high. New York: Alliance for Affordable Internet (A4AI).

Archetti, C. (2010, September). *Media Impact on Diplomatic Practice: An Evolutionary Model of Change*. Paper presented at American Political Science Association (APSA) Annual Convention, Washington, DC. Retrieved November 17, 2016, from https://www.academia.edu/378891/_Media_Impact_on_Diplomatic_Practice_An_Evolutionary_Model_of_Change_

Archetti, C. (2012). *Why Diplomacy in a Global World is Shaped by Local Media*. Retrieved December 27, 2016, from http://www.e-ir.info/2012/11/02/why-diplomacy-in-a-global-world-is-shaped-by-local-media/

Arora, N. (2016, June 17). Translating Modi's Social Media Prowess Into Effective Governance is Easier Tweeted than Done. *The Wire*. Retrieved from https://thewire.in/43460/the-difficult-task-of-translating-modi-govts-social-media-prowess-into-effective-governance/

Austin, J. L. (1962). *How to do things with words.* London: Oxford University Press. Retrieved October 23, 2016, from http://pubman.mpdl.mpg.de/pubman/item/escidoc:2271128:3/component/escidoc:2271430/austin_1962_how-to-do-things-with-words.pdf

Bagchi, I. (2015, April 7). How Narendra Modi government rescued 3,500 Indians from war zone Yemen. *Times News Network, Economic Times*. Retrieved from http://www.economictimes.indiatimes.com

Baldwin, D. (1997). The Concept of Security. *Review of International Studies*, *23*(1), 5–26. doi:10.1017/S0260210597000053 PMID:10164688

Balzacq, T. (2005). The Three Faces of Securitization: Political Agency, Audience and Context. *European Journal of International Relations*, *11*(2), 171–201. doi:10.1177/1354066105052960

Baran, S.J., & Davis, D.K. (n.d.). *Trends in mass communication theory: Seeking consensus, facing challenges, Mass Communication Chronology - Foundation, ferment and future* (4th ed.). Academic Press.

Baru, S. (2009, February 5). *The growing influence of business and media on Indian Foreign Policy*. Institute of South Asian Studies Insights. No. 49. Retrieved from http://www.isas.nus.edu.sg

Basnyat, P. S. (2009). *Military Media Relation and Security*. Retrieved 13 December, 2016, from http://www.premsinghbasnyat.com.np/topics-details.php?articleid=12&type=0

Basu, I. (2015, April 4). Yemen crisis: India rescued almost 2,000 foreign nationals, says Sushma Swaraj. *Huffpost India*. Retrieved from http://www.huffingtonpost.in/2015/04/20/yemen-crisis-india_n_7098856.html

BBC News. (25 November 2016). *Are you a woman too?* Retrieved from http://www.bbc.com/nepali/news-38104211

Behera, N. C. (2002). *State, People and Security: The South Asian Context*. New Delhi: Har-Anand Publications Pvt. Ltd.

Belknap, M. (2002). The CNN Effect: Strategic Enabler or Operational Risk? *Parameters*, 100–114.

Ben-Zvi, A., & Klieman, A. (2016). *Global Politics-Essays in Honour of David Vital*. London: Routledge.

Berkovitch, J., Kremenyuk, V., & Zartman, I. W. (2009). *The SAGE Handbook of Conflict Resolution*. SAGE Publications.

Bhattarai, U. K. (2014). *Responses on India-Nepal Relations.* Journal 19 of Foreign Policy Research Centre, New Delhi, India. http://www.fprc.in/Pragya-NEPAL-19.pdf

Bhattarai, U. K. (2015). *Madhesi Agitation: Comprehending Consequences on Indo-Nepal Relations.* Retrieved from http://diplomatist.com/dipo201511/article001.html

Bhattarai, U. K. (2016, September 28). *US-India-Nepal Alliance: Countering China.* Retrieved from https://thehimalayantimes.com/opinion/us-india-nepal-alliance-countering-china/

Bhattarai, U. K. (2014). *Conflict to Peace Transition in Nepal.* New Delhi: Adarsh Books.

Booth, K. (2007). *Theory of World Security.* New York: Cambridge University Press. doi:10.1017/CBO9780511840210

Brand, S. T. (2009). *Thought on news media's role in Nepal's democratic process.* Kathmandu: Bodhi. http://www.nepjol.info/index.php/BOHDI/article/view/2810/2494

Briggs, A., & Burke, P. (2009). A Social History of the Media: From Gutenberg to the Internet. Cambridge, UK: Polity Press.

Brown, R. (2003). Spinning the war: Political communications, information operations and public diplomacy in the war on terrorism. In D. K. Thussu & D. Freedman (Eds.), *War and the media-reporting conflict 24/7* (pp. 87–88). Sage Publications. doi:10.4135/9781446215579.n7

Brunton, F. (2013). *Spam: A Shadow History of the Internet.* Cambridge, MA: MIT Press.

Buzan, B., & Hansen, L. (2009). *The Evolution of International Security Studies.* New York: Cambridge University Press. doi:10.1017/CBO9780511817762

Buzan, B., Waever, O., & Wilde, J. (1997). *Security: A New Framework for Analysis.* London: Lynne Rienner Publishers.

Caparini, M. (2005). *Media and the Security Sector: Oversight and Accountability.* Retrieved from www.se2.dcaf.ch

Carpentier, N., (2005). *Media Representations of War and Conflict.* KUB Center Communication for Social Change, the Communications Department of the Vesalius College (VUB) and the Pascal Decroos Fund for Investigative Journalism.

Castells, M. (2001). *The Internet Galaxy: Reflections on the Internet, Business, and Society.* New York: Oxford University Press. doi:10.1007/978-3-322-89613-1

Center for International Governance Innovation. (2013). *Constructive power initiative: Internet governance, cyber security and digital diplomacy*. Toronto: CIGI.

Chakravarti, R. (2009). *Media Coverage of Terrorism and Methods of Diffusion*. New Delhi: MD Publications.

Chand, M. (2013). Thinking smart: A giant leap for India's foreign office. *India Writes*. Retrieved from http://mea.gov.in/in-focus-article.htm?21980/Thinking+Smart+A+giant+digital+leap+for+Indias+foreign+office

Chaudhary, D. R. (2016). India on top 10 ranking of global digital diplomacy: Diplomacy live. *Economic Times Bureau*. Retrieved from http://www.economictimes.indiatimes.com

Chaudhury, R. (2011). Big trouble in the left's last post. *Tehelka Magazine*. Retrieved from http://www.tehelka.com/2011/07/big-trouble-in-the-lefts-last-post/

Chutel, L. (2016, October 19). The mystery of Africa's disappearing Presidents. *Quartz Africa*, 18-23.

Dahal, D. R. (2014). *Media's Role in Nation-Building in Nepal*. Retrieved from http://www.spotlightnepal.com/News/Article/Dev-Raj-Dahal-Nation-Building-Nepal

Dahal, R. K. (2009). *Emerging role of Nepalese diplomacy in regional and global politics*. The Weekly Mirror.

Dahir, A. L. (2017, February). Government dithering prevents millions of Africans from accessing the internet. *Quartz Africa*, 21-27.

Deruda, A. (2014). *The Digital Diplomacy Handbook: How to Use Social Media to Engage with Global Audiences*. Create Space Independent Publishing Platform.

Digital Diplomacy Review. (2016). *Ranking and rating*. Retrieved February 18, 2017, from http://digital.diplomacy.live/ranking-and-rating/

Diplomacy School of Armenia. (2015). *Digital diplomacy: Prospects and challenges*. Yerevan: DSA.

Dominik, R. J. (2011). *The dynamics of mass communication*. New York: Grawhill.

Dr Mitha, T. (2011). *Guidelines to Media-Military relations*. Retrieved from: www.pkarticleshub.com/2011/09/09/guidelines-to-media-military-relations/

Dunne, T. (2012). Media and National Security. KW Publishers Pvt Ltd & Centre for Air Power Studies.

Editorial. (2015, July 7). Just in time. *The Hindu*. Retrieved from http://www.thehindu.org

Elassar, N. (2014). *What is Diplomacy?* Retrieved from http://bestdelegate.com/what-is-diplomacy/

Express Web Desk. (2016, December 14). Sushma Swaraj named in FP's global thinkers 2016 list, PM Modi says 'very proud'. *The Indian Express*. Retrieved from http://www.Indian express.com

Flanagan, M. (2015). Foreword. In Digital Diplomacy & the # G8 (pp. 2-3). London: Portland.

Fletcher, T. (2015). Naked diplomacy. In Digital diplomacy & the # G8 (pp. 9-11). London: Portland.

Floyd, R. (2011). Can securitization theory be used in normative analysis? Towards a just securitization theory. *Security Dialogue*, *42*(4-5), 427–439. doi:10.1177/0967010611418712

Friedman, G. (2008). *The Geo-politics of India: A Shifting, Self-Contained World*. The Himalayan Times of Nepal.

Fuchs, C. (2011). *Internet and Society: Social Theory in the Information Age*. New York: Routledge.

Fung, B. (2012). Digital diplomacy: Why is it tough for embassies to get social media right. *The Atlantic*. Retrieved January 24, from http://www.theatlantic.com/international/archive/2012/10/digital-diplomacy-why-its-so-tough-for-embassies-to-get-social-media-right/263744/

Ghareeb, E. (2000). The New Media and the Information Revolution in the Arab World: An Assessment. *The Middle East Journal*, *54*(3).

Gieboa, E. (2007, October 19). Diplomacy in the media age - Three models of uses and effects. *Diplomacy and Statecraft*, *12*(2). Retrieved from http://www.doi.org/10.1080/09592290108406201

Gilboa, E. (2001). Diplomacy in the media age: Three models of uses and effects. *Diplomacy and Statecraft*, *12*(2), 1–28. doi:10.1080/09592290108406201

GovUk. (2014). Transcript of Ambassador Nigel Baker's interview with Fr. Antonio Spadaro. *Cyberteologia* Retrieved February 24, 2017, from https://www.gov.uk/government/world-location-news/digital-diplomacy-social-media-and-the-holy-see

Graham, M., & Dutton, W. H. (2014). *Society and the Internet; How Networks of Information and Communication are Changing Our Lives*. New York: Oxford University Press. doi:10.1093/acprof:oso/9780199661992.001.0001

Gupta, A. (2010). South Asia in India's National Security Strategy. *Proceedings of the IDSA International Workshop on National Security Strategy*, 6.

Gupta, P. (interviewer), & Verma S. (interviewee). (2015). *Operation Rahat - The story of how India evacuated 7000 people from Yemen.* [Interview transcript]. Retrieved from https://silpnujs.wordpress.com/2015/05/12/interview-with-ambassador-sanjay-verma-on-operation-rahat-indias-rescue-operation-in-yemen/

Gurung, R. (2011). *Journalism in Transition: Media, Information Flows and Conflict in Nepal*. International Alert. Retrieved 18 December, 2016, from http://www.ifp-ew.eu/pdf/201110IfPEWJournTransMediaInfoConflict.Nepal.pdf

Guzzini, S. (2011). Securitization as a Causal Mechanism. *Security Dialogue*, *42*(4-5), 329–341. doi:10.1177/0967010611419000

Hacker, K. L., & Mendez, V. R. (2016). Toward a Model of Strategic Influence, International Broadcasting, and Global Engagement. *Media and Communication*, *4*(2), 69-91 Retrieved January 05, 2017, from http://www.cogitatiopress.com/ojs/index.php/mediaandcommunication/article/view/355

Hansen, L. (2013). *Security as Practice: Discourse Analysis and the Bosnian War*. New York: Routledge.

Hayes, B. (2012). *The other Burma? Conflict, counter-insurgency and human rights in Northeast India, Transnational Institute*. Amsterdam, The Netherlands: TNI. Retrieved from https://www.tni.org/files/download/theotherburma-webspreads.pdf

Heng, S. M. L. (2016). Diplomacy and image building: India rides on its soft power. *Observer Research Foundation, Issue Brief, November 2016,* (163). Retrieved from http://cf.orfonline.org/wp-content/uploads/2016/11/IB-163.pdf

Heng, S. M. L. (2016). *Diplomacy and Image-Building: India Rides on Its Soft Power.* Retrieved from http://www.orfonline.org/research/diplomacy-and-image-building/

Hocking, B., Melissen, J., Riordan, S., & Sharp, P. (2012, October 18). *Future for Diplomacy, Integrative Diplomacy in the 21st Century*. Netherlands Institute of International Relations 'Clingendael'. Retrieved from http://www.clingendael.org

HT Correspondent. (2016, July 14). Operation sankat mochas: Indians rescued from South Sudan to reach Delhi today. *Hindustan Times*. Retrieved from http://www.hindustantimes.com/india-news/op-sankat-mochan-over-500-indians-to-be-evacuated-from-south-sudan/story-RzrZ3gsFipBAWGe70pe4WP.html

Hussain, N. (2008). The Role of Media in National Security: A Case Study of 1998 Nuclear Explosions by Pakistan. SASSI Research Report, 13(20), 5.

Indian Public Diplomacy. (n.d.). Retrieved from http://www.en.m.wikipedia.org

Indo Asian News Service. (2014, October 13). *India's foreign policy a big draw on new and social media*. Retrieved from http://mea.gov.in/articles-in-indian-media.htm?dtl/24089/Indias+foreign+policy+a+big+draw+on+new+and+social+media

Internet Usage Statistics. (2017). *Internet World Stats: Usage and Population Statistics*. Retrieved from http://www.internetworldstats.com/stats.htm

Internews. (2011). *Media and Telecoms Landscape Guide*. Retrieved December 3, 2016, from https://www.internews.org/sites/default/files/resources/nepal_media_landscape_guide_final_011011_19.12.12.pdf

Issac, A., & Balan, S. S. (2017, March 30). As "Take Off" suggests, did a malayali businessman help in rescuing nurses from Iraq? *The NEWS Minute*. Retrieved from https://www.thenewsminute.com/article/take-suggests-did-malayali-businessman-help-rescuing-nurses-iraq-59511

Jeffrey, R. I. (2007). Deconstructing the Terrorism-News Media Relationship, Crime Media Culture. *Sge Publication, USA*, *3*(2), 218.

Jelena. (2010, January 16). *What is e-diplomacy anyway?* Retrieved from https://www.diplomacy.edu/blog/what-e-diplomacy-anyway

Joshi, M. (2016, December 23). The Modi government has dismantled India's Foreign Policy [Weblog comment]. Retrieved from http://www.thewire.com

Juneja, K. (2015). *Why operation rahat is a major achievement for India*. Observer Research Foundation. Retrieved from http://www.huffingtonpost.in/kabir-taneja/why-operation-rahat-is-a-_b_7023266.html

Kate, T. (2016). *The West Africa Ebola crisis*. New York: Ebola Deeply.

Kaur, H., & Kumar, A. (2017a). *A paradigm shift in foreign policy*. Retrieved from http://www.dailypioneer.com/columnists/oped/a-paradigm-shift-in-foreign-policy.html

Kaur, H., & Kumar, A. (2017b, August 10). A Paradigm Shift in Foreign Policy [Weblog comment]. Retrieved from http://www.dailypioneer.com

KC, B. (2014). *Political Inclination of Journalists and Its Influence on News*. Kathmandu: Centre for Media Research (CMR) - Nepal. Retrieved November 23, 2016, from http://research.butmedia.org/wp-content/uploads/2014/10/PoliticalInclination.pdf

Khanal, R. (2011). *Geo-Politics and Socio-Political Development in Nepal*. The Shivapuri Journal.

Kluz, A., & Firlej, M. (2015). *The impact of technology on foreign affairs*. FPA: Foreign Policy Association. Retrieved January 12, 2016 from http://foreignpolicyblogs.com/2015/12/22/the-impact-of-technology-on-foreign-affairs-five-challenges/

Kluz, A., & Firlej, M. (2015, December 22). The Impact of Technology on Foreign Affairs - Five Challenges [Weblog comment]. Retrieved from http://www.foreignpolicyblogs.com

Kluz, A., & Mikolas, F. (2015). *The impact of technology on foreign affairs - Five challenges*. Foreign Policy Association. Retrieved from www.foreignpolicyblog.com

Koirala, B. (2011). *Economic Management: Fault lines and ways to Resolve. A panel discussion held by Nepal Administrative Staff College*. Kathmandu: Jawalakhel.

Kumar, D. (2001). *Soldiers and Scribblers – Media in Information Warfare: A Case Study of India*. Occasional Paper, Institute of Defence Studies and Analyses.

Kumar, K. J. (2012). *Mass communication in India*. Mumbai, India: JAICO Publishing House.

Kurbalija, J. (2016, November 7). *25 points for digital diplomacy*. Retrieved from https://www.huffingtonpost.com/entry/25-points-for-digital-diplomacy_us_581c78bae4b0334571e099ec

Leach, J. (2015). Diplomacy – facing a future without borders. In Digital diplomacy & the # G8 (pp. 15-17). London: Portland.

Lind, S. (2004). Article. *Military Review*, *84*(5), 13.

Livingston, S. (1977). *Clarifying the CNN Effect: An Examination of Media Effects According to Type of Military Intervention*. Research Paper R-18. The Joan Shorenstein Center, Harvard University.

Lockyer, A. (2003). The Relationship between the Media and Terrorism. Strategic and Defence Studies Center.

Mallapur, C. (2015). PM Narendra Modi wields soft power to befriend Chinese. *Business Standard*. Retrieved from http://business-standard.com/article/current-affairs/pm-narendra-modi-wields-soft-power-to-befriend-chinese-115050500321_1.html

Manor, I. (2015). Between two digital divides. *Exploring digital diplomacy*. Retrieved January 24, 2017, from https://digdipblog.com/2016/01/27/between-two-digital-divides/

Manor, I. (2015). In digital diplomacy, a narrowing digital divide. *Exploring digital diplomacy*. Retrieved January 24 from https://digdipblog.com/2015/01/19/divide/

Manor, I. (2016). *Digital diplomacy in Africa: A research agenda*. USC Center on Public Diplomacy.

Massolin, P. (1996). Context and content: Harrold innins, Marshal macluhan, and George grant and the role of technology in modern society. *Past Imperfect (Edmonton, Alta.)*, *5*, 81–118. Retrieved from http://www.journals.library.ualberta.ca

McDonald, M. (2008). Securitization and the Construction of Security. *European Journal of International Relations*, *13*(4), 563–587. doi:10.1177/1354066108097553

McQuail, D. (2005). McQuails mass communication theory, new media - New theory (5th ed.). Vistar Publication.

McQuails, D. (2015). *Mass communication theory, New media - new theory* (5th ed.). New Delhi: Vistar Publication.

Mehta, A. K. (2006). *The Royal Nepal Army: Meeting the Maoist Challenges*. New Delhi: Rupa. Co.

Melissen, J. (2005). The New diplomacy: Between theory and practice. In M. Jan (Ed.), *The New public diplomacy. Soft power in international relations* (pp. 3–27). Hampshire: Palgrave Macmillan. doi:10.1057/9780230554931_1

Metzger, E. T. (2012). Is it the medium or the message? Social media, American public relations & Iran. *Global Media Journal*, *15*, 1–16.

Moharir, V. (2009). *India Rising: The Role of Indian Diaspora in Accelerating India's Transition as a Global Power*. The Hague, The Netherlands: Foundation for Critical Choice for India, Pravasiya Bhartiya Divas. Retrieved from https://www.indiawijzer.nl/indian_diaspora/indian_diaspora_nl/pbde_paper_dr_vasant_moharir.pdf

Murphy, M. (2013, July 3). How has social media affected diplomatic reporting? *DiPLO*. Retrieved from http://www.diplomacy.edu.in

Murphy, M. (2013, July 3). *How has social media affected diplomatic reporting?* Retrieved November 26, 2016, from https://www.diplomacy.edu/blog/how-has-social-media-affected-diplomatic-reporting

Nanavatty, R. K. (2009). Army-Media Relations in Sub-conventional Conflict. *Centre for Land Warfare Studies Journal*, 136. Retrieved from: http://www.claws.in/images/journals_doc/1400825447R%20K%20Nanavatty%20CJ%20SSummer%202009.pdf

Nandy, C. (2014, July 5). Evacuation of Indians from Iraq is a momentous diplomatic victory. India World. *Times of India.* Retrieved from https://blogs.timesofindia.indiatimes.com/nandygram/evacuation-of-indian-nurses-from-iraq-is-a-momentous-diplomatic-victory/

Nepali Telecom. (2012). *Only 3 Percent Household Have Internet Access in Nepal.* Retrieved from http://www.nepalitelecom.com/2012/11/only-3-percent-household-have-internet-access-in-nepal.html

Netherlands, Institute of International Relations. (2015). *Diplomacy in the digital age. Clingedael Report.* The Hague: Clingendael Institute.

New Media Institute. (2014). Bailey Socha, Barbara Eber-Schmid. *Defining New Media Isn't Easy*. Retrieved from https://www.facebook.com/permalink.php?story_fbid=200470393410745&id=200469916744126

Nye, J. (1990). Soft Power. *Foreign Policy*, *80*(80), 153–171. doi:10.2307/1148580

Nye, J. Jr. (2004). Soft Power and American Foreign Policy. *Political Science Quarterly*, *119*(2), 256. doi:10.2307/20202345

Organization for Economic Co-operation and Development. (2011). Understanding the digital divide. In *OECD Digital Economy Papers 49*. Paris: OECD Publishing.

Organization for Economic Co-operation and Development. (2016). *People trust in government.* Retrieved January 20, 2017, from http://www.oecd.org/gov/trust-in-government.htm

Pandita, R. (2014). *The Central Reserve Police Mess.* Retrieved from http://www.thehindu.com/opinion/op-ed/the-central-reserve-police-mess/article6686784.ece

Panigrahi, S. (2017, May 26). Three years of Modi government, what India has achieved on foreign policy front [Weblog comment]. Retrieved from http://www.opindia.com

Permyakova, L. (2014, January 2). The Future of digital diplomacy. *Russia Direct*, 23-30.

Press Council Nepal. (2016). *41st Annual Report*. Kathmandu. Retrieved 25 December, 2016, from http://www.presscouncilnepal.org/np/wp-content/uploads/2016/10/Final-Yearly-Report.pdf

Press Council of India. (n.d.). *Military-Media Interface: Changing Paradigms New Challenges*. IDSA. Retrieved from: http://www.idsa-india.org/an-aug-400.html

Press Council. (1994). *Pen and Sword - Towards More Openness*. Retrieved from: http://presscouncil.nic.in/OldWebsite/history.htm

Rachman, G. (2016). *Easternisation*. London: The Bodley Head.

Rai, A. K. (2000). *Military-Media Interface: Changing Paradigms New Challenges*. IDSA. Retrieved from: http://www.idsa-india.org/an-aug-400.html

Rai, A. K. (2003, January). *Diplomacy and the news media: A comment on the Indian experience. Strategic analysis, volume 27*. Institute for Defence Studies and Analysis. Retrieved from http://www.idsa.in

Ray, G. N. (2009). *Terrorism-New Challenges and Media*. Press Academy of Andhra Pradesh.

Reddy, K.J. (2002). *Present Turmoil Godhra and After: Role of Media*. Inaugural function of Indian First Foundation.

Reljic, D. (2004). *News Media and the Transformation of Ethnopolitical Conflicts*. Berghof Research Centre for Constructive Conflict Management. Retrieved 15 November, 2016, from http://www.berghof-foundation.org/fileadmin/redaktion/Publications/Handbook/Articles/reljic_handbook.pdf

Report of UN Special Rapporteur on Extrajudicial Execution to the UN Human Rights Council A/HRC/4/20/Add.1 (Para. 18), Asian Centre for Human Rights. (2010). India Human Rights Report 2009.

Riedel, B. (2015). *JFK's Forgotten Crisis*. Washington, DC: The Brookings Institution Press.

Ritambhara. (2013, April 30). On Indian Public Diplomacy, E-International Relations [Weblog comment]. Retrieved on September 18, 2017 from http://www.e-ir.info

Rito, L. (2013). *Diplomacy and its practices. Digital diplomacy*. ISPD: Protocol and Diplomacy. Retrieved 24 January 2017, from http://ispdnetwork.org/2014/08/diplomacy-and-its-practice-v-digital-diplomacy/

Rose, L. E. (1971). *Nepal: Strategy for Survival*. London: University of California Press.

Sandre, A. (2015). *Digital Diplomacy: Conversations on Innovation in Foreign Policy*. London: Rowman and Littlefield.

Saran, S. (2017, May 29). In year four, Modi's foreign policy needs some course corrections [Weblog comment]. Retrieved from http://www.thewire.com

Saxena, S. (1997). *Defence Journalism in India*. New Delhi: Manas Publication.

Sehgal, R. (2009). Terror on TV, or by TV? *InfoChange News & Features*. Retrieved from: http://infochangeindia.org/agenda/reporting-conflict/terror-on-tv-or-by-tv.html

Shankar, A., & Verma, J. P. (2002). Role of Media in War and Terrorism. New Delhi: Sunrise Publications.

Sharma, S. (2009). Media and the Security Sector: Shifting Relations. In B. Sapkota (Ed.), *The Nepali Security Sector: An Almanac*. Geneva Centre for the Democratic Control of Armed Forces and the Centre for European Studies.

Shenhav, S. R., Sheafer, T., & Gabay, I. (2010). Incoherent narrator: Israeli public diplomacy during the disengagement and the elections in the Palestinian Authority. *Israel Studies*, *15*(3), 143–162. doi:10.2979/isr.2010.15.3.143

Shorter, C. R. (2014). *Digital Diplomacy in an Era of Rising Social Powers: How New Media Impacted the Practice of Public Diplomacy by Empowering Citizens and Terrorist Organizations*. London: Webster University.

Shukla, T. (2014, July 1). Govt. readies aircraft evacuation plan for Iraq, Govt. prepares plan to deploy aircraft to bring back Indians stranded in Iraq if the need arises. *Livemint*. Retrieved from http://www.livemint.com/Politics/nQ9bvIapoTAGVdtCraIuoI/Govt-readies-aircraft-evacuation-plan-for-Iraq.htm

Sileshie, S. K. (2014). Challenges and opportunities of Facebook as a media platform in Ethiopia. *JMCS: Journal of Media Communication Studies*, *6*(7), 99–110.

Slaughter, A. M. (2009). America's Edge, Power in Networked Century. *Foreign Affairs*. Retrieved from http://www.foreignaffairs.com

Spencer, G. (2005). *The media and peace: From Vietnam to the "war of terror"*. Springer. doi:10.1057/9780230505506

Starr, H. (2016). *On Geopolitics*. New York: Routledge.

Statista: The Statistics Portal. (2018). *Most famous social network sites worldwide as of January 2017, ranked by number of active users (in millions)*. Retrieved from https://www.statista.com/statistics/272014/global-social-networks-ranked-by-number-of-users/

Sulovic, V. (2010). *Meaning of Security and the Theory of Securitization.* Belgrade Centre for Security Policy. Retrieved 19 December, 2016, from http://www.bezbednost.org/upload/document/sulovic_(2010)_meaning_of_secu.pdf

Taureck, R. (2006). Securitization Theory and Securitization Studies. *Journal of International Relations and Development*, *9*(9), 53–61. doi:10.1057/palgrave.jird.1800072

Thakur, R. (2012, June 18). Effective diplomacy in the age of social media. Opinion. *The Japan Times*. Retrieved from http://www.japantimes.co.jp

The Pioneer. (2016). *Digital Diplomacy: India Ranked Seventh by Diplomacy.* Retrieved from http://www.dailypioneer.com/nation/digital-diplomacy-india-ranked-seventh-by-diplomacy-live.html

Tiedeman, A. (2005). Islamic republic of Iran broadcasting: Public diplomacy or propaganda? *Al Nakhalali: The Fletcher School Online Journal for Issues Related to South West Asia and Islamic Civilization*, *5*(1), 1–7.

Toffler, A., & Toffler, H. (2006). *War and Anti-War*. New Delhi: Natraj Publishers.

Tripathi, R. (2015). Netting Jihadis Online. *India Today*. Retrieved from: http://indiatoday.intoday.in/story/jihadi-group-intelligence-agencies-islamic-state-chakravyuh/1/412233.html

Uhlig, C. (2015). *Moving towards Securitization. How the Paris Attacks were Used to Justify Extraordinary Measures*. Linnaeus University. Retrieved 19 December, 2016, from http://lnu.diva-portal.org/smash/get/diva2:824877/FULLTEXT01.pdf

United States Government Publishing Office. (1994). *1994 Public Papers 273 - Electronic Mail Message to Prime Minister Carl Bildt of Sweden*. Retrieved from https://www.gpo.gov/fdsys/granule/PPP-1994-book1/PPP-1994-book1-doc-pg273/content-detail.html

Upadhya, S. (2016). *Nepal and the Geo-Strategic Rivalry between China and India*. New York: Routledge.

van Dijk, T. A. (1992). *Power and the News Media. In Program of Discourse Studies* (p. 9). University of Amsterdam.

Vijaykumar, N. (2016, October 17). How Sushma Swaraj means hope for Indians around the world. *The Week*. Retrieved from http://theweek.in

Vohra, N.N. (2008). National Governance and Internal Security. *Journal of Defence Studies, 2*(1), 7.

Vultee, F. (2007). *Securitization as a Theory of Media Effects: The Contest Over the Framing of Political Violence.* Retrieved 22 November, 2016, from https://mospace.umsystem.edu/xmlui/bitstream/handle/10355/4792/research.pdf?sequence=3&isAllowed=y

We Are Social. (2017). *Digital in 2017: South East Asia.* Retrieved 20 February, 2017, from https://www.slideshare.net/wearesocialsg/digital-in-2017-southeast-asia

Whelpton, J. (2005). *A History of Nepal.* London: Cambridge University Press. doi:10.1017/CBO9781107050860

Williams, L. (2015). Disruptive diplomacy. In Digital diplomacy & the # G8 (pp. 12-14). London: Portland.

Wilson, G.I., Sullivan, P., & Kempfer. (2003). *4GW: Tactics of the Weak Confound the Strong*. Retrieved from www.Military.com

WPPGov. (2016). Executive Summary. The Government and public sector practice. *The Leaders' Reporter*, p. 2.

Xavier, C. (2016, December). India's expatriate evacuation operations - Bringing the diaspora home. *Carnegie India*. Retrieved from http://www.carnegieendowment.org

YKA Staff. (2016, March 11). *10 times Sushma Swaraj used Twitter like a boss and helped Indians from around the world*. Retrieved from http://www.youthkiawaaz.com

Zoker, Y. (2015, July 23). Here is how Kenyans on Twitter are responding to CNN's coverage of Obama's first presidential visit to Kenya. *OkayAfrica*, 16-22.

About the Contributors

Swati Jaywant Rao Bute is working as an Associate Professor and teaches subjects related to communication and journalism and actively involved in research and publication. She has nine years experience in academics and seven years experience in industry. She holds Doctorate in Communication and Journalism and have done short duration Visiting Fellowship from New Delhi based Government Think Tank, working in the area of security and defence. She worked with Government organisation as a faculty of Health Communication and was a member of important committees for developing curriculum for different National level health programs. She worked with All India Radio (Public Broadcasting Service of India) for 6 years as a casual compère. She did her post graduation in Communication and Journalism with specialisation in Science Communication. Her area of interests are communication studies and research, International Affairs and Media, Social media communication, Health communication, Advance communication technology and audiences behaviour, Development communication, Electronic media, Cross cultural communication and Science communication.

* * *

Umesh Kumar Bhattarai is an Ex- Brigadier General of Nepal Army. He changed the track to academics from military profession in the year 2012. Besides of PhD in Conflict Management under the Political Science domain, he is also Master in Science (Defense Studies) from Madras University India and Master in Public Administration from Tribhuvan University, Nepal. He is experienced of diplomatic assignment as Counsellor/ Military Adviser at the Permanent Mission of Nepal to the United Nations, New York. In teaching experience—he was Senior Instructor at Nepal Army Command and Staff College, Shivapuri and Visiting Faculty for Master's Program in International Relations and Diplomacy of Tribhuvan

University, Nepal. Presently he is Visiting Scholar at Lumbini Buddhist University, Nepal teaching subjects like Environmental Peace and Research Methodology. He had been to research fellow at the Institute for Defense Studies and Analyses, New Delhi, India. To his credit—he has written number of articles and book on conflict, peace and development.

Floribert Patrick C. Endong (PhD) is a research consultant in the humanities and social sciences. He is a reviewer and editor with many scientific journals in the social sciences. His current research interest focuses on international communication, digital media, media laws, international relations, culture and religious communication He is author of numerous peer-reviewed articles and book chapters in the above-mentioned areas of interest.

Krishna Bharadwaj Hotur, born on November 2nd, 1991, has completed his BBA LL.B (Hons.) from JSS Law College, Mysore in the year 2014, LL.M. (Gold Medallist) from Karnataka State Law University's Law School, Huballi and Post Graduate Diploma in Human Resource Management from Alagappa University both in June, 2015. Currently he is pursuing his Ph.D. from National Law School of India University, Bangalore. He is also an Associate Editor and Member of the Siddhartha Legal Research Society. He has published more than a dozen of his articles on diverse subjects in various journals including international journals. He has also participated in many national and state level conferences and workshops as well.

Ramakrishnan Ramani is a research scholar at the Department of Defence and Strategic Studies at the University of Madras. His doctoral thesis is on the issue of Military–News Media relations in context to Fourth Generation Warfare in India. Since November 2013, he has authored and published close to nine academic papers on International Relations, Military–Media Relations and Environmental Security. He has also presented papers in international conferences. On the professional front, Ramakrishnan heads the global marketing and communication department for a Swiss-based data security company.

Aakriti Sethi is currently an MPhil research scholar at United States Studies Program, Centre for Canadian, US and Latin American Studies (CCUSLAS), School of International Studies (SIS) at Jawaharlal Nehru University (JNU), New Delhi. After her masters in Geopolitics and International Relations from Manipal University, Karnataka, she worked as a research intern at the United States Centre at Institute for Defence Studies and Analyses (IDSA), New Delhi. Her area of interest includes US foreign policy, smart and soft power, various dimensions of diplomacy, media and propaganda studies, US and Asia Pacific, US-China relations, US domestic politics, and Indian foreign policy. She has written various online articles, journal articles and newsletter covers on these respective themes.

Sudeep Uprety is a Nepal based researcher specialising in development communications research and teaching. Sudeep has a Masters in Conflict, Peace and Development Studies from Tribhuvan University, Nepal and has carried out several studies related to media research on conflict and security, disaster response, crisis communications, health, gender and adolescence, among others. Sudeep currently works as Research Uptake and Impact Coordinator for Gender and Adolescence: Global Evidence (GAGE) programme, managed by Overseas Development Institute (ODI) based in London, UK. Sudeep also teaches Development Communications at National College, affiliated with Kathmandu University. He has blogs published in reputed knowledge management portals such as London School of Economics, Research to Action and Scaling-Up Nutrition.

Index

www.ingramcontent.com/pod-product-compliance
Lightning Source LLC
LaVergne TN
LVHW081322300926
849161LV00008B/1851